T0323199

THE
TRIUMVIRATE

By the same author

Titanic: Psychic Forewarnings of a Tragedy (Patrick Stephens, 1988)

Lost at Sea: Ghost Ships and Other Mysteries, with Michael Goss (Prometheus Books, 1994)

Titanic: Safety, Speed and Sacrifice (Transportation Trails, 1997)

'Archie': The Life of Major Archibald Butt from Georgia to the Titanic (Lulu.com Press, 2010)

A Death on the Titanic: The Loss of Major Archibald Butt (Lulu.com Press, 2011)

On Board RMS Titanic: Memories of the Maiden Voyage (The History Press, 2012)

Voices from the Carpathia (The History Press, 2015)

Titanic Memoirs (three volumes; Lulu.com Press, 2015)

The Titanic Files: A Paranormal Sourcebook (Lulu.com Press, 2015)

Titanic: The Return Voyage (Lulu.com Press, 2020)

'Those Brave Fellows': The Last Hours of the Titanic's Band (Lulu.com Press, 2020)

The Titanic Disaster: A Medical Dossier (Lulu.com Press, 2021)

'There's Talk of an Iceberg': A Titanic Investigation (Lulu.com Press, 2021)

Letters from the Titanic (The History Press, 2023)

Fate Deals a Hand: The Titanic's Professional Gamblers (The History Press, 2023)

Titanic Collections, Volume 1: Fragments of History – The Ship (The History Press, 2023)

Titanic: Her Books and Bibliophiles (Lulu.com Press, 2024)

Titanic Collections, Volume 2: Fragments of History – The People (The History Press, coming 2024)

THE
TRIUMVIRATE

CAPTAIN EDWARD J. SMITH, BRUCE ISMAY, THOMAS ANDREWS AND THE SINKING OF TITANIC

GEORGE BEHE

The History Press

Cover illustrations: J. Bruce Ismay, Captain Edward J. Smith, Thomas Andrews (Author collection); *Titanic* sinking (*Titanic*, Filson Young, London: 1912)

First published 2024

The History Press
97 St George's Place, Cheltenham,
Gloucestershire, GL50 3QB
www.thehistorypress.co.uk

British Library Cataloguing in Publication Data.
A catalogue record for this book is available from the British Library.

ISBN 978 1 80399 335 5

Typesetting and origination by The History Press
Printed and bound in Great Britain by TJ Books Limited, Padstow, Cornwall.

Trees for LYfe

CONTENTS

ACKNOWLEDGEMENTS

I'm very grateful to my friends Don Lynch, Dr Paul Lee, Michael Poirier, Kalman Tanito, Randy Bigham, Tad Fitch, John Lamoreau, Daniel Parkes, Gerhard Schmidt-Grillmeier, John Maxtone-Graham, Olivier Mendez, Malte Fiebing-Petersen, Jack Kinzer, Peter Engberg, Lars-Inge Glad, Gavin Bell and the late Phil Gowan for contributing a number of the survivor accounts and photographs that appear in this book.

INTRODUCTION

This book started out with a simple premise – i.e., to thoroughly document the activities of the *Titanic*'s Captain Edward J. Smith during his vessel's maiden voyage. However, I soon realised that Smith's activities were intimately intertwined with those of two other 'top players' in the *Titanic* story – shipbuilder Thomas Andrews and White Star Line chairman Joseph Bruce Ismay. With that being the case, I expanded my coverage to include all three men – men whose post-disaster reputations differ from each other as greatly as night differs from day.

The fact that Captain Smith was the *Titanic*'s commander caused his decisions during the maiden voyage to be alternately praised or criticised by generations of *Titanic* researchers. By contrast, the activities of Thomas Andrews (one of the *Titanic*'s designers) resulted in his being universally regarded as a genuine hero, while the actions of Bruce Ismay were widely condemned by the general public and served to tarnish his reputation for the remainder of his life.

This book will document the words and actions of Smith, Andrews and Ismay throughout the entirety of the *Titanic*'s maiden voyage, beginning with the vessel's departure from Southampton and continuing right through to her last few moments afloat. After describing each man's activities during the first four days of the maiden voyage, we'll examine the *Titanic*'s collision with the iceberg and will explore in detail how Captain Smith and Thomas Andrews went about determining the full extent of the damage their ship had just sustained. We'll look at Smith's eventual decision to evacuate his passengers from the sinking ship, and will then follow him and Andrews from place to place as they assist in alerting the *Titanic*'s passengers as well as loading and launching the lifeboats. Finally, we'll show how Captain Smith and Thomas Andrews spent their final few minutes of life on board the *Titanic*, and will attempt to document the exact manner in which the two men met their individual fates. (It may come as a surprise for readers to learn that the so-called 'legend' of Captain Smith attempting to save a child is corroborated by a primary source, the existence of which few people are currently aware.)

In addition to monitoring the activities of Captain Smith and Thomas Andrews, we'll be following the activities of Bruce Ismay throughout the *Titanic*'s maiden voyage and sinking in order to determine whether or not he truly deserves the unfortunate reputation that has been pinned to his coat-tails ever since the disaster.

This book won't be telling the story of Smith, Andrews and Ismay by describing their bare-bones activities in general terms. Instead, we'll be utilising the words of the three men themselves as well as offering accounts of their activities as observed by eyewitnesses who had *personal interactions* with the three men during the *Titanic*'s maiden voyage. In other words, we'll be telling the stories of Captain Smith, Thomas Andrews and Bruce Ismay by utilising the voices of people who were *there*.

Through the years I've always been interested in figuring out exactly how Captain Smith and Thomas Andrews first determined that the *Titanic* had received her death blow while colliding with the iceberg. Hollywood always depicts an intense private conference between the two men during which Andrews explains to Smith why the ship cannot possibly remain afloat, but is this what really happened? Was Captain Smith truly 'catatonic' during the entire evacuation process, as one present-day author has claimed? How did Captain Smith and Thomas Andrews meet their individual fates when the *Titanic* went down? How did Bruce Ismay come to survive the disaster when the ship's captain and builder both lost their lives? Were rumours of Ismay's supposed cowardice based in fact? We'll examine each of these questions (and others) as our story gradually unfolds.

While examining our various eyewitness accounts, one thing will quickly become apparent to the reader: different eyewitnesses to the same event or conversation often remembered things slightly differently. (Although the gist of their stories is usually the same, the exact wording or exact locations or exact times of occurrence of the events in question often are not.) For instance, did Captain Smith issue certain orders to the occupants of a specific lifeboat before that boat was lowered to the ocean's surface, or did he use his megaphone to call out his orders after the lifeboat had already begun rowing away from the ship's side? Although some of these questions are unanswerable due to conflicting accounts, I have done my best to illustrate each of these inconsistencies and have assigned a 'probable' time and location to each of our described events. Even so, and as author Walter Lord once pointed out, 'It is a rash man indeed who would set himself up as final arbiter on all that happened the incredible night the *Titanic* went down'.

At any rate, I have done my best to tell the story accurately, but I invite readers to examine the eyewitness accounts and evaluate the actions of Edward J. Smith, Thomas Andrews and Bruce Ismay for themselves.

George Behe
Grand Rapids, Michigan

Joseph Bruce Ismay; Captain Edward
J. Smith; Thomas Andrews. (Author's
collection)

1

PRELUDE TO THE MAIDEN VOYAGE

We'll begin our presentation by reading the reminiscences of a number of people who were personal friends of Captain Edward J. Smith and who did their best to describe the kind of man he was …

★

'Captain Smith loved the sea,' remembered Mrs Ann O'Donnell, a friend of Smith's since childhood:

> From his boyhood days until he was placed in command of the great-est liners in the world, he felt a strong attachment for the sailor's life. He was a kindly, thoughtful and genial man. He never rose above his position, and I never knew him to forget that once he was listed on the ship's books as merely an able seaman. He never forgot his friends and loved to cherish memories of the days spent in the little town in England.

'Capt. Smith was one of the bravest then that ever lived,' Mrs O'Donnell went on:

> He was never known to have flinched in the face of the most seri-ous danger. The utmost confidence was always placed in him by the

owners of the ships he commanded. He was thoroughly reliable and conscientious, and was loved by everyone who knew him. They could not help it, for he seemed to be a man who was a friend to all who understood him.[1]

Charles Lightoller was destined to serve with Captain Edward J. Smith as the *Titanic*'s second officer. Captain Smith, or 'E.J.' as he was familiarly and affectionately known, was quite a character in the shipping world, Lightoller wrote later:

Tall, full whiskered and broad. At first sight you would think to yourself, 'Here's a typical Western Ocean Captain. Bluff, hearty, and I'll bet he's got a voice like a foghorn.' As a matter of fact, he had a pleasant quiet voice and invariable smile. A voice he rarely raised above a conversational tone – not to say he couldn't; in fact, I have often heard him bark an order that made a man come to himself with a bump. He was a great favorite, and a man any officer would give his ears to sail under. I had been with him many years, off and on, in the mail boats, *Majestic*, mainly, and it was an education to see him con his own ship up through the intricate channels entering New York at full speed. One particularly bad corner, known as the South-West Spit, used to make us fairly flush with pride as he swung her round, judging his distances to a nicety; she heeling over to the helm with only a matter of feet to spare between each end of the ship and the banks.[2]

'Capt. Smith was a man who had a very, very clear record,' agreed Joseph Bruce Ismay, chairman of the White Star Line. 'I should think very few commanders crossing the Atlantic have as good a record as Capt Smith had, until he had the unfortunate collision with the *Hawke*.'[3]

Sixth Officer James Moody had an equally high opinion and equally respectful attitude towards Captain Smith: 'Though I believe he's an awful stickler for discipline, he's popular with everybody,' Moody wrote in a letter to his sister.[4]

'During most of my service I have been on ships with Captain Smith, of course, starting when he was a junior officer,' Bathroom Steward Samuel Rule remembered. 'A better man never walked a deck. His crew knew him to be a good, kind-hearted man, and we looked upon him as a sort of father.'[5]

'Captain Smith ranked all men in the service, and he ranked them because of carefulness, prudence, skill and long and valued service,' said the White Star Line's Captain John N. Smith, who spoke with Smith on the same day he'd been given command of the brand-new *Olympic*:

> He came down to the pier and clapped his hand on my shoulder. 'Captain,' he said, 'they are making brave ships these days, and I am in charge of the bravest of them, but there will never be boats like the sailing ships we used to take out of Liverpool. Those were the clippers that made old England the queen of the seas.' He said that the senior captain of the White Star fleet was a kindly, humorous, grave man, watchful from long sailing of the sudden and treacherous seas; gentle to those under him, but strict in the hour of duty.[6]

Captain David Evans, who had served as Captain Smith's chief officer on the *Majestic*, spoke very highly of Smith and said he was the finest type of British sailor – a splendid fellow to get along with, although the strongest disciplinarian. If there was any man he would choose to sail a ship across the Atlantic, Captain Evans said Smith would be that man.[7]

★

Professional sailors weren't the only people who had a favourable opinion of Captain Smith.

'All the passengers were eager to meet Captain Smith,' remembered Mrs L. B. Judd, who once sailed with him on the *Baltic*:

> He was so different from the captain of the *Finland*, which vessel I took from New York to Antwerp on the outward trip across. The captain of the *Finland* was jolly and had plenty of time to converse with the passengers, but Captain Smith had little to say. He avoided talking with us although he was very courteous.

'Every morning he would have an inspection of the crew,' Mrs Judd went on:

He made it a practice of speaking a kindly word to each man. It seemed to me that they would do anything for him. Captain Smith was always occupied. He spent but little time in his office, being at his post continually. The passengers did not meet him at meal time as he dined alone in a private apartment. He was my ideal of a captain. He was too occupied to say more than a few words when spoken to. From his accent I gathered that he was of Scotch descent.[8]

★

Howard Weber, president of the Springfield, Illinois, First National Bank, chatted with his friend Captain Smith on the *Olympic* while returning from his last trip abroad.

'The *Titanic* will soon be ready for the water,' Smith told Mr Weber. 'I expect to be given her charge, but somehow I rather regret to leave my present boat, the *Olympic*.'

'I knew Captain Smith, not as an acquaintance, but as a good friend,' Weber related later:

> We always made it a point to be together on trips across the ocean, and he took pride in informing me of new appliances which the ships upon which he was placed had ... Captain Smith was a congenial old man, and one people could not help liking. I was with him last time last year when we crossed the ocean on the *Olympic*. The captain at that time said he expected to be put on the new *Titanic*, but expressed himself as preferring just a little to stay with the *Olympic* ... Officers of the White Star Line and Captain Smith himself believed just as sincerely as anything that the boat [*Titanic*] could not sink.[9]

George W. Chauncey, president of the Mechanics Bank, said, 'I was a passenger on board the *Olympic* on her first eastward voyage, when Captain Smith was in command of her. I met the captain and found him a fine gentleman and a first-class mariner. He inspired everybody on board with confidence.'[10]

Mr J. E. Hodder Williams was another good friend of Captain Smith. 'He was amazingly informed on every phase of present-day affairs,' Mr Williams wrote:

and that was hardly to be wondered at, for scarcely a well-known man or woman who crossed the Atlantic during the last twenty years but had at some time sat at his table. He read widely, but men more than books. He was a good listener, on the whole, although he liked to get in a yarn himself now and again, but he had scant patience with bores or people who 'gushed'. I have seen him quell both ...

He had lived his whole life on the sea and ... used to laugh at us for talking as if we knew anything of its terrors in these days of floating hotels. He had served his apprenticeship in a rough school, and knew the sea and ships in their uncounted moods. He had an infinite respect − I think that is the right word − for the sea.

Absolutely fearless, he had no illusions as to man's power in the face of the infinite. He would never prophesy an hour ahead. If you asked him about times of arrival, it was always 'if all goes well'. I am sure now that he must have had many terrible secrets of narrowly averted tragedies locked away behind those sailor eyes of his.[11]

Mr Hodder Williams continued with a few more reminiscences about his old friend:

Late in the evening the captain's boy would come with an invitation to his [Smith's] room on the bridge, and I learned something of the things hidden away behind an exterior that some thought stern and grim. Those keen eyes of his had pierced far into the ugly side of life as it flaunts itself on the monster liner, but they had never lost their power of pity.

I saw him angry once, and that was when a passenger made a slighting remark about one of the captain's old officers having gone wrong. 'How do you know that's true?' he asked, sharply. 'If you want to, you can always hear enough stories about every officer to ruin his reputation.' And later on I found that Captain Smith knew that the story was all too true, and that he had given up one of his few, so highly prized days between trips to journey to this man's home and try to arrange for him to have a fresh start.

I could tell, too, of the time when he promised to sit by the operating table when a serious operation was to be performed on an old comrade, who felt that he could go through with it only if the captain were there all the time, and how he kept that promise to the letter.[12]

W. W. Sanford of New York City agreed:

He was the kind of man who is at his best in a crisis ... I recall the last time I saw him we talked, principally of politics, in his cabin on the *Olympic*. He was a keen follower of the politics of this country and England, and his ideas were always worth listening to. He was a strong advocate of clean politics.

I cannot imagine Captain Smith taking chances ... His company might do so, but Captain Smith never. He was a shrewd, careful commander.[13]

'There never was a braver or better officer than Captain Smith,' said Irish businessman J. E. Graham, who made five crossings with Smith. 'Although bravest of the brave, he was at all times cautious.'[14]

'I have never known Captain Smith to take an unnecessary risk,' wrote Joseph Francis Taylor:

He was always cool and thoughtful, attending to every detail of navigation and never flinching when he had to undergo hardships in his line of duty. Whenever we were off the Grand Banks of Newfoundland ... he had the ship creep along slowly and he used every device known to ward off danger. The toot of a horn on another ship would cause him to stop his own craft dead and take locations before going on.

I believe that Captain Smith would allow no suggestion [from another person] to cause him to run into danger. In his long and honorable career at sea he met with but one mishap ... the result of circumstances over which he had no control. The former accident I refer to is when the *Olympic* had trouble because of the suction created when she left port. For the benefit of those who have been misled by pictures supposed to be of Captain Smith, I will say this: He was 5 feet 11 inches in height, weighed about 200 pounds, wore a short gray Van Dyke beard and a mustache, and was the picture of vigor and alertness.

He resembled none of the Santa Claus style of pictures I have observed in a certain paper ... He was a man who seemed to live on the bridge of his ship through life.[15]

Captain Anning, former captain of the White Star liner *Persic*, said that Captain Smith was 'a man absolutely devoid of nervousness. He was one of the smartest navigators on the Atlantic. He had had a splendid career, serving at different periods in the Pacific trade between San Francisco, Japan and China before being transferred to the Atlantic.'[16]

'Capt. E. J. Smith, commodore of the White Star fleet, believed he had been hoodooed,' said retired English businessman J. P. Grant, 'and several months ago told me that if he would have another accident with a liner of which he had the command he would resign his ship and retire into private life.'

'Captain Smith was recognized as one of the ablest sea captains of the Atlantic, and White Star officials had the utmost confidence in him,' Mr Grant went on:

> Within the last three years, however, he seemed to be unfortunate in his commands. He was in the *Olympic* when this ship met with three accidents in one year. It was first struck by the British man-of-war *Hawke*, and the White Star line had to spend $500,000 to repair it. It then lost a blade of a screw by running into a submarine wreck and had to put into Belfast for repairs. When the ship left the Belfast harbor it ran aground.
>
> It shows what great confidence his superiors had in him, because he retained his command of the *Olympic* until he was transferred to command the *Titanic* on its maiden voyage. In all these mishaps it was always found that Captain Smith was not to blame, but he came to fear his luck and often spoke about it to me.[17]

★

Captain Smith was a versatile man who had other talents besides seamanship. His friends Mr and Mrs Henry Buckhall were members of Long Island's Nassau Country Club, and it was there they discovered that the good captain played a very respectable game of golf.[18] Mr Buckhall said:

> Captain Smith had nothing of the old salt in appearance ... He was over six feet in height, well proportioned, fair complexion, and had the appearance of a military or naval officer. His manner was quiet and his address pleasing. It was not necessary for him to be severe in his tone on shipboard to command respect. His whole appearance did

that, and as a prominent lady remarked, when introduced to him, 'His countenance inspired confidence.' He was very little in evidence on shipboard, being only where his duty called him. The large circle of friends among ocean travelers that he had was not created by his catering to their society.

He concluded:

Last fall, on Captain Smith's return to New York after the collision with the *Hawke*, about one hundred of his friends gave him a dinner at the Metropolitan Club as an expression of their sympathy and confidence in him … Captain Smith made a very modest speech thanking his friends for their esteem. Besides good wishes, a purse of several thousand dollars was presented to him.[19]

★

But good seamanship, political savvy and good 'golfmanship' were insufficient to protect Captain Smith from every eventuality, as a 1909 American newspaper article made clear:

Captain Smith of the *Adriatic* … and the ship's surgeon, Dr [William] O'Loughlin were invited to Marblehead to spend a few days. As they started ashore yesterday, they went to the customs office on the pier and offered the valises they carried for inspection.

Each officer was carrying a box of cigars, upon which the seals had been broken. In spite of their protests, these cigars were confiscated. In the doctor's valise was a bottle of whisky. This suffered the same fate.[20]

'Having fitted out this magnificent vessel, the *Titanic*, we proceeded to man her with all that was best in the White Star organization,' White Star Line chairman Bruce Ismay said later:

and that, I believe, without boasting, means everything in the way of skill, manhood and *esprit de corps*. Whenever a man had distinguished himself in the service by means of ability and devotion to duty, he was earmarked at once to go to the *Olympic* or *Titanic*, if it were possible to spare him from his existing position, with the result that, from Captain Smith, Chief Engineer Bell, Dr O'Loughlin, Chief Purser McElroy, Chief Steward Latimer, downwards, I can say without fear of contradiction, that a finer set of men never manned a ship, nor could be found in the whole of the Mercantile Marine of the country, and no higher testimony than this can be paid to the worth of any crew.[21]

★

Captain Smith and Dr William O'Loughlin were good friends and had an excellent working relationship, and one day Dr O'Loughlin told his colleague, Dr J. C. H. Beaumont, how he came to be transferred from the *Olympic* to the *Titanic*. Beaumont later wrote:

Dr O'Loughlin, 'Old Billy' as we called him, had been for many years in the service, and I followed him up to the *Olympic*. Whether he had any premonition about the *Titanic* ... I cannot say. But I do know that during a talk with him in the South Western Hotel he did tell me that he was tired at this time of life to be changing from one ship to another. When he mentioned this to Captain Smith the latter chided him for being lazy and told him to pack up and come with him. So fate decreed that 'Billy' should go on the *Titanic* and I to the *Olympic*.[22]

Just before the *Titanic* was delivered from Belfast to Southampton to prepare for her maiden voyage, Harland & Wolff's managing director John Kempster asked Captain Smith if the traditional old-time seaman's courageous fearlessness in the face of death still existed. Smith replied with emphasis, 'If a disaster like that to the *Birkenhead* happened, they would go down as those men went down.'[23]

★

On 2 April the *Titanic*, under the command of Captain Edward J. Smith, completed her sea trials in Belfast.

★

On 3 April the *Titanic*, under the command of Captain Smith, was midway on her delivery voyage from Belfast to Southampton.

*

On 4 April, at 1.15 a.m., the *Titanic* docked after completing her delivery trip from Belfast to Southampton, where preparations would continue for the vessel's 10 April maiden voyage. Later that day, crewmen began signing onto the vessel in preparation for the voyage.

On 6 April 1912 Benjamin Steele, the Marine Superintendent at Southampton Docks, sent Captain Smith a message describing a possible danger to his future navigation of the *Titanic*:

> Please note the following reports: *Rotterdam*, March 27 *Rotterdam* (3) from New York reports March 20 in lat. 40.24 N., long. 64.41 W. passed a piece of mast standing perpendicular, height about 10 feet, apparently belonging to submerged wreckage.[24]

*

On 8 April 1912 a lifeboat drill was held on the *Titanic* at Southampton, and the crew lined up in two rows on the boat deck while volunteers were called for. Someone in the second row pushed Fireman George Beauchamp from behind and, when he stumbled forward, he was thought to be a volunteer and was picked to man one of the boats during the drill.[25]

*

A standard form letter advocating safe and prudent navigation practices was issued by the White Star Line to each of its captains:

> Captain [Edward J. Smith]
> Liverpool
>
> Dear Sir,
> In placing the steamer [*Titanic*] temporarily under your command, we desire to direct your attention to the company's regulations for the safe and efficient navigation of its vessels and also to impress upon you

in the most forcible manner, the paramount and vital importance of exercising the utmost caution in the navigation of the ships and that the safety of the passengers and crew weighs with us above and before all other considerations.

You are to dismiss all idea of competitive passages with other vessels, and to concentrate your attention upon a cautious, prudent and ever watchful system of navigation which shall lose time or suffer any other temporary inconvenience rather than incur the slightest risk which can be avoided.

We request you to make an invariable practice of being yourself on deck and in full charge when the weather is thick or obscure, in all narrow waters and whenever the ship is within sixty miles of land, also that you will give a wide berth to all Headlands, Shoals and other positions involving peril, that where possible you will take cross bearings when approaching any coast, and that you will keep the lead going when approaching the land in thick or doubtful weather, as the only really reliable proof of the safety of the ship's position.

The most rigid discipline on the part of your officers must be observed and you will require them to avoid at all times convivial intercourse with passengers or each other, the crew also must be kept under judicious control and the lookout men carefully selected and zealously watched when on duty, and you are to report to us promptly all instances of inattention, incapacity or irregularity on the part of your officers or any others under your control.

Whilst we have confidence in your sobriety of habit and demeanor, we exhort you to use your best endeavors to imbue your officers and all those about you with a due sense of the advantage which will accrue not only to the Company but to themselves by being strictly temperate, as this quality will weigh with us in an especial degree when giving promotion. The consumption of coals, water, provisions and other stores, together with the prevention of waste in any of the departments, should engage your daily and most careful attention, in order that you may be forewarned of any deficiency that may be impending, that waste may be avoided, and a limitation in quantity determined on, in case you should deem such a step necessary, in the interest of prudence.

Should you at any time have any suggestion to make bearing upon the improvement of the steamers, their arrangement, equipment or any other matter connected with the service on which they are engaged, we shall always be glad to receive and consider same.

In the event of a collision, stranding or other accident of a serious nature happening to one of the Company's steamers, necessitating the holding of an Enquiry by the Managers, written notice of the same will be given to the Commander, who shall immediately on receipt of such notice hand in a letter tendering the resignation of his position in the Company's Services, which letter will be retained pending the result of the Enquiry.

We have alluded, generally, to the subject of safe and watchful navigation, and we desire earnestly to impress on you how deeply these considerations affect not only the well-being, but the very existence of this Company itself, and the injury which it would sustain in the event of any misfortune attending the management of your vessel, first from the blow which would be inflicted to the reputation of the Line, secondly from the pecuniary loss that would accrue, (the Company being their own insurers), and thirdly from the interruption of a regular service upon which the success of the present organization must necessarily depend.

We request your cooperation in achieving those satisfactory results which can only be obtained by unremitting care and prudence at all times, whether in the presence of danger or when by its absence you may be lured into a false sense of security; where there is least apparent peril the greatest danger often exists, a well-founded truism which cannot be too prominently borne in mind.

We are,
Yours truly
[White Star Line][26]

★

A newspaper interview with Glenn Marston (a friend of Captain Smith's) described his interactions with Smith during an earlier voyage of the White Star liner *Olympic*:

Chicago, April 18 – That Captain Edward J. Smith of the *Titanic* knew that the steamer was not properly equipped with lifeboats and other life-saving devices, and that he protested against the lack of precaution, but without success, to the officials of the line, is the statement of Glenn Marston, a friend of the captain who is stopping in Chicago at the Brevoort Hotel.

Mr Marston is connected with the Public Service magazine and just returned from Europe, where he made an investigation of the government-owned utilities.

He has been a friend of Captain Smith for a number of years and on his trip abroad both crossed and returned on the *Olympic*, a companion ship of the *Titanic*, although slightly smaller in tonnage, which was commanded by Captain Smith.

According to Mr Marston, Captain Smith had always insisted that the steamers that he commanded should carry an equipment of boats and rafts sufficient to take care of every passenger and every member of the crew in case of disaster at sea.

He had been successful in his demands until he took command of the *Olympic*, when he was unable to induce the officials of the line to carry more boats than were included in the original plans of the ship.

He was also unable to induce the company officials to equip the *Titanic* with additional lifeboats when he took command of that ship.

'Captain Smith knew that the *Titanic* did not carry enough lifeboats and rafts,' said Mr Marston last night. 'When he went to Belfast, where the *Titanic* was built, just after he was notified that he was to take command he noticed the small number of life-saving devices and was not satisfied, he told me. I got into a discussion with him when I was returning on the *Olympic*, on what I believe was his last trip on that ship before he took command of the *Titanic*.

'I noticed the small number of boats and rafts aboard for the heavy passenger-carrying capacity of the ship and remarked on it to Capt Smith,' said Mr Marston.

'Yes,' he replied, 'If the ship should strike a submerged derelict or iceberg that would cut through into several of the watertight compartments, we have not enough boats or rafts aboard to take care of more than one-third of the passengers.

'The *Titanic*, too, is no better equipped. It ought to carry at least double the number of boats and rafts that it does to afford any real protection to the passengers. Besides there always is danger of some of the boats becoming damaged or swept sway before they can be manned.'[27]

Mr Marston asked Captain Smith why the company took such a chance, and whether it was to save money:

> 'No,' the captain is quoted as replying. 'I don't think it's from motives of economy, as the additional equipment would cost only a trifle when compared to the cost of the ship, but the builders nowadays believe that their boats are practically indestructible as far as sinking goes, because of the watertight bulkheads, and that the only need of life-boats at all is for purposes of rescue from other ships that are not so modernly constructed, or to land passengers in case of the ship going ashore. They hardly regard them as life-saving equipment.
>
> 'Personally, I believe that a ship ought to carry enough boats and rafts to carry every soul aboard it. I have followed the sea now for forty years, and have attributed my success in not having an accident, until we were rammed by the *Hawke* in the Solent at Southampton, and I was exonerated in that case, to never taking a chance.
>
> 'I always take the safe course. While there is only one chance in a thousand that a ship like the *Olympic* or *Titanic* may meet with an accident that would injure it so severely that it would sink before aid would arrive, yet if I had my way, both ships would be equipped with twice the number of lifeboats and rafts. In the old days it was different from today. With the mergers and Trusts in the steamship business, now the captain has little to say regarding equipment. All of that has been taken out of his hands and is taken care of at the main office.'[28]

In another interview, he said:

> 'In the cases of ocean steamers,' Captain Smith continued, 'there is not one of the transatlantic liners that could not carry enough boats and rafts to carry every passenger aboard. Of course, such equipment would take up space, but it would make but little difference in the vessel's tonnage.'[29]

'What wind or weather would you fear, supposing your ship were in danger?' a friend of Captain Smith's asked him at dinner on the night before the *Titanic* sailed.

'I fear no winds or weather,' Smith replied. 'I fear only icebergs.'[30]

★

'Remember, upon the conduct of each depends the fate of all.'
— Alexander the Great.

'Everybody, soon or late, sits down to a banquet of consequences.'
— Robert Louis Stevenson.

2

10–14 APRIL

10 April 1912

At about 7.30 a.m. on the morning of 10 April 1912, Captain Edward J. Smith, wearing a bowler hat and long overcoat, boarded the new White Star liner *Titanic* in Southampton, England.[1] Captain Smith went directly to his cabin to receive the sailing report from Chief Officer Henry Wilde, and at 8 a.m. the Blue Ensign was hoisted at the ship's stern while the crew began to assemble on deck for muster. The ship's articles – the 'sign-on list' – for each department was distributed to the respective department heads.

On this morning Captain Smith was kept busy meeting and assisting the various officials whose approval was required before the vessel could put to sea. Captain Benjamin Steele, the White Star Line's Marine Superintendent, supervised the muster as each man was scrutinised by one of the ship's doctors. Another company representative examined each department's final rosters and handed them to Captain Steele, who took them to Captain Smith for his examination and approval.

While the *Titanic*'s passengers were in the process of boarding the great vessel, the local Board of Trade inspector, Captain Maurice Clarke, was making his final check of the ship. Despite a rigorous inspection that even required the lowering of two of the ship's lifeboats, Clarke's final report never mentioned the existence of a fire that was currently burning in one of the ship's coal bunkers. Even so, Captain Smith was probably assured by Chief Engineer Joseph Bell that the situation was under control, and that any potential damage would be confined to a small portion of the transverse bulkhead without endangering the soundness of the hull.

While signing the final documents, Captain Steele received the formal Captain's Report from Smith, stating: 'I hereby report this ship loaded and ready for sea. The engines and boilers are in good order for the voyage, and all charts and sailing directions up-to-date. Your obedient servant, Edward J. Smith.' There were handshakes all around, after which the two officials left the bridge.[2]

At one point during the morning hours, young Roy Diaper accompanied his father on board the *Titanic* to have a few words with Captain Smith before the vessel left Southampton on her maiden voyage. Diaper remembered:

My ... impression I got then was of a tall man completely bearded and he was wearing a frock coat; he had on a peaked cap ... it had a small brim and small top. I remember my father speaking to him. Captain Smith didn't speak to me, but he bent down and shook me by the hand. There was a tremendous bustle going on, and Captain Smith was surrounded by people.[3]

Marine artist Norman Wilkinson was paying his own visit to the Southampton docks on the morning of 10 April. He wrote later:

On reaching the jetty at the top of Southampton Water I saw the new White Star liner *Titanic*. She was to sail on her maiden voyage that afternoon. I said to my friend, 'What a bit of luck. I know the captain. We will go aboard and look around the ship.'

The quartermaster at the head of the gangway said that Captain Smith was on board and took us along to his cabin. He was nearly 60 years old with 40 years' service in the Line and radiated Edwardian confidence. He gave me a warm welcome but said that he was extremely busy and would hand us over to the Purser, who would show us round. We made a thorough tour of the splendid ship. Over the mantelpiece in the smoking-room was a painting I had done as a commission for Lord Pirrie of Harland & Wolff of Belfast, who had built her. The subject of the picture was Plymouth Harbour.[4]

Captain Smith's wife Eleanor and their daughter Helen also paid a brief visit to the *Titanic* that morning and visited the bridge before going ashore again. The family of Bruce Ismay, president and managing director of the White Star Line, toured the ship as well before bidding farewell to him and returning ashore.[5]

At around 10.30 a.m. representatives of the press were escorted to the *Titanic*'s boat deck, where they encountered Captain Smith standing near the bridge. Two press photographers snapped pictures of Smith on the port boat deck standing alongside the quarters of First Officer William Murdoch and Second Officer Charles Lightoller, and one photographer snapped two additional photos of the *Titanic*'s captain as he stood outside the vessel's navigating bridge.[6]

Fifth Officer Harold Lowe was also participating in the ship's pre-voyage activities and preparations. 'The general boat list passed through my hands in being sent to the captain for approval,' he recalled. 'I glanced at this list casually, and remember from this glance that there were three seamen assigned to some of the boats and four to others.'[7]

As the *Titanic*'s noon sailing time approached, the various officials took their leave of the ship and all gangways except one were pulled ashore. Thomas Andrews, the managing director of Harland & Wolff, remained on board the *Titanic* in order to monitor the ship's performance during the maiden voyage and make any necessary repairs that might be required before the vessel reached New York. Presently Andrews accompanied Bruce Ismay onto the bridge, where both men exchanged brief greetings with Captain Smith and Chief Officer Henry Wilde. Pilot George Bowyer also conferred with the *Titanic*'s master about the draughts, turning circles and manoeuvrability of the great liner.

At twelve noon Captain Smith gave the order to sound the *Titanic*'s whistles and cast off her mooring lines. Five tugs eased the great vessel out into the turning circle and, before casting off, they manoeuvred her bows into a position facing down the River Test. The engine telegraph rang down to the engine room for the ship's screws to be engaged, and as the two huge bronze wing propellers began turning slowly, the *Titanic* eased ahead and gradually began to pick up speed.

While the *Titanic* was in the process of leaving Southampton harbour, she nearly suffered a collision with the liner *New York* when the latter vessel broke her mooring lines and was pulled away from the dock and into the channel towards the passing White Star liner. Quick work by attending tugs averted the collision, and after the danger was past a group of first-class passengers are reported to have discussed the incident with Captain Smith.

'They tell me,' said one of the group, 'that the ship is absolutely unsinkable.'

'Yes,' replied Captain Smith:

that is correct. The whole ship is built of watertight compartments. Should one be smashed, it would fill with water, but this wouldn't affect the rest of the ship. The crowd on board this ship is as safe as if it were on land – safer, for that matter, since on land, especially in your New York, one is apt to be run down with one of those automobiles. I never feel as safe on land as I do on water. You have to deal only with nature on water, and nature is usually kindly and regular in her habits. If you study your charts, you know pretty well just what she is going to do.[8]

★

That afternoon first-class passenger Robert Daniel was on deck with some friends and was taking special note of several well-known people nearby. Daniel 'pointed out some prominent people' whose number included Captain Smith, artist Frank Millet and others.[9]

As for Thomas Andrews, his subsequent days on board the *Titanic* were soon to settle into a regular routine and began at 7 a.m. when Steward Henry Etches knocked at his cabin door (A-36, at the aft end of A deck) carrying some fruit and a cup of tea. Etches knew this light breakfast would be the beginning of a busy day for Andrews, during which he would continue to add to an unending series of notes of 'any improvements that could be made' to the brand-new White Star liner. In looking around the cabin, Etches could see that Andrews 'had charts rolled up by the side of his bed, and he had papers of all descriptions on his table during the day,' and the steward knew that Andrews would spend his entire day 'working all the time' until evening arrived. 'He had a separate cabin, with bathroom attached – the only cabin,' Etches recalled.[10]

Bruce Ismay likewise knew that Thomas Andrews would be kept busy throughout the *Titanic*'s entire maiden voyage.

'He was about the ship all the time, I believe,' Ismay recalled later:

Naturally, in a ship of that size, there were a great many minor defects on board the ship, which he was rectifying. I think there were probably three or four apprentices on board from Messrs. Harland & Wolff's shipbuilding yard, who were there to right any small detail which was wrong … A door might jam, or a pipe might burst, or anything like that, and they were there to make it good at once.[11]

Even so, Thomas Andrews and Bruce Ismay never had any detailed discussions about the *Titanic* while the vessel was at sea. 'The only plan which Mr Andrews submitted to me,' Ismay testified later, 'was a plan where he said he thought the writing room and reading room was unnecessarily large, and he said he saw a way of putting a stateroom in the forward end of it. That was a matter which would have been taken up and thoroughly discussed after we got back to England.'[12]

First-class passenger Antoinette Flegenheim was well aware of the fact that Captain Smith, Bruce Ismay and Thomas Andrews were all on board the *Titanic* during the maiden voyage. 'Not only was the best commander of the fleet at the helm,' she said later:

but the chairman of the line was there, as well as the chief draughts-man of the company that had built this fine ship. And to the latter many went to express their congratulations for having designed such a wonder. Some others, myself included, went to him with less excitement, to suggest adjustments, tweakings. Things that required his attention, really, for as much as *Titanic* closed perfection, it never actually fully reached it. Complaints were not scarce.[13]

But Thomas Andrews didn't wait for complaints and suggestions to be brought to him – he actively sought them out, as Stewardess Violet Jessop remembered:

Perhaps we felt proprietary about this last ship because, in our small way, we were responsible for many changes and improvements ... There were things of seemingly small importance to the disinterested but of tremendous help to us, improvements that would make our life aboard less arduous and make her more of a home than we had hitherto known at sea.

It was quite unusual for members of the catering department to be consulted about changes that would benefit their comforts or ease their toil, So when the designer paid us this thoughtful compliment, we realized it was a great privilege; our esteem for him, already high, knew no bounds.[14]

Indeed, *Titanic*'s victualling staff was so grateful for Thomas Andrews' show of concern for their welfare that they decided to do something about it. Jessop continued:

Rather diffidently, they asked this always approachable man to honour them by a visit to the glory hole, which he did to receive their warm-hearted thanks ... His gentle face lit up with real pleasure, for he alone understood – nobody else had bothered to understand – how deeply these men must feel to show any sentiment at all; he knew only too well their usual uncouth acceptance of most things, good or bad.[15]

'I was proud of him,' Stewardess Mary Sloan said of Thomas Andrews:

He came from home and he made you feel on the ship that all was right. It was good to hear his laugh and have him near you. If anything went wrong it was always to Mr Andrews one went. Even when a fan stuck in a stateroom, one would say, 'Wait for Mr Andrews, he'll soon see to it,' and you would find him settling even the little quarrels that arose between ourselves. Nothing came amiss to him, nothing at all. And he was always the same, a nod and a smile or a hearty word whenever he saw you and no matter what he was at.[16]

During his typical workdays on board the *Titanic*, Thomas Andrews wore a set of blue coveralls whenever he went down into the engineering department, with a second set of coveralls being reserved for his trips to the boiler rooms; one or the other of these two sets of coveralls could often be seen thrown onto Andrews' bed whenever they were not in use. During his own workday, Steward Etches knew he might meet Mr Andrews 'in all parts [of the ship], with workmen, going about. I mentioned several things to him, and he was with workmen having them attended to. The whole of the day he was working from one part of the ship to the other.'[17]

Meanwhile, down in the *Titanic*'s boiler rooms, the stokers sliced and scraped as they shovelled coal into the ship's hungry furnaces. 'My recollection is that between Southampton and Cherbourg we ran at 60 revolutions,' Bruce Ismay recalled later.[18]

Despite the fact that the coal fire burning in one of the *Titanic*'s bunkers was being kept a secret, word of its existence was gradually leaking out and making its way to the passenger decks. 'The first day at sea passengers heard reports that the *Titanic* was afire,' Mrs Thomas Brown reported later. 'The officers denied it, but I was told on good authority that there was a fire in one of the coal bunkers and a special crew of men were kept at work day and night to keep it under control. I believe this to be true.'[19]

After the *Titanic* touched at Cherbourg, France, on the evening of 10 April, Thomas Andrews penned another quick letter to his wife. 'We reached here in nice time and took on board quite a number of passengers,' he wrote. 'The two little tenders looked well, you will remember we built them about a year ago. We expect to arrive at Queenstown about 10.30 a.m. tomorrow. The weather is fine and everything shaping for a good voyage. I have a seat at the Doctor's table.'[20]

That evening Mrs Elisabeth Lines was in the *Titanic*'s first-class dining room when she noticed a nearby man reposing in the 'seat of honor' that she supposed was reserved for the ship's captain. 'He sat at the head table, and I supposed he was Captain Smith,' Mrs Lines testified later. 'I asked my table steward in the dining room if that were not the captain and he said yes, the first evening that we were out.'[21]

This was not the last time that Mrs Lines would see Captain Edward J. Smith during the *Titanic*'s maiden voyage …

11 April 1912

After departing Cherbourg on the evening of 10 April, *Titanic* steamed through the night towards Ireland, and on the morning of 11 April Thomas Andrews wrote another letter to his wife that was later posted at Queenstown. He reported that everything on board the ship was going splendidly and that he was pleased to have received so much kindness from everyone on board.[22]

That morning a general inspection of the *Titanic*'s watertight doors took place, and a drill was conducted in order to make sure they were all operating properly. 'I saw them closed at bulkhead door inspection on the day after we left Southampton,' Steward John Hart testified later. 'The Chief Officer came round with Mr Andrews, the man representing Harland & Wolff's.' It was Hart's duty to close one of the watertight doors on E deck, and it was his understanding that these manual tests were conducted 'in case anything should go wrong with the machinery leading from the bridge in closing those doors'.[23]

It was Bruce Ismay's understanding that the *Titanic*'s engines were making seventy revolutions during her crossing to Ireland,[24] but the vessel's speed that morning was not his only concern. Indeed, Ismay reportedly had a tendency to involve himself in the daily operations of the White Star ships he happened to be travelling on, a tendency that was later recalled by a British army officer who had shared an earlier voyage with the White Star chairman: 'Ismay was continually telling the officers what to do ... Even the stewards were taking his orders about trivial duties. Of course, when he was on the *Titanic*, the captain would have regarded his suggestions as orders.'[25]

Several *Titanic* passengers likewise noticed Ismay's tendency to insert himself into the normal chain of command regarding routine shipboard operations, but in these particular cases his actions were motivated by kindness. 'I remember that Mr Ismay had given Mr [James Clinch] Smith one of the ship's suites deluxe,' Archibald Gracie remembered later.[26]

Emily Ryerson had a similar experience. 'My husband had told me when we came on at Cherbourg that Mr Ismay had been very kind and had offered us an extra stateroom, which we had, and an extra steward who waited on us,' she remembered.[27]

★

The *Titanic* touched at Queenstown at 11.30 a.m. to pick up additional passengers and mail from the two tenders that came alongside her for that purpose, and an enterprising newspaper photographer boarded the great vessel, corralled Captain Smith and Chief Purser Hugh McElroy and asked them to pose for a photograph. The two men dutifully stood outside the starboard side of the officers' quarters while the photographer snapped away,[28] and Henry Evans, the Commodore Pilot at Liverpool, also came aboard and visited Captain Smith briefly while passengers and mail were being brought aboard.[29]

In the meantime, Ismay's penchant for 'getting involved' in the *Titanic*'s routine operations apparently took hold yet again when he invited Chief Engineer Joseph Bell to his cabin for a private conference regarding the possibility of driving the *Titanic* at full speed on 15 or 16 April.

'I wanted to know how much coal we had on board the ship, because the ship left after the coal strike was on, and he told me,' Ismay said later:

> I then spoke to him about the ship and I said it is not possible for the ship to arrive in New York on Tuesday. Therefore, there is no object in pushing her. We will arrive there at 5 o'clock on Wednesday morning, and it will be good landing for the passengers in New York, and we shall also be able to economize our coal ... I said to him then, we may have an opportunity of driving her at full speed on Monday or Tuesday if the weather is entirely suitable.[30]

In the light of Ismay's curious claims, one wonders if he was somehow unaware of the fact that for the past year *Titanic*'s elder sister *Olympic* had been making routine arrivals in New York on Tuesday nights instead of Wednesday mornings. In any case, what Ismay didn't realise while talking with Engineer Bell was that – even without utilising her full complement of twenty-nine boilers – by the night of 14 April the *Titanic* would have needed to *decrease* her speed in order to *avoid* arriving in New York on Tuesday night.[31]

'When we got on the *Titanic*,' second-class passenger Ruth Becker recalled, 'we heard people say we were going to get there in about

4 or 5 days, that Captain Smith was going to make his maiden voyage a record one.'[32]

Several *Titanic* passengers were among the people who disembarked at Queenstown and boarded the tender that would carry them ashore. Among them was Father Frank Browne and – as he looked up from the deck of the tender – he could see Captain Smith peering down from his position on the *Titanic*'s bridge. Browne quickly raised his hand-held camera and snapped the last surviving photograph of the *Titanic*'s master.[33]

After the Queenstown tender pulled away from the *Titanic*'s side on the afternoon of 11 April, the big White Star liner turned her bows westwards and headed towards the United States. At the same time, word was reportedly passed in the *Titanic*'s engine department that it was intended for the vessel to make a speedy passage to New York. 'We had orders to fire her up from the start at Queenstown, where, of course, we started to make the run,' Fireman John Thompson said later:

> We understood we were to beat all records on our maiden trip. I heard that these orders came from the engineering department. Of course, there was no time in a fire room to talk of where orders came from. There was nothing for firemen to do but work.[34]

'When we left Queenstown, we were running at 72 revolutions,' Ismay recalled, 'and I believe that the ship was worked up to 75 revolutions, but I really have no accurate knowledge of that.'[35]

On the evening of 11 April, passengers Edwin and Marion Kenyon went to dinner in the *Titanic*'s first-class dining room to celebrate their wedding anniversary. It was there that they met Captain Edward J. Smith for the very first time. As Marion Kenyon recalled:

> When we came down to dinner the captain's table was the first inside of the dining saloon, and the next was the first mate's, [Charles] Lightoller. Well, our table was bedecked with flowers, and Captain Smith coming in a few moments later, came over and asked, 'Is this a bride and groom?' And we explained to him it was just an anniversary. He congratulated us, and in a short time the steward brought over a huge bottle of wine. Well, none of us drank, but we took a sip anyhow, and we sent the bottle back to his table so that they would have some. Cute too. That

was our introduction to Captain Smith. He seemed always to stop us
and call us the bride and groom. It really was a lovely friendship. He was
a middle-aged man with whiskers and was kind-eyed, was very lovely
and gentlemanly in every manner, I remember that so well.[36]

Marian Thayer had closer contact with Captain Smith during the
maiden voyage:

My husband, my son and I were the only persons at the captain's table
in the Saloon … The captain usually took his meals in the Saloon, but
did not do so for about the first day and a half after sailing. I noticed that
the captain never took any alcoholic liquor of any kind at any meal.[37]

Saloon Steward Fred Ray later gave a more specific description of where
Captain Smith's table was located in the first-class dining saloon: '[It
was] in the centre of the saloon, the sixth table on the forward end of
the saloon; back toward the bow of the ship.'[38]

Whenever evening approached during the course of the maiden
voyage, Thomas Andrews always took a brief break from his daily
duties to prepare himself for dinner. 'I used to see him again when he
dressed at night,' Steward Etches recalled later. 'That would be about
a quarter or 20 minutes to 7, as a rule. He was rather late in dressing.'[39]
In the first-class dining saloon, Andrews usually shared a table with
Mr and Mrs Albert Dick, Dr William O'Loughlin, Dr John Simpson
and Mr and Mrs Frederick Hoyt.[40] (According to Eleanor Cassebeer,
she, Harry Anderson and a Mr and Mrs 'Lord' (Hoyt?) shared the
same table.)[41]

Steward Thomas Whiteley took special note of the individual dining
arrangements of Captain Smith, Thomas Andrews and Bruce Ismay
during the maiden voyage. 'Captain Smith dined as usual at the head of
his own table,' he recalled:

Mr Andrews on his right: on his left a very beautiful woman, who
always wore white furs of great richness, but whose name I did not
know. Mr Ismay during the whole trip sat at one of the small tables
for two persons. Throughout the voyage he was always served by the
head waiter; always he dined alone.[42]

The seating arrangements in the *Titanic*'s first-class dining saloon weren't necessarily chiselled in stone, however. 'Mr Andrews dined with me one night,' Ismay recalled later. 'We had no conversation, really, in regard to the ship.'[43] During the course of one evening, Ismay dined in the restaurant with Captain Smith as well.[44]

Saloon Steward Thomas Whiteley later gave a description of a specific dinner that took place in the first-class dining saloon sometime during the *Titanic*'s maiden voyage:

It was the gayest night of the trip among the diners. We had made great time, and the probability was the trip would be a record-breaker … I believe it was soon after half past six when the passengers strolled in. Mr Ismay sat alone at a table a few feet away from the table of Mr and Mrs Astor, and he was in a corner. The Astor table was to the right and the captain's table was in the center just abutting the Astor table. At the Astor table sat Dr O'Loughlin, the ship's surgeon, and his assistant. There were some other people there, but I don't know who they were.

Soon after the dinner was served, the fun commenced. Wine was served at the Astor table, and the conversation was very animated. The captain talked and joked with Mr Astor, and Mr Ismay spoke [to the room's occupants?]. The one topic of conversation was the new boat, and the speed she was making.

I did not see the captain drink anything, and I don't think he ever indulged. As dinner progressed the gaiety increased, and I believe some bets were made as to the speed of the boat. At one time Dr O'Loughlin stood up, and raising a glass of champagne, cried 'Let us drink to the mighty *Titanic*.' With cries of approval, everybody stood and drank the toast.

I believe it was generally believed by all of those at the tables that the *Titanic* would reach New York late Tuesday or early Wednesday morning, and the captain and other officers were planning a big banquet after the landing in anticipation of the trip being a record-breaker.

The dinner broke up shortly before nine o'clock and the men retired to the smoking room, while some of the women went to their staterooms, and others strolled along the promenade. We cleared the dining room about ten o'clock, and soon after I went to bed.[45]

★

Unfortunately, relaxing at the dinner table during his evening meals did not bring an end to Thomas Andrews' own workday. 'He was very late in going to bed,' Henry Etches observed. 'I never saw him in the smoke room or in any other of these rooms. I happened to meet him at different parts of deck E more often than anywhere else.'[46]

Even so, it was easy for passengers and crewmen to tell that Thomas Andrews was a family man. 'I was talking to him on the Friday night [12 April] previous as he was going into dinner,' Stewardess Mary Sloan recalled. 'The dear old doctor [William O'Loughlin] was waiting for him on the stair landing, and calling him by his Christian name Tommy. Mr Andrews seemed loth to go, he wanted to talk about home, he was telling me his father was ill and Mrs A. was not so well.'[47]

Miss Sloan congratulated Mr Andrews on the beauty and perfection of the *Titanic*, but Andrews gave an unexpected reply.

'There's one thing I don't like about her,' he said.

'And what might that be?' asked Dr O'Loughlin.

'Just,' said Mr Andrews, 'that the further she's taking us to our journey's end the further she's taking us from home.'[48]

'I looked at him,' Miss Sloan remembered, 'and his face struck me at the time as having a very sad expression.'[49]

Thomas Andrews definitely had strong feelings about the way the *Titanic* was steaming further away from Ireland with each passing day. Violet Jessop wrote in later years:

Often during our rounds we came upon our beloved designer going about unobtrusively with a tired face but a satisfied air … He never failed to stop for a cheerful word, his only regret that we were 'getting further from home.' We all knew the love he had for that Irish home of his and suspected that he longed to get back to the peace of its atmosphere for a much-needed rest and to forget ship designing for a while.[50]

In later years, passenger Albert Dick told how he and his wife struck up a shipboard friendship with Thomas Andrews. 'He showed us all over the ship,' Dick remembered, 'explaining the fine points of her design and her various safety devices. I remember him showing us the watertight doors and saying, "See, you're safe on this ship." I believed him.'[51]

Albert Dick's wife Vera later told a reporter how she and her husband dined with Thomas Andrews on board the ship; the reporter wrote that Andrews:

> spoke of the *Titanic*'s great potential as he had on previous occasions when he had taken the Dicks on tour and shown them her safety devices and sixteen watertight compartments. He had concurred with many others that the world's largest and most luxurious ship was unsinkable.[52]

At one point during the maiden voyage, Albert Dick and Thomas Andrews found themselves discussing the topic of shipbuilding in the first-class smoking room. When the conversation turned specifically to the *Titanic*, Mr Andrews told Dick that: 'I believe her to be as nearly perfect as human brains can make her.'[53]

According to Eleanor Cassebeer, Thomas Andrews sat next to her in the *Titanic*'s first-class dining saloon and said something to her that was completely unexpected. 'Another thing that is not generally known,' Mrs Cassebeer recalled:

> is that the *Titanic* was not ready to sail at the time she did. Mr Andrews told me so himself and said that the only reason they allowed her to go when she did was that the sailing date had already been fixed and they just simply had to start. While the ship was fitted up most sumptuously, one could not help but notice that she was not prepared to sail.[54]

According to Mrs Cassebeer, Andrews also told her that, even if the *Titanic* should be cut into three parts, she would still float.[55]

Mrs Jacques Futrelle had a similar experience in talking with Thomas Andrews. 'No one had the slightest fear, however,' Mrs Futrelle recalled, 'for Mr Andrews, who had some part in the construction of the vessel, (he called it his baby) had laughingly assured us that at last man had constructed an unsinkable craft.'[56]

During the early days of the maiden voyage, first-class passenger Henry Frauenthal noticed that Captain Smith and his officers likewise exhibited supreme confidence in the safety of their brand-new vessel. He noted:

> The notion that the *Titanic* was unsinkable had taken hold everywhere ... The crowd contained many women and men of delightful personality. The days and evenings were charmingly spent. Captain Smith and his officers seemed to be at pains to make everybody comfortable and gay. If anybody ventured an opinion that we might sink, that person would have been hooted down.[57]

For his own part, first-class passenger Hugh Woolner had not yet seen the *Titanic*'s master with his own eyes. 'I asked somebody to point him out to me,' he said later. 'Naturally, one is interested to know the appearance of the captain, and I knew him by sight ... I saw him at breakfast and, I think, at dinner one evening in the saloon, but I am not quite definite about dinner; I think so.'[58]

Bruce Ismay apparently didn't strive to be noticed by his fellow passengers, but several people have provided us with brief glimpses of the man during the early part of the maiden voyage. 'I did not know Mr Ismay by sight,' the Countess of Rothes said later, 'until one night at dinner in the restaurant he came in late, and someone pointed him out to me as being the managing director of the line.'[59]

'There were a great many prominent people on the passenger list,' Jack Thayer remembered:

> and because it was her maiden voyage there were on board many of those responsible for the building of the ship and the management of the steamship line. Some of these were: Thomas Andrews, one of the ship's designers; Archie Frost, the builders' Chief Engineer, including his approximately twenty assistants; J. Bruce Ismay, President of the International Mercantile Marine Company and Chairman of the Board and Managing Director of the Oceanic Steam Navigation Company, Limited, owners of the White Star Line; all observing the performance of the ship, and all of whom were often with my Father and myself, during the few days we were aboard the ship.[60]

'I do not think I saw Mr Ismay but one evening, I think, while the band was playing after dinner,' Charles Stengel said later.[61]

On the other hand, Colonel John Jacob Astor actively sought out Ismay and Captain Smith during the early days of the maiden voyage. '[The Colonel] was interested in the maiden performance of the new *Titanic*, for anything mechanical interested him,' Madeleine Astor's sister said later, 'and he frequently consulted the log and heard from Captain Smith and Mr Ismay of how the great ship was behaving.'[62]

While conducting his routine rounds of the ship, Captain Smith occasionally found himself interacting with some of his passengers. 'My father showed me the gymnasium,' young Washington Dodge remembered, 'and I sat on a mechanical exercise bicycle but my feet did not reach the pedals. At the foot of a wide staircase, he introduced me to a friendly bearded man who was Captain Smith.'[63]

Occasionally the *Titanic*'s master could also be seen walking the decks in the company of various passengers. 'During the voyage father, mother and I walked round the promenade deck on many occasions and sometimes with Captain Smith himself,' second-class passenger Edith Brown remembered. 'He was such a nice man, and my father got along with him fine.'[64]

Little Eva Hart also encountered Captain Smith while she and her father were strolling on the *Titanic*'s second-class promenade deck:

He was on deck when my father and I were on deck (I imagine he went all over the ship), and he was very nice; he had a beard like my own grandfather, and he admired a doll I had. I had this beautifully-dressed doll, and I had a big teddy bear, too, which a lot of the children used to play with, and he admired my doll. I remember talking with him and my father telling me he was the captain.[65]

'He seemed very large to me,' Eva went on:

I don't know if he was, but he was very upright and he had a beard, and he looked different from all the other sailors (in my eyes), which he was, and he was very nice. I met him perhaps three or four times. My father spoke to him several times, and a couple of times I was with my father, and he [Smith] took us somewhere, and I'm quite sure it

wasn't the bridge, but he took us somewhere which was where passengers didn't normally go, and I of course wasn't at all interested at
seven years of age, but he was very nice ... He was very nice to me.[66]

Twelve-year-old Robertha Watt was another young second-class
passenger who encountered Captain Smith on the *Titanic*'s upper decks.
'I saw him', she remembered, 'but we were just little kids, and we didn't
get to see him that much.'[67]

12 April 1912

It was at about 1.30 on the afternoon of 12 April that Elisabeth Lines
noticed Captain Smith and Bruce Ismay seated together enjoying each
other's company. 'I passed through the lounge after luncheon to my
state room and the Captain and Mr Ismay were sitting there,' she testified later:

> I saw the gentlemen sitting there with their liqueurs, I saw the steward
> bring them as he came and asked me if I would have any. It was the
> steward to serve all those things, you know that is a customary thing
> on a steamship; it was no special order ... Captain Smith was in uni-
> form ... I heard them discussing ships ... I passed through the lounge
> again to go to the elevator and go up on deck from my stateroom, they
> were there. I went two or three times all the way round the deck and
> came down to my state room, they were still there. I remained in my
> state room reading for perhaps half an hour or three quarters of an
> hour and went out into the lounge to get a cup of tea, and the Captain
> and Mr Ismay were just leaving it.[68]

At one point during the maiden voyage, May Futrelle found herself
conversing with Captain Smith on a subject that, in retrospect, struck
her as being very significant. 'The *Titanic* did not have a searchlight,'
she wrote later:

> I remember asking the captain the reason for this one day, and he said
> the darkness which followed a flash was very confusing and that it

had been found impracticable to carry a search light. It seems to me, however, that a searchlight would have shown up the iceberg.[69]

★

At 5.46 p.m. on 12 April the *Titanic* had received a wireless message from *La Touraine*:

From *Touraine* to Captain *Titanic*. My position, 7 p.m., GMT, lat. 49.28, long. 26.28 W. Dense fog since this night. Crossed thick ice-field lat. 44.58, long. 50.40' 'Paris'; saw another ice-field and two icebergs lat. 45.20, long. 45.09 'Paris'; saw a derelict 40.56 long. 68.38, 'Paris.' Please give me your position. Best regards and bon voyage. Caussin.[70]

At 6.21 p.m. the following reply from Captain Smith was transmitted to *La Touraine*:

To Capt., *La Touraine*, Thanks for your message and information. My position 7 p.m. G.M.T. lat. 49.5, long. 23.38 W Greenwich. Had fine weather. Compliments, Smith[71]

It was Fourth Officer Boxhall who had worked out *Titanic*'s position for Captain Smith and showed him *La Touraine*'s position. 'I remarked to Capt Smith, that those positions were of no use to us, because they were absolutely north of our track,' Boxhall recalled:

I plotted all these positions out … and I said, 'They are out of our way' … The captain saw me, and he was there alongside of me where I was putting the positions down, or shortly after I put them down, anyhow, he read the telegram and looked at it, and these positions satisfied him.[72]

Still, there was a bit of uncertainty among the officers about the meaning of the reference to 'Paris' in *La Touraine*'s ice warning. They finally decided the French vessel's wireless operator was referring to Paris' longitude and that he was keeping French time instead of Greenwich Mean Time. 'We had some discussion on board the ship – the captain,

Mr Wilde, and myself,' Fourth Officer Boxhall remembered. 'I forget the difference in longitude between Paris and the British meridian, but we allowed for that.'[73] The officers knew that the longitude of Paris was important in determining the exact time and location in which *La Touraine* had sighted ice.

'All the ice I remember plotting out was to the northward of the track,' Fourth Officer Boxhall explained later:

If it had been on the track or to the southward I should have seen fit then to call the Captain's special attention to it at the time I put it on [the chart]. But I just merely remarked to him that I had put down the ice we had had reported; whenever I did put it on the chart, I remarked to him that I had done so. But if it had been so close to the track as that I should have thought it an immediate danger to the ship. I should have pointed it out specially to him, and I never had reason to do that.[74]

★

Captain Smith was in possession of several additional wireless messages whose ice positions needed to be recorded on the *Titanic*'s charts. 'The captain gave me some wireless messages from Southampton, I think, that we had had before we had sailed, and asked me to put these positions on the chart,' Boxhall testified later.[75]

On the evening of 12 April, Captain Smith had his evening meal in company with Bruce Ismay. 'I think he dined with me on Friday night,' Ismay recalled. 'He left us immediately after dinner. I went into my own room with the people who were dining with me, and we sat in my room and played bridge. But I never saw the captain after we left the restaurant. He never came near my room.'[76]

13 April 1912

Third Officer Herbert Pitman performed his usual bridge duties throughout the *Titanic*'s maiden voyage, and during his regular afternoon watch on Saturday, 13 April he noted that Captain Smith made repeated appearances on the bridge. 'He used to pay periodical visits to the bridge,' Pitman recalled. 'He may have been up there a half a dozen times in a [two-hour] watch.' During his visits Captain Smith never made any mention to Pitman of the presence of ice located on the steamer track.[77]

Meanwhile, Fireman John Thompson and his mates were hard at work deep in the belly of the *Titanic*. 'I was in the engine room on Saturday afternoon,' Thompson remembered, 'and I saw Second Engineer Ferguson [Farquharson] chalk up on the blackboard the number of [engine] revolutions. He made it seventy-seven, and that would be about twenty-two knots.'[78]

At about 1.30 that afternoon, Elisabeth Lines was having coffee in the *Titanic*'s lounge when she saw Captain Smith and Bruce Ismay enter the room and seat themselves at the same corner table where she'd seen them the previous day. Smith and Ismay spent the next two hours in the lounge within earshot of Mrs Lines, and eventually the two men began comparing *Titanic*'s daily runs with those that had been achieved by the *Olympic* on her own maiden voyage.

'At first I did not pay any attention to what they were saying,' Mrs Lines testified later:

> They were simply talking and I was occupied, and then my attention was arrested by hearing the day's run discussed, which I already knew had been a very good one in the preceding twenty-four hours, and I heard Mr Ismay – it was Mr Ismay who did the talking – I heard him give the length of the run, and I heard him say 'Well, we did better today than we did yesterday, we made a better run today than we did yesterday, we will make a better run tomorrow. Things are working smoothly, the machinery is bearing the test, the boilers are working well.' They went on discussing it, and then I heard him make the statement: 'We will beat the *Olympic* and get in to New York on Tuesday.'

Mrs Lines made special note of Ismay's manner and tone of speech during his conversation with Captain Smith:

> It was very positive, one might almost say dictatorial ... He asked no questions ... Mr Ismay did the talking, I did not hear Captain Smith's

voice. I saw him nod his head a few times ... [Ismay] asked no questions. He made assertions, he made statements. I did not hear him defer to Captain Smith at all.

Finally, Ismay finished talking to Captain Smith and the two men stood up. 'Come on, Captain, we will get somebody and go down to the squash courts,' Ismay said as the two men left the reception room.[79]

'I know that the ship was going faster every day,' Charles Stengel said later, 'as my stateroom was near the engines and I noticed that the vibration was getting quicker and that the boilers were working free.'[80]

It was at 2 p.m. on 13 April that the *Titanic*'s firemen finally succeeded in emptying coal bunkers 9 and 10[81] on the starboard side of boiler room 5 and extinguishing the coal fire that had been burning there since before the vessel left Belfast. The heat from the fire had slightly warped a small section of one of the bunker's transverse metal bulkheads, and it seems probable that Thomas Andrews was one of the men who later examined the damaged bulkhead.

'The chief engineer, Mr Bell, gave me orders: "Builder's men wanted to inspect that bulkhead,"' Leading Fireman Fred Barrett testified later.[82]

The day wore on, and *Titanic* continued to speed onward towards New York.

'Now a very curious thing happened on the Saturday night,' second-class passenger Esther Hart later wrote:

We had made splendid progress, and although I was still far from easy in my mind, I was as content as I could be off the land. I heard someone remark with glee that we were making a bee line for New York. I knew we were going at a tremendous speed, and it was the general talk – I cannot say what truth there was in it – that the Captain and officers were 'on' something good if we broke the record.[83]

14 April 1912

At 9.12 a.m. on Sunday 14 April, *Titanic* received a message from the *Caronia*:

Captain, *Titanic:* West-bound steamers report bergs, growlers and field ice in 42N from 49 to 51 W April 12. Compliments Barr[84]

This message was shown to Captain Smith, whose reply to the *Caronia* was transmitted at 10.28 a.m.:

Captain *Caronia* Thanks for message and information. Have had variable weather throughout. Smith[85]

As it was the Sabbath, Captain Smith conducted religious services at 10.30 a.m. in the first-class dining saloon for the spiritual benefit of the *Titanic*'s first-class passengers. Eleanor Cassebeer remembered:

On Sunday morning we assisted at a religious ceremony in the restaurant, which was presided over by our dear captain, a tall man, very polite, who sported a white beard. It was easy to say, by giving him a single look, that his life had been entirely devoted to the sea.[86]

After attending a church service in second class that was conducted by Purser Hugh McElroy, Madeleine Mellinger and her mother headed down towards their cabin to get ready for lunch. 'We'd gone right down on this [E] deck, and all of a sudden some [watertight?] doors opened!' Madeleine remembered later:

I didn't even know they were doors; they opened and these gentlemen came through – everyone was a gentleman to me – they came through with all their gold braid and Sunday clothes and I said to mother, 'Who are those people?' And she said, 'They must be officers,' and then somebody said, 'That's the Captain!'[87]

To passengers in second class, the presence of the *Titanic*'s captain was completely unexpected. 'I saw Captain Smith and his officers coming towards us in full regalia, lots of gold braid,' Madeleine recalled in later years:

and I knew him as he looked so much like Edward VII [with his?] beard small. I asked what they were doing & was told they were inspecting the Airtight Compartments & doors. That was his last inspection, eh? and those doors where he was that a.m. were only about forty feet from our cabin.[88]

It was undoubtedly during this same inspection tour that Captain Smith surprised the *Titanic*'s steerage passengers when he suddenly walked into the ship's third-class areas. 'I saw Captain Smith only once during the voyage and that was the day before the accident,' Gunnar Tenglin recalled. 'He came into the third cabin quarters and told some of the crew who had been loafing there to keep out, and threatened to impose a fine of $5 on each member of crew who was found among the passengers.'[89]

Even though he was usually good-natured, Captain Smith was definitely capable of putting his foot down if he thought circumstances warranted it. While travelling on the *Olympic* with Captain Smith the previous year, Matt Flynn (the new comptroller of Kansas City) had observed this fact with his own eyes. 'I met Captain Smith, and he impressed me as being a strict disciplinarian,' Flynn said later:

He was of the impressive, fine-looking type of a captain that appeals so strongly to passengers. As an example of his strict discipline, I saw him lecture severely, before other officers of the crew, a steward of the second cabin who had overlooked some small detail of the daily inspection of the boat.[90]

Eventually Captain Smith returned to the upper decks after completing his inspection tour. 'Late Sunday morning, as I was sitting on deck, Captain Edward Smith was talking nearby to a few passengers when a steward came out and handed him a message,' Helen Ostby remembered in later years. 'Captain Smith looked at it, but then continued talking for a while with the passengers. I have always felt this might have been one of the several messages received that day warning of ice ahead.'[91]

The *Titanic*'s daily run from 13 to 14 April was recorded at noon, and everyone was pleased with the new vessel's performance.

'During the 24 hours ending the 14th the ship's run was 546 miles,' Archibald Gracie remembered, 'and we were told that the next 24 hours would see even a better record posted. No diminution of speed was indicated in the run, and the engines kept up their steady running.'[92]

Shortly before the noontime end of her daily run, however, at 11.47 a.m. the *Titanic* received a wireless message from the *Noordam* via the *Caronia*:

Captain SS *Titanic:* Congratulations on new command. Had moderate westerly winds, fair weather, no fog. Much ice reported in lat. 42.24 to 42.45 N and long. 49.50 to 50.20 W. Compliments Krol[93]

At 12.31 p.m. Captain Smith's reply was sent to the *Noordam*:

Captain, *Noordam* Many thanks had moderate variable weather throughout. compts. Smith[94]

In the meantime, Second Officer Lightoller had arrived on the bridge at 12.30 p.m. to relieve First Officer William Murdoch for lunch. Fifteen minutes later Captain Smith made an appearance carrying the *Caronia*'s 11.47 a.m. ice message. 'Captain Smith came on the bridge during the time that I was relieving Mr Murdoch,' Lightoller remembered. 'In his hands he had a wireless message, a Marconigram. He came across the bridge, and holding it in his hands told me to read it … I particularly made a mental note of the meridians – 49 to 51.'

This was the first news Lightoller had received that *Titanic* was heading towards an icefield. 'I knew that we should not be in the vicinity of the ice before I came on deck again [at 6 p.m.],' the second officer said later. 'I roughly ran that off in my mind.'[95] Lightoller relayed that information to First Officer Murdoch when the latter returned from lunch, and Murdoch replied, 'All right.'[96]

In the meantime, Thomas Andrews and Bruce Ismay spent at least part of their Sunday socialising with some of their fellow first-class passengers.

'Sunday, April 14th, dawned bright and clear,' Jack Thayer recalled:

It looked as if we were in for another very pleasant day. I spent most of that day walking the decks with my mother and father. We had short chats with many of the other promenaders, among whom I particularly remember J. Bruce Ismay, Thomas Andrews and Charles M. Hays, who was President of the Grand Trunk Railway of Canada; with all of whom we spent quite a lot of time.[97]

At 1.49 p.m. *Titanic* received an ice message from the *Amerika* reporting 'two large icebergs' in 41.27N, 50.8W, a position that was south of *Titanic*'s own latitude.[98] (Of course, this meant that northern ice had now drifted southwards right across the *Titanic*'s own track.) Junior wireless operator Harold Bride remained unaware of the existence of this message, however, and it's uncertain when (or if) the ice warning was ever delivered to the bridge.[99] Captain Smith appears to have relied on Fourth Officer Boxhall to monitor pertinent data from all wired ice warnings and record that data onto the charts located in the *Titanic*'s two chart rooms.

'The captain generally gave the messages to me to put in the positions he had to put on the charts,' Boxhall remembered later. 'He seemed to give them to me when I was on deck.'[100]

It was at 1.54 p.m. that *Titanic* received a message from the *Baltic* stating that the Greek steamer *Athenai* had reported the presence of ice in lat. 41.51N, long. 49.52W.[101] At 2.57 p.m. the following reply from Captain Smith was sent to the *Baltic*:

Commander *Baltic*
Thanks for your message and good wishes. Had fine weather since leaving.
Smith[102]

Shortly afterwards, Captain Smith was walking along (probably) the A deck promenade when he found himself approaching Bruce Ismay; in passing, Smith silently handed Ismay the ice warning from the *Baltic* that had been received shortly before. Ismay glanced at the Marconigram's message, stuffed it in his pocket and then went down to lunch,[103] but he seems to have shown the *Baltic* ice warning to Mr and Mrs John Thayer and their son Jack later that same afternoon. 'I remember Mr Ismay showing us a wire regarding the presence of ice and remarking that we would not reach that position until around 9 p.m.,' Jack Thayer wrote in later years.[104] (It seems likely that Ismay learned this 9 p.m. time determination from Captain Smith, since it's doubtful he calculated it himself.)

Ismay may have mentioned the *Baltic* ice warning to Mrs Jacques Futrelle that same afternoon, because she still recalled the Marconigram's importance twenty years later: 'Bruce Ismay, the president of the line, was on the ship, and he said that Captain Smith showed him a radiogram seven hours before the crash warning him that he would strike an ice field at about 11.30.'[105]

Meanwhile, down in the *Titanic*'s boiler rooms, the stokers continued to fire the ship's active boilers at a breakneck pace in order to keep the engine revolutions at their maximum. 'We were running at seventy-four,' Fireman John Thompson remembered, 'and all Sunday we never dropped below seventy-seven revolutions. I wasn't in the fire room when she struck [the iceberg], but I was there before and we were hitting it up, and so surely she must have been making that speed when we struck.'[106]

Rumours of icebergs located somewhere ahead of the ship were circulating among the *Titanic*'s passengers on 14 April, and Daisy Minahan had something to say about Captain Smith's reaction. 'There is one thing I want to say about the way the *Titanic* was speeding,' Miss Minahan said later:

> We had been cautioned that the icebergs were drifting in the waters, and someone asked the captain if he meant to slow down. He said no; that if anything, the boat would be given more speed. A bulletin was posted just a short while before the accident saying that the boat was then making the fastest time of the whole trip and that if we kept up the speed we would land in New York ahead of record time.[107]

Imanita Shelley heard the same thing about Captain Smith's preferred method of avoiding the ice danger:

> In the early evening of the accident it had been getting colder and colder, so that all knew we must be getting close to the ice belt. It was reported that wireless messages had been received warning of the proximity of the great bergs. Several of the first-cabin passengers, whom I met afterward on board the *Carpathia*, told me of having gone to the captain and asked him whether he was not going to slow up while running through the ice belt, and he had replied in every case that he intended to put on more speed and get through.[108]

During that same afternoon Lillian Bentham heard Captain Smith discussing the ship's speed with one of her fellow second-class passengers: 'From Saturday noon until Sunday noon the ship had made 546 miles. Before the accident I heard him say to one of the men: "We are going to make it 550 today."'[109]

At one point during the afternoon Martha Stephenson had occasion to look at the *Titanic*'s bulletin board, upon which notices of interest were posted for the benefit of her passengers. 'Then [I] read the chart and noticed we had made a run of five hundred and forty-seven miles,' she wrote later. 'After lunch we spoke to Penrose, our room steward, about the run and he said it was nothing to what we would do on Monday, when they expected to do five hundred and eighty.'[110]

Helen Candee heard a similar approximate figure for the *Titanic*'s expected mileage during the next twenty-four hours. 'Yes, we were trying to make 570 miles that day,' she recalled, 'and we were steaming at top speed.'[111]

Captain Smith's avowed intention to increase *Titanic*'s speed seems to have had a separate motivation besides the mere bettering of the *Olympic*'s maiden voyage crossing time. Indeed, Smith had already clarified his reasoning on the subject to his friend Henry Martyn Hart during an earlier voyage on another White Star liner. 'I sailed home in the *Britannic*, with Captain Edward Smith, with whom I became very friendly,' Hart wrote in his autobiography:

> One day, standing on the bridge, we were in the neighborhood of ice, and I asked him what his custom was in such water. He said, 'I go as fast as I can, for by so doing I shorten the time of danger, and if we are so unfortunate as to strike a berg, it would only be a matter of three minutes' difference in going down, between low speed and high speed.' He had evidently held to his custom when he captained the *Titanic*.[112]

An uncertain report that surfaced later alleged that on Sunday afternoon first-class passenger George Widener engaged in conversation with Bruce Ismay in one of the *Titanic*'s public rooms. Widener had heard about the existence of several Marconi messages warning of a large icefield that lay directly ahead of the *Titanic*, and he reportedly remarked to Ismay that it was getting colder outside and asked if this wasn't a sign the vessel was getting close to the icefield. Mr Widener expressed his own opinion that it might be a wise precaution for the *Titanic*'s officers to decrease the vessel's speed until she was clear of the danger zone.

'Oh, there is no danger,' Ismay insisted as he casually dismissed Widener's topic of conversation. 'Well,' Widener replied, 'if there is an ice pack in the course of this vessel we should slow down. I for one don't wish to be a passenger on a vessel to hit an iceberg.'

George Widener is said to have told his wife about his conversation with Ismay later that same afternoon, but Ismay's final response to Widener's misgivings is not on record.[113]

It was also on Sunday, 14 April that John B. Thayer and his son Jack found themselves in Ismay's company. During the course of their conversation the question of the *Titanic*'s speed and arrival time in New York came up, and Ismay informed the Thayers that the ship's speed was scheduled to be increased very soon. 'Two more boilers are to be opened up today,' he told his two friends.[114]

Later that day Ismay said much the same thing to Mrs Arthur Ryerson as he pulled out the ice warning from the *Baltic* that Captain Smith had handed to him earlier. 'We are in among the icebergs. We are not going very fast, 20 or 21 knots, but we are going to start up some extra boilers this evening.'[115]

Emily Ryerson later repeated Ismay's conversation to Major Arthur Peuchen and to Mrs Walter Douglas, the latter of whom took special care to recall Mrs Ryerson's exact words:

'Sunday afternoon Mr Ismay, whom I know very slightly, passed me on the deck,' Mrs Ryerson said. 'He showed me, in his brusque manner, a Marconigram, saying, "We have just had news that we are in the icebergs." "Of course, you will slow down," I said. "Oh, no," he replied, "we will put on more boilers and get out of it."'[116]

Mrs Ryerson also made an observation about the way Ismay presented himself during the conversation. 'Mr Ismay's manner was that of one in authority & the owner of the ship & that what he said was law,' she wrote later.[117]

'During the 24 hours ending the 14th the ship's run was 546 miles,' Colonel Archibald Gracie recalled, 'and we were told that the next 24 hours would see even a better record posted. No diminution of speed was indicated in the run, and the engines kept up their steady running.'[118] Later, Colonel Gracie wrote that: 'The captain had each day improved upon the previous day's speed, and prophesied that, with continued fair weather, we should make an early arrival for this maiden trip.'[119]

Other passengers agreed with Colonel Gracie's recollection. 'The general impression prevailing aboard the vessel,' Mrs Frank Warren recalled, 'was that the speed in the fourth day would be better than that shown on any preceding day and that we would arrive in New York sometime Tuesday afternoon.'[120]

'On Sunday we had a delightful day,' Mrs Walter Douglas remembered. 'Everyone in the best of spirits; the time the boat was making was considered very good, and all were interested in getting into New York early.'[121]

'It is useless to deny that the *Titanic* was out to break the trans-Atlantic record,' Dorothy Gibson said later. 'Everybody knew it; it was the talk of the voyage.'[122]

★

At one point during the afternoon of 14 April, several passengers noticed Captain Smith walking the decks in company with Bruce Ismay. 'Have you noticed those two men laughing as they walk the deck?' Hugh Woolner asked fellow passenger Helen Candee one day. 'They are our captain, and the head of the line. Admiral of the White Star Fleet and the head of the line, Bruce Ismay.'

'[Edward] Kent would say they should not look so happy on a voyage across the North Atlantic,' Mrs Candee replied, regarding the likely opinion of a fellow first-class passenger.

'With weather like this?' Woolner replied:

Those two men – look at them; they are standing at the rail looking at the ship scoot through the water. Now they seem to congratulate each other. And well they may. Did you see the run the ship made yesterday? This ship is not only the biggest afloat but she is developing a speed that will show her to be the fastest.[123]

'The captain and the head of the line promenaded together like chums in a winning team, sure and elated,' Mrs Candee noted. 'They were discovering that their ship was not only the biggest, the most luxurious ever built, but, by heavens, she was the fastest. So they put her to it. The engines were tickled, and speed increased.'[124]

In regard to the *Titanic*'s best speed as compared to that of the *Olympic*, Ismay later testified that: 'I should call the *Olympic* a good 22-knot ship. She can do better under very favourable circumstances; I think she can work up to 22½ or perhaps 22¾ as a maximum.' As for the *Titanic* herself, Ismay said that: 'We were hoping that she would do a little bit better than that.' (When asked if he meant *Titanic* might be a quarter of a knot faster than the *Olympic*, Ismay replied, 'Yes, something like that, a little bit better, so we were told by our shipbuilders.')[125]

'The work [in the boiler rooms] was so terrific that a number [of us] had decided not to return on the *Titanic* had she reached New York,' Fireman John Thompson declared later:

> It is customary on the big liners to give little breathing spells to the men, but there were no such spells on the *Titanic*. We never had chance to let up a minute when on duty, for Mr Ferguson [Farquharson] was always at our heels telling us to work harder and faster.[126]

Up on the *Titanic*'s open decks, however, it was beginning to turn chilly, and Mrs Candee, Hugh Woolner and their friends rose from their deck chairs on the promenade deck. 'We all scattered indoors to seek warmth, and again met Captain Smith and Mr Ismay,' Mrs Candee remembered. 'And they both showed the same gratulatory smiles cutting through happy looks. It came time for my bridge game and I left the group, cozily indoors.'[127]

Late on the afternoon of 14 April, Cosmo and Lucy Duff Gordon and Laura Francatelli were walking on the outer deck when they noticed that the temperature was becoming noticeably colder as the day wore on. 'I have never felt so cold,' Lady Duff Gordon said to her husband as she shivered in her furs. 'Surely there must be icebergs around.'

Cosmo Duff Gordon poked fun at his wife's comment, and an approaching ship's officer sought to reassure her as well. 'Captain Smith, who happened to be passing, assured us that we were far from the ice zone,' Lucy Duff Gordon remembered. 'Miss Francatelli, my secretary, and I went into my cabin to get warm, but it was no use. When we three went down to dinner, we kept on our thick clothes.'[128]

'When Sunday evening came,' Archibald Gracie recalled:

we all noticed the increasing cold, which gave plain warning that the ship was in closer proximity to icebergs or icefields. The officers, I am credibly informed, had been advised by wireless from other ships of the presence of the icebergs and dangerous floes in that vicinity. The sea was as smooth as glass, and the weather clear. It seems that there was no occasion for fear.[129]

At six o'clock that evening Second Officer Lightoller arrived on the bridge to relieve Chief Officer Wilde. Presently, after remembering the ice message that Captain Smith had shown to him at 12.45 p.m., Lightoller turned to one of his subordinate officers. 'I directed the Sixth Officer to let me know at what time we should reach the vicinity of the ice,' Lightoller said later. 'The junior officer reported to me, "About 11 o'clock".'

'As a matter of fact,' Lightoller said later:

I have come to the conclusion that Mr Moody did not take the same Marconigram which Captain Smith had shown me on the bridge because on running it up just mentally, I came to the conclusion that we should be to the ice before 11 o'clock, by the Marconigram that I saw ... I roughly figured out about half-past nine.

Moody was busy making other calculations by the time Lightoller came to this realisation, though, so the senior officer decided not to interrupt Moody by voicing his own opinion. Lightoller likewise decided not to offer his observation to Captain Smith when the latter appeared on the bridge.[130]

When Third Officer Pitman arrived on the bridge at 6 p.m. for his two-hour watch, he saw 'the commander and the second officer' there. Pitman spent most of his two-hour watch making calculations in the

Titanic's chart room, but he did notice Captain Smith's renewed presence on the bridge sometime prior to 7 p.m.[131]

Fifth Officer Harold Lowe also arrived on the bridge at 6 p.m. for his own two-hour watch. 'From 6 to 8,' Lowe recalled:

> I was busy working out this slip table ... and doing various odds and ends and working a dead-reckoning position for 8 o'clock p. m. to hand in to the captain, or the commander of the ship ... I handed [Captain Smith] the slip report ... [I laid it] on his chart-room table ... We simply put the slip on the table; put a paper weight or something on it, and he comes in and sees it. It is nothing of any great importance.[132]

It was shortly after 7.37 p.m. that Marconi operator Harold Bride arrived on the bridge carrying an unofficial wireless ice warning he'd just intercepted when the Leyland liner *Californian* transmitted it to the *Antillian*:

> To Captain, *Antillian*, 6.30 p.m., apparent time; ship, latitude, 42.3 north; longitude, 49.9 west. Three large bergs five miles to southward of us. Regards – Lord.[133]

Bride testified later:

> In the first place the *Californian* had called me ... with an ice report ... I was rather busy just for the minute, and I did not take it. She did not call again. She transmitted the ice report to the *Baltic*, and as she was transmitting it to the *Baltic* I took it down. I took it to the [officer on watch]; but it was not official because it was not intended for me afterwards.[134]

Later that evening Major Arthur Peuchen encountered Captain Smith below decks. 'I passed him in one of the companionways some place, just about dinner time,' Peuchen recalled. 'I cannot be very certain as to the hour; around 7 o'clock, I imagine. I generally come out to dress about 7 o'clock.'[135]

At about 7.15 p.m. Bruce Ismay happened to see Captain Smith walking through the *Titanic*'s first-class smoking room on some unknown errand. 'I was sitting in the smoking room,' Ismay recalled:

when Capt. Smith happened to come in the room for some reason – what it was I do not know – and on his way back he happened to see me sitting there and came up and said, 'By the way, sir, have you got that telegram which I gave you this afternoon?' I said, 'Yes.' I put my hand in my pocket and said, 'Here it is.' He said, 'I want it to put up in the officers' chart room.' That is the only conversation I had with Capt. Smith in regard to the telegram. When he handed it to me, he made no remark at all.[136]

Ismay then arose from his chair and went down to dinner.[137]

Mr and Mrs Jacques Futrelle had already finished eating an early dinner, and it might have been around this time that they encountered Captain Smith and asked a special favour of him. 'It was Sunday – a very dull monotonous Sunday night,' May Futrelle recalled in later years:

We had a brilliant dinner at 6 o'clock. The women wore their Paris gowns. The men were in full dress. Then we all sat around and were bored stiff. They asked the captain for permission to break the boredom by playing cards. There was no grand ball. There was nothing but dullness.[138]

In the meantime, Eleanor Cassebeer was down in her first-class cabin preparing to go to dinner wearing a white dress with an ermine collar and her pearls. While on her way to the first-class dining room, Mrs Cassebeer happened to encounter Thomas Andrews, who complimented her by exclaiming: 'Now that's the way a lady should look!'[139]

Stewardesses Katherine Gold and Annie Martin were eating their own dinner that evening when an unexpected visitor arrived in their mess-room. It was Thomas Andrews, who had come 'to ask us if there were any improvements in the ship we could suggest'.[140]

On Sunday evening Thomas Andrews reportedly sat at the same dinner table with Mr and Mrs Fred Hoyt, Dr William O'Loughlin, Dr John Simpson and Mr and Mrs Albert Dick.[141] According to Mrs Dick, Andrews monopolised the dinner conversation by talking about his wife, his daughter, his mother and his family and home in Belfast.[142]

Eleanor Cassebeer had a slightly different memory of the table's dining companions:

I sat at the table at Dr O'Loughlin's left side … with Mr Thomas Andrews opposite me. Mr and Mrs [Fred] Hoyt sat beside Mr Andrews, and I think next came a Mr and Mrs Lord [?], and then a Mr and Mrs Albert Dick. My dinner companion was Mr [Harry] Anderson who sat right next to me.[143]

Interestingly, Ismay later testified that he and Dr O'Loughlin dined by themselves that evening. 'I was all alone,' he recalled, 'so I asked Dr O'Loughlin to come and dine with me, and he dined with me in the restaurant at half-past 7 … No other persons were present excepting the doctor and myself.'[144]

Lucy Duff Gordon confirmed the fact that Ismay and Dr O'Loughlin dined by themselves at the same small table. 'Bruce Ismay, Chairman of the White Star Line, was dining with the ship's doctor next to our table,' she remembered:

and I remember that several men appealed to him as to how much longer we should be at sea. Various opinions were put forward, but none dreamed that the *Titanic* would make her harbor that night. Mr Ismay was most confident, and said that undoubtedly the ship would establish a record.[145]

Renée Harris, who had broken her arm in a fall earlier that day, was also planning to have dinner in the *Titanic*'s restaurant that evening. 'When I entered the Ritz Room I had a reception from all the diners, most of whom I had not met,' she recalled in later years:

It made me feel that a broken arm was an asset … I had just sat down at our table when Captain Smith came into the room. I had not before met the captain. In passing our table, he stopped, complimented me on my spirit, and went to an unoccupied place at the Ismay table. He was not there five minutes, for on his passing me again I asked him if he wasn't going to stay to enjoy the festivities. He answered that he was going back to the bridge because of the presence of icebergs in the region where we were. Captain Smith had not indulged in any drinking bout, as has been the general impression. On the contrary, he was one hundred percent on his job.[146]

Captain Smith had come to the restaurant that evening as guest of honour at a dinner hosted by George and Eleanor Widener. The members of the Widener party seated themselves at a long table that extended into an alcove not far from the entrance, and Mahala Douglas noticed that Smith was seated at the head of the table, with Eleanor Widener to his right and Major Archibald Butt on his left.[147]

Other diners were seated nearby in the restaurant as well.

'My brother, his wife, and myself went to the cafe for dinner at about 7.15 p.m. (ship's time),' Daisy Minahan recalled:

When we entered there was a dinner party already dining, consisting of perhaps a dozen men and three women. Capt. Smith was a guest, as also were Mr and Mrs Widener, Mr and Mrs Blair [Thayer], and Maj. Butt. Capt. Smith was continuously with his party from the time we entered until between 9:25 and 9:45, when he bid the women good night and left.[148]

Miss Minahan was seated so close to Captain Smith's party that she could even overhear snatches of their conversation.[149]

Mrs Walter Douglas remembered:

The tables were gay with pink roses and white daisies, the women in their beautiful shimmering gowns of satin and silk, the men immaculate and well-groomed, the stringed orchestra playing music from Puccini and Tchaikovsky. The food was superb: caviar, lobster, quail from Egypt, plover's eggs, and hothouse grapes and fresh peaches.[150]

'It is true that a supper was given that night at which Capt. Smith took wine,' Catherine Crosby said later. 'We were surprised, because we thought that if an officer did that he would have his papers taken away from him. As far as we know, however, none of the officers was intoxicated.'[151]

Emma Bucknell and Margaret Brown had also noticed Captain Smith as he entered the restaurant and seated himself at a long table reserved for a private party. 'Shouldn't he be on the bridge?' whispered Mrs Bucknell. 'I've heard rumors of icebergs and such.' 'Nonsense,' Mrs Brown replied. 'He often dines with first-class passengers.'[152]

Major Arthur Peuchen had also heard rumours about the nearby icefield, but his later claim that Captain Smith and Bruce Ismay dined together for three hours that night was mistaken. Still, it's possible Peuchen did see Captain Smith in the restaurant that evening and that he shared Mrs Bucknell's misgivings about Smith's absence from the bridge. 'I know as a matter of cold fact,' claimed Peuchen:

> that on Sunday night from 7.30 o'clock until nearly 10.30 Ismay and Captain Smith with several other men were having a dinner party in one of the salons, and I thought to myself at that time: 'Wouldn't it be a pretty situation if something would happen to this ship just now and her captain would be discovered at a dinner table – out of uniform and in evening garments?'[153]

As one of the guests at the Widener dinner, Marian Thayer had a closer view of the proceedings than did Major Peuchen and a few other passengers. 'My husband and I were guests at a dinner in the restaurant on Sunday evening, the 14th of April, given by Mr and Mrs Widener,' she recalled later. 'Captain Smith was there, also Major Butt and others. We entered the restaurant at 7.35 p.m.'[154]

'At 7.30 p. m., as usual, my husband and I went to dinner in the café,' Mary Eloise Smith recalled:

> There was a dinner party going on, given by Mr Ismay to the captain and various other people on board ship. This was a usual occurrence of the evening, so we paid no attention to it. The dinner did not seem to be particularly gay; while they had various wines to drink, I am positive none were intoxicated at a quarter of 9 o'clock, when we left the dining room.[155]

Eleanor Widener confirmed Mrs Smith's impression regarding alcoholic beverages at the Widener table. 'On the night of Sunday, the 14th of April, 1912, my husband and I gave a dinner at which Capt. Smith was present,' she wrote later. 'Capt. Smith drank absolutely no wine or intoxicating liquor of any kind whatever at the dinner.'[156]

Lucy Duff Gordon was another passenger who saw Captain Smith dining with the Widener party that evening:

Further along the room the Wideners and the Thayers (American multi-millionaires both of them) were dining with the Captain and others, and there was a great deal of laughter and chatter from their table. It was the last time I saw them. At another table sat Colonel Jacob Astor and his young bride. They were coming back to New York after a honeymoon in Europe, and I thought how much in love they were – poor things, it was the last few hours they were to have together.[157]

Antoinette Flegenheim heard later rumours that Captain Smith had drunk freely of alcoholic spirits that evening. 'Some said the captain was drunk and that this was one of the reasons why we were going at full speed amongst icebergs,' she recalled:

> I cannot personally account for the commander on the last night, because I saw no sign of him at all in the saloon, but later on the *Carpathia* one lady [Marian Thayer] from Haverford who told me she had dined with the captain that night in the restaurant, said he drank no alcohol and had left early to go back on duty.[158]

'There is our Captain,' Mrs Churchill Candee said to her own table companions. 'That signifies his peace of mind,' replied Colonel Archibald Gracie. 'Mr and Mrs Widener are with him; and I think the other man is the President's Aide, Archie Butt, a great favourite,' Edward Kent observed.

'It was Kent who told us this,' Mrs Candee remembered later:

> He seemed always to know who people were. A hot toddy made us happy and jolly to an unusual degree, and [Edward] Colley called merrily, 'Set 'em again? Yes? That is just the right answer to my remark. Here, Steward.' In the near distance I saw a little commotion on the captain's table, everyone standing. Gracious but firm, Mrs Widener was saying goodnight.[159]

It was between 8 and 8.15 p.m. when Bruce Ismay and Dr O'Loughlin finished their dinner, and when they rose from their table they noticed that Captain Smith and the Widener party were still seated together at their own large table. 'They were sitting at the table when I went out of the room,' Ismay testified later.[160]

After finishing his dinner, Captain Smith and his fellow dinner guests left the restaurant and repaired to the reception area beside the stairway to have coffee. 'I am sure that our party, including Captain Smith, left the restaurant, to have coffee, before 8.30 p.m., as the dinner was served very quickly,' Marian Thayer wrote later. 'We went out into the hall by the companionway for that purpose.'[161]

Cosmo Duff Gordon hadn't noticed Captain Smith's presence at the Widener dinner, but he did notice him after the dinner concluded. 'I saw him just after dinner just outside,' he remembered. 'I think he was in evening uniform.'[162]

Fernand Omont later heard about the captain's post-dinner coffee gathering from his friend Pierre Maréchal. 'Monsieur Maréchal remarked to me that the captain was with a party and seemed very happy and very confident in his boat,' Omont recorded later.[163]

In the meantime, Elmer Taylor and Fletcher Lambert-Williams decided to head for the lounge as well. 'Williams was a democratic sort of chap, did not hesitate to move among the high, the less high or lowly,' Mr Taylor wrote later:

> so after dinner he selected a table for coffee in the Reception Room next to a table at which Captain Smith was entertaining a party. We were close enough to hear Captain Smith tell his party the ship could be cut crosswise in three places and each piece would float. That remark confirmed my belief in the safety of the ship.[164]

'That is Captain Smith and Mr Ismay,' Joseph Loring said to his brother-in-law George Rheims as he pointed to two men who were taking coffee with a group of people in the lounge. Mr Rheims noted that Smith and Ismay remained seated in the lounge for about ten minutes before they finally arose and headed for the door.[165]

'Captain Smith had left our party and gone towards his own quarters by a quarter of nine o'clock, at the latest,' Marian Thayer remembered.[166] Mrs Thayer later spoke with fellow passenger Charles Stengel about Captain Smith's sobriety at the dinner. 'I have a distinct recollection of a Mrs Thorne [Thayer] stating, while talking about the captain being to dinner, that she was in that party,' Mr Stengel testified later, 'and she said, "I was in that party, and the captain did not drink a drop. He smoked two cigars, that was all."'[167]

William Sloper was playing bridge with three companions in the *Titanic*'s lounge when he looked up and saw a group of people walking past his table. What he saw tended to corroborate Mrs Thayer's own statement about Captain Smith:

While we were playing, the *Titanic*'s Captain Smith, a tall, distinguished-looking man with white hair and a full, close-cropped white beard, Commodore of the White Star Line fleet, passed our table about 10 p.m. [sic] on his way to the bridge from a private banquet at which he had been the guest of honor. Captain Smith was accompanied by Bruce Ismay, another tall, handsome man in his late forties, whose firm in London, Ismay, Imrie & Company, owned the White Star Line. Bruce Ismay was at the time its managing director. In the same party passing our table was also the designer of the *Titanic* [Thomas Andrews] and Major Archibald Butt, President Taft's military attaché at the White House, John Jacob Astor, returning home from his honeymoon with his young bride, Madeleine Force Astor. In the party also was Mr Charles M. Hays, president of the Grand Trunk Railway, and Clarence Moore of Washington whose wife was a member of the Swift family of Chicago of meat packing fame. There were several others in the party whose names I did not know, but all of these gentlemen were perfectly sober and gave no indication of having had too much wine to drink at the banquet as was suggested by some of the witnesses at the subsequent investigation of the sinking of the *Titanic* held in Washington some weeks afterward.[168]

Mr and Mrs Walter Douglas had eaten their own dinner in the restaurant at the same time as Captain Smith and the Widener party.

'We did not leave the tables until most of the others had left, including Mr Ismay, Mr and Mrs Widener, and their guests, and the evening was passed very quietly,' Mrs Douglas remembered. 'As we went to our stateroom – C-86 – we both remarked that the boat was going faster than she ever had. The vibration as one passed the stairway in the centre was very noticeable.'[169]

★

It's unknown if it was Captain Smith who told Bruce Ismay that the *Titanic* would be reaching the ice zone at about 9 p.m. Be that as it may, Smith arrived on the *Titanic*'s bridge at 8.55 p.m. and checked in with Second Officer Lightoller, who had relieved Chief Officer Henry Wilde at 6 p.m.[170]

'We spoke about the weather,' Lightoller recalled:

> calmness of the sea; the clearness; about the time we should be getting up toward the vicinity of the ice and how we should recognize it if we should see it – freshening up our minds as to the indications that ice gives of its proximity. We just conferred together, generally, for 25 minutes. Capt. Smith made a remark that if it was in a slight degree hazy there would be no doubt we should have to go very slowly.

Captain Smith conversed with his second officer until about 9.25 p.m., at which time he left the bridge with a final admonition. 'If it becomes at all doubtful, let me know at once,' Smith instructed his second officer. 'I will be just inside.'[171]

'Yes, sir,' Second Officer Lightoller replied.[172]

Even though Captain Smith was no longer on the outer bridge, Second Officer Lightoller knew he would not go to bed with the threat of an unseen icefield lying ahead of his vessel. 'He would just remain in his navigating room where his navigating instruments are,' Lightoller said later, 'chart books, etc., where he would be handy to pop out on the bridge.'[173]

At around 9.30 p.m. (the time he calculated that the *Titanic* would reach the icefield), Second Officer Lightoller decided to take some precautions. 'I told the sixth officer, Mr Moody, to ring up the crow's nest and tell them to keep a sharp lookout for ice, particularly small ice and growlers,' he testified later. 'That was received and replied to – and also to pass the word along …[174] until daylight – to keep a sharp look out till daylight.'[175]

★

At 9.52 p.m. a wireless message from the *Mesaba* reached the *Titanic*, warning her and all east-bound ships that:

> lat. 42N to 41.25, long. 49W to long. 50.30 saw much heavy pack ice and great number large icebergs also field ice. Weather good, clear.[176]

Just like the earlier ice warning received from the *Amerika*, the *Mesaba's* ice warning confirmed the fact that drifting ice and icebergs were now present in (as well as south of) the *Titanic's* own latitude. It's unknown if Captain Smith ever saw this message, because he never mentioned its receipt to Fourth Officer Boxhall or sent a reply of acknowledgement to the *Mesaba*.[177]

Titanic's three as-yet-unused main boilers had already been connected to the ship's engines at 7 p.m. as planned,[178] and – under the influence of all twenty-four main boilers – the ship's speed had increased to around 22.5 knots at that time. Fireman John Thompson was on duty in one of the *Titanic's* boiler rooms when these last three main boilers were brought online – an event that added to the stokers' workload:

> The first three days out I was in the engine room, and I was then transferred to the stoke room. I watched the gauges, and they were always getting higher, showing that we were increasing our speed all the time. Whenever anyone from the engine room came in the stokehold we always asked about the speed. In fact, that was the only thing we talked about. Then Sunday they put in those additional boilers. That doubled our work. They carried 215 pounds of steam all the time. The boilers could not stand any more.[179]

Quartermaster Sidney Humphreys agreed with Thompson's assessment and later told a reporter that the *Titanic* was 'hooked up' on the night of 14 April and was going as fast as she was capable of achieving utilising twenty-four boilers.[180]

Meanwhile, up on the ship's higher decks, passengers were becoming aware of the increase in *Titanic's* speed. 'After undressing and climbing into the top berth,' second-class passenger Lawrence Beesley wrote later, 'I read from about quarter-past eleven ... During this time I noticed particularly the increased vibration of the ship, and I assumed that we were going at a higher rate of speed than at any other time since we sailed from Queenstown.'[181]

Charles Stengel noticed the same thing from his own cabin. 'I called my wife's attention to the fact that the engines were running very fast,' he remembered. 'That was when I retired, about 10 o'clock. I could hear the engines running when I retired, and I noticed that the engines were running fast. I said I noticed that they were running faster than at any other time during the trip.'[182]

'When we retired to our room that evening, we spoke of the increased vibration of the ship,' first-class passenger Alice Silvey agreed, 'and Mr Silvey said that the speed had been increased. The sea was as smooth as glass, the stars shining and a more beautiful evening could not be imagined.'[183]

Meanwhile, down in the *Titanic's* restaurant on B deck, Mrs Lucian Smith was getting ready to call it a day. 'My husband was with some friends just outside of what I know as the Parisian Café,' she remembered:

I stayed up until 10.30, and then went to bed. I passed through the coffee room, and Mr Ismay and his party were still there. The reason I am positive about the different time is because I asked my husband at the three intervals what time it was. I went to bed, and my husband joined his friends.[184]

Up on the *Titanic's* bridge, Fourth Officer Boxhall was serving on the 8 p.m. to 12 p.m. watch and was busy assisting Captain Smith with navigational concerns even though the latter had left the outer bridge at 9.25 p.m. 'From nine o'clock to the time of the collision, Captain Smith was around there the whole of the time,' Boxhall remembered:

I was talking to him on one or two occasions … sometimes in the officers' chart room and sometimes at his chart-room door … I was discussing some stellar bearings I had had. I was also standing at his chart room door while he pricked off the 7.30 stellar position of the ship [on his chart].[185]

Fourth Officer Boxhall remembered that it was around 10 p.m. when Captain Smith recorded the *Titanic's* 7.30 p.m. position on the ship's navigation chart.[186] 'I saw [the captain] frequently during the watch ... On and off, most of the watch,' Boxhall remembered:

> Sometimes [he was] out on the outer bridge. I would go out and report. I was working observations out, if you understand, most of that watch working out different calculations and reporting to him; and that is how it was I came in contact with him so much ... Sometimes [he was] in his chart room and sometimes on the bridge, and sometimes he would come to the wheelhouse, inside of the wheelhouse ... I did not know that the captain was anywhere away from the bridge the whole watch. I mean to say from the bridge taking the whole bridge together; all the chart rooms, and the open bridge. They are all practically on one square, and I do not think the captain was away from that altogether.[187]

In later weeks, disturbing accounts from many survivors claimed that the *Titanic*'s lookouts sighted and reported the presence of three 'early' icebergs that passed near the ship during the twenty-five-minute interval between 11.15 p.m. and the *Titanic*'s encounter with the fatal iceberg at 11.40 p.m. These reports of 'early' icebergs were never investigated by the two subsequent inquiries into the disaster, but the existence of a significant number of these reports – plus the fact that *Titanic* is *known* to have passed right through a charted belt of outlying icebergs prior to the actual collision – makes one wonder whether the accepted accounts of the officers' activities on the *Titanic*'s bridge that night are truly complete.[188]

At 11.40 p.m. two crewmen were preparing to begin their nightly duties on the boat deck and were close enough to see what was taking place on the *Titanic*'s bridge. 'The first officer of the watch was Murdoch,' the two men said later. 'He was on the bridge. Captain Smith may have been near at hand, but he was not visible to us who were about to wash down the decks. Hichens, quartermaster, was at the wheel. Fleet was the outlook [lookout].'[189]

It's uncertain exactly what Captain Smith was doing at 11.40 p.m., but undoubtedly he was looking forward to a quiet, uneventful night. Sadly, it wasn't meant to be.

3

11.40 P.M.–12 A.M., 15 APRIL

Bump … bump … bump …[1] Captain Edward J. Smith was immediately alert to the sudden vibration caused by *Titanic*'s collision with an iceberg. 'The skipper came from the chart room onto the bridge,' Quartermaster Robert Hichens remembered.[2] Captain Smith now stood beside Fourth Officer Boxhall and queried First Officer William Murdoch, who had been in charge of the *Titanic*'s bridge while Smith was working in the chartroom.

'What have we struck?' Captain Smith demanded.

'An iceberg, Sir,' Murdoch replied. 'I hard-a-starboarded and reversed the engines, and I was going to hard-a-port round it but she was too close. I could not do any more.'[3]

'Close the watertight doors,' Captain Smith ordered.

'They are already closed,' Murdoch replied, and when Smith asked if the warning bell had been rung before the watertight doors were closed, the first officer replied 'Yes.'[4]

Captain Smith, First Officer Murdoch and Fourth Officer Boxhall then hurried over to the starboard bridge wing and stared aft at the rapidly receding iceberg as it gradually disappeared in the darkness behind the stricken vessel.[5] Presently Smith sent Fourth Officer Boxhall below decks to search for damage, and he also ordered Quartermaster Olliver to instruct the carpenter to sound the ship.[6]

A number of firemen who were quartered below decks in the *Titanic*'s bow had felt the collision as soon as it occurred, and these men were now slowly gathering on the ship's forward well deck to look at the large piles of ice fragments that had fallen onto that deck after being dislodged from the iceberg. These crewmen soon realised that Captain Smith was not yet aware of the gravity of the situation.

'When we first went on deck to see what was the matter, not one of us realized the seriousness of the position,' an unnamed fireman recalled. 'In fact, we had a smoke and chat until Capt. Smith called out, "Go down boys, and come up again [later.]" Many of us went to our bunks and were about to turn in when a leading hand called out that the water was up to the winding stairs, and we knew that the position was serious.'[7]

Presently, Fourth Officer Boxhall completed his brief inspection trip below decks and returned to the *Titanic*'s bridge. 'I went on to the bridge and reported to the Captain and First Officer that I had seen no damage whatever,' Boxhall testified later.[8]

In later years, Boxhall went into a little more detail about the things he told Captain Smith. 'I've been down below, Sir,' said the fourth officer, 'right down as far as I can go without removing hatches or the tarpaulin or anything, right through the third-class accommodation forward, and I don't see any signs of any damage, not even a glass port broken.'

'Did you see the carpenter anywhere, Mr Boxhall?' asked Captain Smith.

'No, sir, I didn't,' Boxhall replied.

'I do wish you'd go down and find him,' said Smith, 'and tell him to sound the ship round forward and let me know right away.'

Fourth Officer Boxhall obeyed his captain's order and started back down towards the lower decks. 'Well, I didn't get down all the ladders down to the fore deck, when I met the carpenter coming up, absolutely out of breath,' Boxhall recalled, 'and he said, "Mr Boxhall, the forepeak hatch has blown off and number one tarpaulin is ballooning up. She's evidently making water fast." So I said, "Alright, go up to the captain (he is on the starboard wing of the bridge) and tell the captain."'[9]

'He went on the bridge to the captain,' Boxhall remembered:

and I thought I would go down forward again and investigate; and then I met a mail clerk, a man named [John] Smith, and he asked where the

captain was. I said, 'He is on the bridge.' He said, 'The mail hold is full'
or 'filling rapidly.' I said, 'Well, you go and report it to the captain and I
will go down and see,' and I proceeded right down into the mail room.
I looked through an open door and saw these men working at the racks,
and directly beneath me was the mail hold, and the water seemed to be
then within two feet of the deck we were standing on.[10]

'It was rising rapidly up the ladder and I could hear it rushing in,'
Boxhall went on:

I stayed there just for a minute or two and had a look. I saw mail-bags
floating around on deck. I saw it was no use trying to get them out so
I went back again to the bridge. I met the Second Steward, Mr Dodd,
on my way to the bridge … and he asked me about sending men down
below for those mails. I said 'You had better wait till I go to the bridge
and find what we can do.'[11]

By now the *Titanic*'s engines were stopped and the ship had drifted
almost to a complete stop, but Captain Smith chose to be optimistic
about the amount of damage his ship had sustained.

'The captain telegraphed half speed ahead,' Quartermaster Alfred
Olliver remembered. Presently Olliver was sent away on several brief
errands, and it was only after returning to the bridge after one of these
errands that he realised the engine telegraph had again been rung to
'stop' during his brief absence.[12]

After feeling the vibration of the collision from her stateroom, first-
class passenger Eleanor Cassebeer was in the process of lacing up her
boots when Harry Anderson knocked at her cabin door and urged her
to accompany him up to the boat deck. 'The elevators being condemned,
we had to mount the steps to the top deck,' she recalled. 'At the purser's
office level we bumped into Mr Andrews, the ship's designer, whom I
knew well. He seemed to be extremely busy, and when he passed us he
didn't even say a word to me.'[13]

Thomas Andrews may have been on his way to the *Titanic*'s bridge to
confer with Captain Smith, but no eyewitness account of their meeting
and subsequent discussion has come to light.

Meanwhile, Mrs Cassebeer and Mr Anderson continued making their own way to the boat deck, where they eventually walked all the way forward and observed the ice fragments that had fallen from the iceberg onto the ship's forward well deck. Here the two passengers again encountered Thomas Andrews. 'In answer to many questions, [Mr Andrews] assured everybody that we were absolutely safe and that the *Titanic* was absolutely unsinkable,' Mrs Cassebeer remembered. 'He said that she could break in three separate and distinct parts and that each part would stay afloat indefinitely.'[14]

Mr and Mrs Albert Dick were apparently among this same group of passengers who encountered Thomas Andrews on the forward boat deck. Mr Dick remembered:

He was on hand at once and said that he was going below to investigate … We begged him not to go, but he insisted, saying he knew the ship as no one else did and that he might be able to allay the fears of the passengers. He went. As the minutes flew by, we did not know what to do or which way to turn. Captain Smith was everywhere doing his best to calm the rising tide of fear … But in the minds of most of us there was … the feeling that something was going to happen, and we waited for Mr Andrews to come back.[15]

It was apparently around this same time that another first-class passenger was getting ready to make an investigatory trip to the *Titanic*'s bridge after his wife felt the vibration of the collision and urged him to find out what was going on. 'Immediately I roused Jacques, telling him I feared something serious had happened,' May Futrelle recalled:

He got up and dressed. Meanwhile the doors of other staterooms were opening. People were putting their heads out and asking what was the matter. Nobody knew. My husband was well acquainted with Captain Smith, in fact, with all the ship's officers. He said, 'I'll go ask the captain,' and immediately left the suite. I stayed with Mrs Henry B. Harris, the wife of the theatrical man who was lost, while he was gone. In twenty minutes or so Jacques came back, announcing that the ship had struck an iceberg but that men were making repairs and that the ship would soon proceed. I was skeptical.

'Who told you that?' I asked him.
'The captain himself,' he replied.[16]

Down in cabin B-56, Bruce Ismay had also been awakened by the collision. Ten minutes later, after a steward was unable to enlighten him about what had happened, Ismay donned a coat and 'went up on the bridge, where I found Capt. Smith. I asked him what had happened, and he said, "We have struck ice." I said, "Do you think the ship is seriously damaged?" He said, "I am afraid she is."' Ismay then turned and headed back in the direction of his cabin.[17]

Meanwhile, John B. Thayer and his son Jack were walking around on A deck after someone told them that the ship's engines had stopped because the *Titanic* had struck an iceberg. 'We were joined shortly by J. Bruce Ismay, managing director of the White Star Line, and some engineers who had designed and constructed the ship,' Jack Thayer remembered. 'They [the engineers] immediately went on a tour of the ship, taking some twenty-five minutes. I visited the swimming pool and post office department. Water was coming in very rapidly.'[18]

While on his way back to his own cabin, Ismay encountered Chief Engineer Joseph Bell in the main companionway. 'I asked if he thought the ship was seriously damaged,' Ismay said later, 'and he said he thought she was, but was quite satisfied the pumps would keep her afloat.'[19] After finally reaching his cabin, Mr Ismay began putting on a suit of clothes over his pyjamas.[20]

Meanwhile, Third Officer Pitman undoubtedly contributed his own damage assessment to Captain Smith after he made certain observations while on the *Titanic*'s forward well deck. He recalled:

I saw a little ice there … I went further, to the forecastle head, to see if there was any damage there. I could not see any at all. On my return, before emerging from under the forecastle head, I saw a crowd of firemen coming out with their bags, bags of clothing. I said, 'What is the matter?' They said, 'The water is coming in our place.' I said, 'That is funny.' I looked down No.1 hatch, then, and saw the water flowing over the hatch. I then immediately went to the boat deck.[21]

4

12–12.20 A.M.

Captain Smith seems to have waited patiently on the *Titanic*'s bridge while awaiting damage reports from his officers and crewmen, but shortly after midnight he apparently realised his ship was listing.

'He also came back to the wheelhouse and looked at the commutator in front of the compass, which is a little instrument like a clock to tell you how the ship is listing,' helmsman Robert Hichens recalled. 'The ship had a list of five degrees to the starboard.'[1]

Fourth Officer Boxhall finally completed his second inspection trip and reported back to the bridge to tell Captain Smith what he'd seen in the ship's flooding mail room. The *Titanic*'s master said 'all right' and then issued the order for crewmen to start clearing the lifeboats and ready them for loading.[2]

Standing nearby, Quartermaster Robert Hichens heard the captain tell someone, 'Get all the boats out and serve out the belts.'[3]

Captain Smith had previously sent Quartermaster Alfred Olliver down to the engine room to deliver a written note to Chief Engineer Joseph Bell, and at around midnight Olliver returned to the bridge bearing Bell's reply that he would obey the captain's written order as soon as possible.

'As soon as I delivered that message [to Captain Smith],' Olliver recalled, 'the chief officer sent me to the boatswain of the ship and told me to tell the boatswain to get the oar lines and to uncover the boats and get them ready for lowering, and I done so, and came back on the bridge.'[4]

Seaman Joseph Scarrott had just come up from alerting the next group of crewmen that their watch was about to begin. 'Needless to say, I found them all awake,' he wrote in later years:

> At 12 we got the order: 'All hands on deck. Clear away and turn out all boats.' I was at work on boat 14 when Captain Smith gave that never-to-be-forgotten order 'Men, you know your duty – get the women and children into the boats.'[5]

First-class passenger Gilbert Tucker had been awakened by the collision and had gone up to the boat deck shortly afterwards after he felt the ship's engines stop:

> I walked forward and got up to the navigator's bridge ... Though there was considerable broken ice littering the forecastle decks, the stem of the ship did not seem to be damaged at all, and there was no looming ice-cliff in sight. I started back to my cabin, and in the main companionway I ran across Captain Smith with a group of his officers. As I passed, he was giving orders to call all hands, get lifebelts on them and prepare to lower away the boats. This determined me to get myself and my friends ready for anything that might happen, and I told them what was going on, went in my own cabin for some more clothes, some money and my watch. As I looked at the watch then it was about 11:15 [actually 12:02 a.m.].[6]

When Fourth Officer Boxhall heard the order to summon all hands and prepare the lifeboats for lowering, he assembled a group of deckhands to get the boats uncovered and prepared for sea.[7] Third Officer Pitman assisted in this endeavour.[8]

An unnamed deck hand later reported that he was asleep in his bunk in the crew quarters when:

> I was awakened by someone shouting orders for all hands to turn out on deck to clear away the lifeboats. We were told to put on lifebelts. When we came up, the captain would not allow us on the boat deck

for about half an hour. Then we were told to come up and lower the boats, putting in women and children first.[9]

In the meantime, Captain Smith was getting ready to begin his own inspection tour below decks, but before doing so he paid a brief visit to the Marconi wireless cabin on the boat deck. 'We've struck an iceberg, and I'm having an inspection made to tell what it has done for us,' Smith told wireless operators Jack Phillips and Harold Bride. 'You better get ready to send out a call for assistance. But don't send it until I tell you.'[10]

Helen Ostby had just left cabin B-36 and was coming upstairs on her first post-collision trip to the upper decks. 'With the Warrens, we went up to the boat deck by the main staircase,' she remembered. 'I remember seeing Captain Smith and one or two other officers coming down it, to explore the ship and see what damage had been done. The officers looked very sober. They didn't stop to talk to the passengers at all.'[11]

After descending to B deck, Captain Smith seems to have made a brief detour to cabins B-52, 54 and 56, the cabins to which Ismay had returned after concluding his first trip to the *Titanic*'s bridge. It was now about 12.05 a.m. 'I heard Captain Smith come down to the room of Mr Bruce Ismay – managing director of the company – which was only a few feet away from mine,' Stewardess Katherine Gold recalled. 'I heard the captain say to Mr Ismay, "We had better get the boats out."'[12]

First-class passenger Quigg Baxter was just coming out of his mother's cabin B-58 when he encountered Captain Smith coming out of the next-door cabin after conferring with Ismay.

'It is all right, Baxter,' the captain said reassuringly. 'Nothing serious at all. Go right back to bed.'[13] However, as Captain Smith hurried away, Ismay reportedly spoke to Baxter and advised him to get his womenfolk into the lifeboats.[14] Baxter's mother and sister, who'd been alarmed by the collision, were not comforted by this news, and ten minutes later a stewardess came into the cabin, put lifebelts on the two ladies and told them they had only three minutes to get out.[15]

One deck below, Karl Behr left cabin C-148 and began ascending the grand staircase when he encountered Captain Smith coming down the same stairway; the *Titanic*'s master passed Behr without saying anything to him.[16]

Elizabeth Shute was in cabin C-25 when she noticed that:

> An officer's cap passed the door. I asked: 'Is there an accident or danger of any kind?' 'None, so far as I know,' was his courteous answer, spoken quietly and most kindly. The same officer then entered a cabin a little distance down the companionway and, by this time distrustful of everything, I listened intently and distinctly heard: 'We can keep the water out for a while.' Then, and not until then, did I realize the horror of an accident at sea.[17]

Steward James Johnstone was down on D deck and estimated that it was roughly fifteen minutes after the collision when Thomas Andrews walked past him in the passageway and headed aft towards the *Titanic's* engine room. Three or four minutes later, Johnstone saw Captain Smith headed along D deck in the same direction.[18]

Down on E deck, Laura Francatelli had been standing in the doorway of her stateroom ever since the collision occurred twenty-five minutes previously. She now 'saw all the officers come down, to inspect the damage, & then starting screwing down the iron doors outside my bedroom; presently a man came rushing up, saying all the hold & luggage & mail had gone'.[19]

It must have been around this same time that Bedroom Steward Alfred Theissinger ran into Captain Smith on E deck. 'He passed me just after I had seen the fireman rushing from the incoming waters,' Theissinger recalled later.[20] Further aft on E deck, Kitchen Clerk Paul Maugé saw Captain Smith descending a stairway leading towards the engine room.[21]

After Captain Smith left E deck, Saloon Steward Charles Mackay saw him emerging from a stairway onto F deck and assumed (perhaps mistakenly) that Smith was headed for the cabin of Chief Engineer Joseph Bell.[22] However, steerage passenger Edward Dorkings apparently discovered Smith's true destination while returning to his cabin to retrieve his lifebelt. 'As I passed the engine room, I saw Captain Smith, standing in the doorway, giving orders to the crew,' Dorkings remembered. 'The perspiration was pouring down his face in streams, but he was calm and collected, and as I recollect him now, he appeared like a marble statue after a rain.'[23]

Ten minutes after Captain Smith appeared on F deck, Steward Mackay saw him retrace his path along the F-deck passageway and ascend the working staircase to E deck.[24]

Barber Augustus Weikman gave two slightly different descriptions of things he saw and heard after he left his quarters and headed towards the upper decks. A newspaper reporter later paraphrased the first version of Weikman's experiences:

> On the way up he met Mr Andrews, the builder of the boat, and in answer to his question as to what the situation was the builder replied 'My God, it's serious.' Mr Weikman also met Captain Smith on the stairway and spoke to him concerning the extent of the damage. The captain made no reply.[25]

Later, Mr Weikman made a written statement at the US Senate *Titanic* inquiry: 'When I was on "E" deck I met the captain returning from "G" deck, who had been there with Mr Andrews.'[26]

Despite Augustus Weikman's speculation about where Captain Smith was supposedly coming from, it seems unlikely that Smith and Thomas Andrews ever encountered each other in the *Titanic*'s engine room (a conclusion supported by Weikman's newspaper interview), because Steward James Johnstone reported seeing Thomas Andrews walking forward by himself through the D-deck dining room before stopping for a moment in the first-class reception room. He remembered:

> I saw him speaking to some ladies and they were all in a bunch and he said he thought it would be all right. He said, 'Be easy, it will be all right.' I asked him, and he said, 'All right.' … He told me to see that the ladies were quiet, or something to that effect, at the foot of the companion.[27]

Johnstone then followed Mr Andrews from D deck down to E deck and saw him descend even further towards the mail room and baggage area located down on the orlop deck.[28]

It must have been during this same period that Thomas Andrews began advising occasional crewmen that the damage to the *Titanic* was serious. Lamp Trimmer Samuel Hemming had just returned to his bunk when the ship's joiner entered the room and announced:

'If I were you, I would turn out, you fellows. She is making water, one-two-three, and the racket court is getting filled up.' At that moment Bosun Alfred Nichols came into the bunk room and called out, 'Turn out, you fellows, you haven't half an hour to live. That is from Mr Andrews. Keep it to yourselves, and let no one know.'[29]

Shortly afterwards, Stewardess Annie Robinson saw a mail clerk walking aft along E deck, and a few minutes later the same mail clerk returned in company with Captain Smith and Purser McElroy. The three men continued walking forward towards the flooding mail room.

Presently Captain Smith and Thomas Andrews returned together along the E-deck passageway, and Stewardess Robinson heard Andrews say, 'Well, three have gone already, Captain' (undoubtedly referring to the three foremost watertight compartments). Stewardess Robinson then hurried to the lower stairway and discovered that seawater had risen to within six steps of the deck she was standing on, so she hurried upstairs to summon help.[30]

Captain Smith and Thomas Andrews apparently climbed part-way up the stairway together and were seen doing so by passenger Albert Dick. 'I saw them coming up from the bottom of the vessel looking anxious,' he remembered.[31]

At that point Smith and Andrews seem to have gone their separate ways, because Pierre Maréchal, who had seen Smith inspecting the ship below decks fifteen minutes previously, now saw him ascending the stairway by himself. 'When he returned after a quarter of an hour, my faith got quite a shock,' Mr Maréchal remembered. 'The captain was as white as a sheet. He went back up to the boat deck and on his way men and women asked him questions anxiously. He told them, "Just to be on the safe side, I suggest that you put on your lifebelts."'[32]

In cabin B-3, Elizabeth Allen and her aunt, Elizabeth Robert, had just been warned by Emilie Kreuchen (Robert's maid) that Kreuchen's own cabin on a lower deck was flooding. 'We concluded then that something must be wrong,' Miss Allen remembered. 'I stepped outside the door to find out, and I met Captain Smith. He told us to dress and go on deck.'[33]

'The steam was blowing with a deafening noise,' Sidney Collett remembered:

They said that we had struck an iceberg and had to look up to see it. I did not see the iceberg myself. I talked to the officers, and the captain ordered us to get the ladies. I ran down, got more clothing and went to Miss [Marion] Wright. She had got up and was out on the deck.[34]

Charles Stengel and his wife had been awakened earlier by the stopping of the *Titanic*'s engines, and after dressing themselves they went up to the boat deck to find out what had happened. He remembered:

There were not many people around there … That was where the lifeboats were. We came down to the next deck [A deck], and the captain came up. I supposed he had come up from investigating the damage. He had a very serious and a very grave face. I then said to my wife, 'This is a very serious matter, I believe.' I think Mr Widener and his wife – I think it was Mr Widener – followed the captain up the stairs, and they returned, and I presume they went to their staterooms. Shortly after that the orders were given to have the passengers all put on life preservers.[35]

He related elsewhere:

I realized the seriousness of the situation immediately because I saw Captain Smith come out of the cabin. He was closely followed by Mr and Mrs George Widener, of Philadelphia. 'What is the outlook?' I heard Mr Widener inquire. 'It is extremely serious, gentlemen,' he said. 'Please keep cool and do what you can to help us.' … It was his face, more than anything else, which made me fearful. He looked like an old, old man. I heard him give instructions to his officers, and they took their stations at the boats.[36]

Stengel never forgot the expression he saw on Captain Smith's face: 'The first inkling I had of danger was when I saw the serious face of Captain Smith as he talked to George Widener.'[37]

James McGough may have been nearby during the Smith–Widener conversation, because his version of their exchange was almost identical to Charles Stengel's. He said later:

> As soon as the vessel had struck the iceberg, Mr and Mrs Widener had sought out Captain Smith.
> 'What is the outlook?' Mr Widener was heard to inquire.
> 'It is extremely serious,' was the quick reply. 'Please keep cool and do whatever you can to help us.' And that is what Mr Widener did.[38]

Spencer Silverthorne was another who saw the *Titanic*'s master coming up from below decks. 'As my friends and I came on deck I saw Captain Smith hurrying to the bridge,' he remembered. 'I had not seen him before that and do not know where he came from. It was not his watch. I heard him say nothing.'[39]

'We saw the captain and the first officer going up to the bridge,' Fernand Omont remembered. 'All around about fifty or sixty women and men were waiting anxiously to know what was happening.'[40]

It was somewhere around 12.20 a.m. when Bathroom Steward Samuel Rule saw Captain Smith finally reappear on the boat deck. 'He was walking back from the engine room, where I heard he had been to consult Mr Bell, the chief engineer,' Rule remembered.[41]

It was at this same approximate time that Elizabeth Allen, her aunt Elizabeth Robert and her cousin Georgette Madill came up from below decks and found themselves standing on the forward boat deck. 'We found other people were moving out and up on the sun-deck,' Miss Allen remembered.

> A good many women were already there … In a few minutes orders were given to take out the boats, and the crew began to get the rigging ready. Captain Smith gave orders for the orchestra to come on deck, and they rushed out past us, down forward near the bridge.[42]

The temperature that night was chilly, so Stewardess Violet Jessop went back to her quarters to get a warmer wrap:

I gathered my eiderdown and went up … On my way I passed a group of officers, still in their mess jackets, hands in pockets, chatting quietly on the companion square as men do who are waiting for something. They smiled at me and I waved back.

Miss Jessop would later specify that these men were Captain Smith, Bruce Ismay, Purser Hugh McElroy and Doctor William O'Loughlin:

'As I turned I ran into Jock [Hume], the bandleader and his crowd with their instruments. Funny, they must be going to play, thought I, and at this late hour! Jock smiled in passing, looking rather pale for him, remarking, "Just going to give them a tune to cheer things up a bit," and passed on.' Presently, after reaching the boat deck, Miss Jessop could hear faint strains of music as the band began to play.[43]

When Algernon Barkworth came up from his cabin onto the upper deck, he saw William T. Stead, who told him that the *Titanic*'s forecastle deck was full of ice fragments that had fallen from the iceberg. Barkworth noted that the ship's foremast was listing heavily to starboard and that Captain Smith was telling the women passengers to put on lifebelts, so he returned to his cabin, changed his clothes and came back on deck.[44]

Shortly after returning to the boat deck, Captain Smith again descended the stairway to A deck, apparently with the intention of alerting the passengers who were gathered there of the need for them to take safety precautions. 'Suddenly Captain Smith ran downstairs [to A deck] calling out "Put on your lifebelts,"' Marie Young wrote later. 'It seemed impossible we could really have understood his words, so full of tragic import, and spoken on such a gigantic "unsinkable" boat as the *Titanic*.'[45]

'The captain came down with the first officer,' Fernand Omont remembered. 'The captain was chewing a toothpick and he said "You had better put your life-preservers on, as a precaution."'[46]

Omont's friend Pierre Maréchal witnessed the same exchange. 'Captain Smith, nevertheless, appeared nervous,' Maréchal recalled. 'He came down on deck chewing a toothpick. "Let everyone," he said, "put on a lifebelt. It is more prudent."'[47]

For his own part, Isaac Frauenthal had already concluded that the *Titanic's* iceberg 'must have been between 90 and 100 feet high, as the boat deck was covered with snow from it'.[48] Right now, though, Frauenthal was among the first-class passengers who were gathered on the forward end of A deck:

Presently I saw the captain appear, apparently from the bridge, and several men approached him. One of them was Colonel Astor, and I heard him say to Captain Smith: 'Captain, my wife is not in good health. She has gone to bed, and I don't want to get her up unless it is absolutely necessary. What is the situation?'

'Colonel Astor, you had better get your wife up at once,' Captain Smith replied quietly. 'I fear that we may have to take to the boats.' [Smith also advised Astor and his wife to don lifebelts.] Colonel Astor never changed expression. He thanked the captain courteously and walked rapidly, but composedly, toward the nearest companionway.[49]

Isaac Frauenthal's brother, Dr Henry Frauenthal, happened to be close by when Captain Smith's conversation with Colonel Astor took place. 'As I came on deck I saw the Captain and heard him telling Colonel Astor that the boat had been injured by an iceberg,' he said later. 'The deck was already well crowded and the passengers were rushing to the deck.'[50]

Mr and Mrs John Snyder also overheard Captain Smith's conversation with John Jacob Astor. Mrs Snyder recalled:

When I came up on deck, I heard Colonel Astor ask Captain Smith if he had not better awaken Mrs Astor … He said he did not wish unnecessarily to disturb her, as she was in delicate health. I did not hear the captain's answer, but I saw Colonel Astor turn pale and hurry below. When he returned a little later, he was supporting his wife and patting her reassuringly on the back. It made me feel better just to see him.[51]

While Dickinson Bishop returned to cabin B-49 for a few minutes, his wife Helen remained on A deck with a group of fellow passengers and saw Colonel Astor speak with Captain Smith as the latter came down the stairway. 'The captain told him something in an undertone,' Mrs Bishop remembered:

He [Astor] came back and told six of us, who were standing with his wife, that we had better put on our life belts. I had gotten down two flights of stairs to tell my husband, who had returned to the stateroom for a moment, before I heard the captain announce that the life belts should be put on. That was about three or four minutes later that the captain announced the life belts should be put on. We came back upstairs and found very few people up.[52]

Mr Bishop's own memories were similar to those of his wife:

When we reached the upper deck we found only a few people there and none of them seemed to be frightened in the least. We stayed there awhile talking. Mr and Mrs John Jacob Astor and Mr and Mrs G. A Harder were in our group. I went downstairs to get some wraps just as Mr Astor started to go up to see the captain. When I returned, I found that the captain had advised him to get life preservers and prepare for the worst.[53]

Caroline Brown remembered:

It was some little time after midnight that Capt. Smith, followed closely by John Jacob Astor, went rapidly along our deck [apparently A deck]… As he passed, Capt. Smith was quite pale and I have since had a feeling that he realized the extent of our danger even at that time. But he seemed perfectly calm and his voice was quite natural as he ordered all on deck to put on lifebelts. His steady, quiet tones were reassuring.[54]

In a different description of Captain Smith, Mrs Brown stated that 'his face was marble white in its paleness, but he seemed perfectly self-possessed and gave several orders in a clear, cool voice that seemed to carry assurance with it'.[55]

Isaac Frauenthal recalled:

What struck me as singular even then was the comparatively small number of people who had come on deck …There weren't enough there when I arrived to fill one boat. The officers seemed to have matters well in hand. I was told that the captain was going through the ship personally arousing passengers and giving instructions about lifebelts and about getting into the boats.[56]

Gladys Cherry was standing among a crowd of passengers who had gathered (apparently) at the forward end of A deck to look down at the ice fragments lying on the forward well deck. Miss Cherry later related that 'suddenly the captain appeared and said: "I don't want to frighten anyone, but will you all go quietly and put on your lifebelts and go up on the top deck?" We all dispersed very calmly and slowly.'[57]

Not long after the collision took place, Karl Behr and Helen Newsom had gone to the cabin of Richard and Sallie Beckwith and urged them to get dressed, but now things appeared to be taking a more serious turn. 'When we were proceeding along the passage someone told us orders were issued to don lifebelts, which we did very calmly,' Behr remembered. 'We met Captain Smith on the main stairways and he was telling everyone to put on lifebelts. Knowing exactly where the lifeboats were, I led my party to the uppermost deck.'[58]

At that point Captain Smith might possibly have made a quick trip aft to the *Titanic*'s first-class smoking room, because Caroline Bonnell later reported seeing him there talking with first-class passenger Stephen Blackwell. According to Miss Bonnell, this meeting between the two men occurred shortly before the women and children were ordered to start boarding the lifeboats.[59]

★

In the meantime, after separating from Captain Smith below decks, Thomas Andrews had resumed his solitary inspection tour of the *Titanic*'s lower decks. It didn't take Andrews long to discover the full extent of the damage the ship had sustained, and he knew he had to relay his news to the captain on the upper deck as quickly as possible. Mrs Frank Warren remembered:

While standing there [on D deck] a Mr Perry [Pirrie; actually Thomas Andrews], I think his name was, one of the designers of the vessel, rushed by, going up the stairs ... He was asked if there was any danger but made no reply. But a passenger who was afterwards saved told me that his face had on it a look of terror. Immediately after that the report became general that water was in the squash court, which was on the deck below where we were standing, and that and that the baggage had already been submerged.[60]

Up on A deck, Dorothy Gibson saw Thomas Andrews hurrying up the stairway towards the bridge and noted that he was making 'three or four steps at a bound. His face was pallid. When I tried to make further inquiry from him, he simply couldn't speak, from his excitement.'[61]

Standing beside Miss Gibson was William Sloper, who later wrote his own description of Mr Andrews' hurried ascent towards the *Titanic*'s bridge:

At this moment the designer of the ship, at whose table in the dining saloon Mrs Gibson and Dorothy had been sitting at meal-time during the voyage, came bouncing up the stairs three steps at a time. Dorothy rushed over to him, and putting her hands on his arm demanded to know what had happened. Without answering and with a worried look on his face, he brushed Dorothy aside and continued up the next flight of stairs to the top deck, presumably on his way to the captain's bridge. Following the designer a moment or two later came one of the bedroom stewards. Raising his voice so that everyone standing in the companionway could hear what he was saying, he called out, 'The captain says that all passengers will dress themselves warmly, bring their life preservers with them and go out onto the top deck.'[62]

Dorothy Gibson was frightened by this news. 'I was paralyzed,' she remembered later. 'Two men – Mr Ismay was one of them – helped fasten on the preservers, and taking our rugs, we hurried to the boat deck.'[63]

'Going on deck again, I met Mr Ismay with the ship's officer,' Archibald Gracie recalled. 'Mr Ismay was smiling serenely and not in the slightest degree perturbed. Presently, however, I noticed people with life-preservers adjusted, which was said to be a mere provision of safety ordered by the captain.'[64]

During his inspection tour below decks, Thomas Andrews had just discovered that – in addition to the three watertight compartments that had 'already gone' – boiler rooms 6 and 5 were also flooding uncontrollably. Andrews knew that this extensive flooding meant the ship could not be saved, and he was hurrying up to the *Titanic*'s bridge to break this shattering news to Captain Smith.

It appears that Bruce Ismay was heading towards the *Titanic*'s bridge at about the same time as Thomas Andrews. 'My mind is a blank as to a trip we took to the boat deck,' Martha Stephenson wrote later, 'when I distinctly remember being beside the gymnasium on starboard side and seeing Mr Ismay come out, noting the fact that he had dressed hurriedly, as his pajamas were below his trousers.'[65]

Passenger Fred Hoyt was apparently standing within earshot of the bridge when Thomas Andrews finally arrived there and made his devastating damage report to Captain Smith. 'Mr Andrews, managing director of the firm of Harland & Wolff, which built the *Titanic*, was on board, and he made a thorough examination,' Hoyt said later. 'When he came back to the upper deck, he said: "She's gone."'[66]

Storekeeper Frank Prentice was standing nearby and noted that Ismay was now back on the *Titanic*'s bridge:

I happened to be up on the boat deck and I saw Thomas Andrews, the designer, Bruce Ismay, the chairman, and Captain Smith, talking together. I heard Ismay say to Andrews: 'What's the position? Is there any news?' And Andrews said: 'Well, Sir, the position is that she's going to sink. There's nothing that can stop us sinking, the water is just coming straight up. The bulkheads won't help her in any way at all.'[67]

5

12.20–12.40 A.M.

It was at that point Captain Smith was forced to issue the order he'd been dreading, because Seaman John Poigndestre heard him say, 'Start putting the women and children in the boats.'[1] Leading Fireman Charles Hendrickson heard Smith give this order as well,[2] and Quartermaster Robert Hichens saw the *Titanic*'s master standing beside collapsible D as he said, 'Women and children first,' with First Officer Murdoch repeating the captain's order in acknowledgement.[3]

'I heard the order given to get the boats out,' Bruce Ismay recalled:

> I walked along to the starboard side of the ship, where I met one of the officers. I told him to get the boats out … I heard Capt. Smith give the order when I was on the bridge … I know I heard him give the order to lower the boats. I think that is all he said. I think he simply turned around and gave the order.[4]

At this point, Captain Smith, Thomas Andrews and Bruce Ismay all went their separate ways, each man doing his best to fulfil his individual responsibilities no matter whether those responsibilities were official or self-imposed. 'As soon as I heard him [Captain Smith] give the order to lower the boats, I left the bridge,' Ismay remembered. '… I assisted, as best I could, getting the boats out and putting the women and children into the boats.'[5]

'I think I saw [Mr Ismay] standing for a moment without his hat on; just a moment, on the port side ... on the boat deck,' Major Arthur Peuchen recalled. 'I should say it would be probably an hour after we had struck the iceberg.' Peuchen noted that the White Star Line's chairman wasn't doing anything in particular at the time he glimpsed him.

'As I went up on deck the next time, I saw Mr Ismay with one of the officers,' Archibald Gracie said later. 'He looked very self-contained, as though he was not fearful of anything, and that gave encouragement to my thought that perhaps the disaster was not anything particularly serious.'[6]

But Ismay didn't remain idle for long, and Charlotte Appleton later vouched for the selfless role he played during the evacuation. 'I saw him on the bridge with Captain Smith,' she remembered, 'doing everything in his power to get the women and children in the lifeboats.'[7]

For his own part, Second Officer Charles Lightoller made a specific observation about Bruce Ismay's location as the latter began assisting the *Titanic*'s officers with the evacuation. 'Mr Ismay, as far as I know, from what I have gathered afterwards, was on the starboard side of the deck wholly, helping out there,' Lightoller testified later.[8] Elizabeth Allen agreed with Lightoller's observation. 'We could see Ismay and Colonel Astor, with Mr Ismay in charge on the starboard side,' she said later. 'He filled one boat after another until all the women were gone.'[9]

★

After receiving Thomas Andrews' devastating news about the ship's impending fate, Captain Smith headed for the *Titanic*'s wireless cabin. Junior Operator Harold Bride later described what happened next:

> 'Send the call for assistance,' ordered the captain, barely putting his head in the door.
>
> 'What call shall I send?' Phillips asked.
>
> 'The regulation international call for help. Just that.'
>
> Then the captain was gone. Phillips began to send 'C. Q. D.' He flashed away at it and we joked while he did so. All of us made light of the disaster.[10]

It was 12.27 a.m.[11]

★

It wasn't long after Captain Smith left the Marconi cabin that Chief Operator Jack Phillips received a reply to his wireless distress signal. It was from the German vessel *Frankfurt*, and Phillips instructed Junior Operator Bride to tell Captain Smith about this communication. Bride left the wireless cabin and soon found the *Titanic*'s commander out on the boat deck. After listening to Bride's news about the *Frankfurt*, Smith asked him for the German vessel's latitude and longitude. 'I told him we would get that as soon as we could,' Bride recalled, after which he returned to the Marconi cabin.[12]

At one point during the evacuation, steerage passenger Luigi Finoli came within earshot of Captain Smith. He remembered:

> The appearance of Capt. Smith ... reassured the passengers, who became quieter ... No one seemed to think then that there was any danger. Capt. Smith, however, ordered all the women passengers to go below and get their wraps. He explained that he was going to place them in the boats so that they would feel safer, and at the same time told us that other boats had received our distress message, and that they were on their way to help us.[13]

Meanwhile, out on the open boat deck, Dr Washington Dodge made an interesting observation about the overall evacuation of the *Titanic* as he watched it unfold:

> I don't think it has been made clear to many the difference in the conditions which obtained on the starboard side of the *Titanic* from those on the port side ... I myself did not visit the port side of the boat deck at all, but from the testimony that has been given it is apparent how different things were there. On a ship like the *Titanic* people on the port side might as well have been at the Battery for all we could see of things happening there. The officers' quarters separated the starboard side from the port side and we could neither hear nor see what was going on over them.
>
> At no time were there many people on the starboard side that night. Why was that? The most plausible reason I can advance is that

the captain was in charge of the launching of the boats to port. Now in times of danger the captain always draws a crowd. The more notable men on board who were known by sight to the other passengers knew Captain Smith personally and remained with him. These men attracted others. In this way the crowd grew and grew on the port side, while at no time was there anything like a crowd on the starboard side. Now this may explain many things. It may explain why the boats were launched from the starboard side more quickly and successfully and why when the last boats on that side were reached, No. 13 and No. 15, the boat taken by Mr Ismay,[14] there were practically no women around, and not many men. When the order to launch the boats was given, Captain Smith took command of the port side and never left there. Chief Officer Murdoch took command of the starboard side. But to keep near the captain appeared to be a controlling motive with many.[15]

Midway through the process of uncovering and clearing the lifeboats, Fourth Officer Boxhall sought out Captain Smith once again and asked if he should send out a wireless distress signal:

'I've already sent a distress signal,' Smith replied. 'What, what position did you send it from?' Boxhall queried.

'From the eight o'clock DR [dead reckoning].'

'Well,' Boxhall replied, 'that was about, she was about twenty miles ahead of that, sir. If you like, I will run the position up from the star position up to the time of the contact with the iceberg.'[16]

Meanwhile, Second Officer Lightoller was busy getting all the lifeboats uncovered and swung out, and Lamp Trimmer Samuel Hemming was hard at work at lifeboat 4. That boat's canvas cover had just been removed when Lightoller sought out Chief Officer Wilde. He testified later:

I asked the Chief Officer should we put the women and children in and he said 'No.' I left the men to go ahead with their work and found the Commander, or I met him and I asked him should we put the women and children in, and the Commander said 'Yes, put the women and children in and lower away.' That was the last order I received on the ship.

Mr Lightoller then proceeded to supervise the work taking place at life-boat 6.[17]

'We lowered the boat [4] in line with the A deck, when I had an order come from the captain to see that the boats were properly provided with lights,' Lamp Trimmer Samuel Hemming remembered. '… I called Mr Lightoller and told him that I would have to leave the boat's fall; so he put another man in my place.'[18]

★

It must have been around this time that first-class passenger Robert Daniel saw fellow passenger Clarence Moore approach Captain Smith:

I was standing near the captain when Mr Moore went to him and asked whether he could be of service in any way.

'Tell me what I can do to help, and I'll do it,' Moore said to Captain Smith.

'The thing to do,' Smith replied, 'is to see that all the women get off the ship in safety and that the men do not crowd into the boats.'

'Count on me,' declared Moore.[19]

'That's what we did,' Robert Daniel said later.[20]

At this point Captain Smith seems to have walked aft along the port boat deck in order to monitor his crewmen's progress in preparing the lifeboats for lowering. 'Ladies, if you will go down to deck A I think you can get in more easily,' Smith announced to Bertha Chambers and a group of female passengers. However, Mrs Chambers soon learned that A deck was enclosed with heavy glass windows that could only be opened by means of a crank whose location was unknown.[21]

Hugh Woolner also heard Captain Smith issuing these instructions while standing between lifeboats 6 and 8.[22] 'I want all the passengers to go down on A deck, because I intend they shall go into the boats from A deck,' Smith told nearby crewmen, who began ushering passengers towards a stairway that led down to the lower deck.

'At last, the women were told to go to the deck below as the lifeboats would be lowered from there,' Caroline Bonnell remembered:

> Mr Wick stood with us, reassuring us all. As the captain went to and fro shouting the order that women must be put into the lifeboats first, many held back, thinking it a greater peril to risk the sea in open boats than to stay behind with their husbands and brothers. We bid a cheerful goodbye to all the men we had met on the way over.
>
> Mr Wick kissed his wife, patted her on the shoulder, bidding us keep up courage, and we left him, smiling, and thinking we would all soon meet again.[23]

After hearing Captain Smith's order for the women to descend to A deck, Hugh Woolner suddenly recalled something important and approached Smith with a pertinent observation:

> I remembered noticing as I came up that all those glass windows [on A deck] were raised to the very top, and I went up to the captain and saluted him and said: 'Haven't you forgotten, sir, that all those glass windows are closed?' He said: 'By God, you are right. Call those people back.' Very few people had moved, but the few that had gone down the companionway came up again, and everything went on all right.[24]

Helen Candee was standing with Hugh Woolner when Captain Smith first issued his order for the women to descend to A deck, but she had her own memory of Smith quickly countermanding that order:

> Captain Smith's big voice called out an order: 'Lower all life-boats to the promenade deck, the deck below. Passengers will take the boats there!' ...
>
> My impulse was to remind him of the plate glass which would prevent passengers. But a captain is to be obeyed, not informed. Woolner and I stopped at the ladder-like stair but could not step upon it because of the stream of men mounting. They were the stokers ... As they came, one by one, on the narrow white stair, they

looked like cut-out black paper silhouettes, and every man touched his cap to the captain...

The stairway being cleared, Woolner and I descended to the promenade deck. It was no surprise to see lifeboats hanging unreachable on the outside of the unbreakable plate-glass. We sought the captain. 'Beg your pardon, Sir, but the plate glass is too heavy to break and boats cannot be reached.'

'My God! I forgot it!' said Captain Smith in anguished humility. Then in the same breath – an order. 'Raise the lifeboats! The passengers will take lifeboats from this deck.' From that moment on the scene changed. People poured up into the high level ... The milling crowd awaited orders.[25]

Mr and Mrs Lucian Smith were standing nearby when Captain Smith issued and then countermanded his own order. 'Then the captain gave the order, "Ladies on deck," indicating a deck that was protected with glass,' Mrs Smith recalled. 'When someone called the captain's attention to the fact that the lifeboats couldn't be lowered from that deck, he ordered us to another deck where the gymnasium was.'[26]

Mrs Smith duly obeyed the order for passengers to return to the boat deck. 'When we got there, Lucian took me to the farthest corner,' she said later. 'By that time I was frightened and a little suspicious, but he told me there was no danger.'[27] Presently Mr and Mrs Smith and Mrs Helen Candee approached lifeboat 6 and stood by to await developments.

After Second Officer Lightoller finished readying the lifeboats for launching, he walked forward towards the bridge while excess steam from the ship's idle boilers roared from the safety valves located atop the ship's funnels. 'Having got the boats swung out, I made for the captain, and happened to meet him nearby on the boat deck,' Lightoller recalled. 'Drawing him into a corner, and, cupping both my hands over my mouth and his ear, I yelled at the top of my voice, "Hadn't we better get the women and children into the boats, sir?" He heard me, and nodded reply.'[28]

'I went to the bridge and asked [Captain Smith] if I should fill No.5 boat with women and get her away,' Third Officer Herbert Pitman remembered, and the *Titanic*'s master replied, 'Carry on,' or words to that effect.[29]

At this point we need to mention a curious interview with survivor Richard Beckwith that makes a brief but significant mention of Third Officer Pitman and Captain Smith. Although Pitman made no mention of the following incident in his inquiry testimony, it's the sober, leisurely, level-headed quality of the overall account (given in Mr Beckwith's own words four days after the *Carpathia* reached New York) that makes us pay special attention to the tiny portion of his interview we will quote here:

On one thing the Hartford survivor agrees – that no one should blame for the accident but the negligence of the ship's officers, and Mr Beckwith heard a tale told to him personally by the ship's third officer that Capt. Smith, whose misfortunes came in the very winter of his life, went 'completely to pieces' when the realization of the seriousness of the crash with the iceberg came to his senses.

'The officer had to take Capt. Smith by the arm,' said Mr Beckwith, 'and lead him up and down the deck, and try to get his senses settled.'[30]

If Richard Beckwith's account is true, Captain Smith's alleged discomposure didn't last long, because Quartermaster Robert Hichens was helping to prepare lifeboat 6 for lowering when he noticed Smith standing close beside the nearby collapsible D: 'I heard the captain say, "Women and children first," and the officer repeated the words from the captain.'[31]

Kitchen Clerk Paul Maugé was standing on the forward boat deck when he saw Captain Smith enforcing his evacuation order by trying to convince a passenger to enter the first lifeboat. 'He said to a lady, "It is all right, lady,"' Maugé remembered, '"… because no lady or gentleman would like to go; everybody thought it would be quite safe."'[32]

Meanwhile, Fourth Officer Boxhall had finally completed his revised calculation of the *Titanic*'s exact latitude and longitude, and he submitted that position to Captain Smith. 'Take it to the Marconi room,' Smith instructed his fourth officer. Boxhall turned and carried the amended position to the Marconi room, where he found Jack Phillips and Harold Bride on duty.

'There was too much noise of the steam escaping, so I wrote the position down for them and left it,' Boxhall testified later. The fourth officer then returned to the boat deck and continued helping to clear the lifeboats.[33]

At 12.37 a.m. wireless operator Jack Phillips was sending out the *Titanic*'s updated position when he received a reply from the Cunard liner *Carpathia*. 'Our captain had left us at this time,' Harold Bride remembered, 'and Phillips told me to run and tell him what the *Carpathia* had answered. I did so, and I went through an awful mass of people to his cabin. The decks were full of scrambling men and women.'[34]

In his official report to the Marconi Company, Junior Operator Bride wrote:

> These communications I reported myself to the captain, who was, when I found him, engaging in superintending the filling and lowering of the lifeboats. The noise of escaping steam directly over our cabin caused a deal of trouble to Mr Phillips in reading the replies to our distress call, and this I also reported to Capt. Smith.[35]

★

Thomas Andrews was busy with his own self-imposed duties during this same time period. Mr and Mrs Albert Dick were still on the *Titanic*'s boat deck when they saw Andrews standing nearby amid a crowd of passengers. 'Quite a number of ladies were standing around him,' Mr Dick remembered:

> Just as we came up, he said earnestly: 'Now there is no occasion for a panic, and there is nothing to get excited about, but you had better go down to your cabins and put on life preservers just as quickly as you can.' He was so earnest about it that we were all impressed and followed his instructions. Everything was orderly and there seemed to be no excitement. To tell the truth, many people seemed to regard it as a drill or joke.[36]

In a different interview, Mr Dick related that Thomas Andrews told the passengers to go down to their cabins and put on their lifebelts. 'There is no need of a panic,' Andrews said reassuringly. 'There are plenty of boats. Get up as quick as you can, however.'[37]

In a third interview Mr Dick said Andrews told the passengers:

> There is no cause for any excitement. All of you get what you can in
> the way of clothes and come on deck as soon as you can. She is torn
> to bits below, but she will not sink if her after bulkheads hold. She has
> been ripped by an underwater peak of ice and it has torn many of her
> forward plates from their bolts.[38]

Mr Dick would recall later that 'It seemed almost impossible that this
could be true, and many in the crowd smiled, thinking this was merely
a little extra knowledge that Mr Andrews saw fit to impart'.[39]

In later years Albert Dick added a couple of extra details to his
memory of Thomas Andrews' announcement to the crowd:

> There was no panic ... Andrews had a megaphone and he began to
> address the passengers. I remember his words. 'Ladies and gentlemen,'
> he said, 'there is no need of panic. Go back to your staterooms and put
> on your lifebelts and warm clothing. Be as quick as you can.'[40]

Despite the fact that he was withholding the alarming truth from most of
the *Titanic*'s passengers, Thomas Andrews was unusually candid with John
B. Thayer and his son Jack. 'There were quite a few people standing around
questioning each other in a dazed kind of way,' Jack Thayer recalled:

> No one seemed to know what next to do. We saw, as they passed,
> Mr Ismay, Mr Andrews, and some of the ship's officers. Mr Andrews
> told us he did not give the ship much over an hour to live. We could
> hardly believe it, and yet if he said so, it must be true, No one was
> better qualified to know.[41]

Years later, Jack Thayer wrote much the same thing while compiling his
personal account of the sinking of the *Titanic*: 'I saw Mr Andrews half
an hour after the collision ... He told my father and I and some others
who were standing on deck that the ship could not live more than two
hours. He had just come up from the bowels of the ship.'[42]

Thomas Andrews seems to have given a similar time estimate to
Captain Smith, because after replying to Smith's question about whether

crewmen were continuing their work of evacuation, Fourth Officer Boxhall asked the *Titanic*'s master, 'Is it really serious?'

'Mr Andrews tells me he gives her from an hour to an hour and a half,' Captain Smith replied.[43]

Presently Thomas Andrews advised first-class passenger Frederick Hoyt that 'the best thing to do was put on lifebelts and get into the first available lifeboat'.[44] Andrews told passenger George Rheims to put on a lifebelt as well, but he didn't take time to explain why he deemed this extraordinary precaution to be necessary.[45]

After informing Captain Smith and a crowd of first-class passengers that the *Titanic* didn't have long to live, Thomas Andrews appears to have hurried below decks again to make sure that all stewards and stewardesses were rousing their passengers and directing them to come up to the boat deck. It's a good thing he did so, because Stewardesses Katherine Gold and Annie Martin were both still in their bunks when a steward knocked at their door and called out, 'Now then, girls, you must get up and dress: the boat has struck.'

'Go away!' Mrs Martin called out in reply. 'You don't pull my leg at this time of night.'

After being assured that the ship was truly in danger, the two stewardesses got up and were starting to dress when Thomas Andrews suddenly appeared at their cabin door. 'Hurry up there,' he urged, 'don't you know the ship is sinking?' (although he added the reassuring comment that the two ladies shouldn't be nervous).

The two stewardesses still failed to appreciate the true gravity of the situation, but they stepped out into the B-deck alleyway partially dressed. 'We ... tried to rouse some of the lady passengers,' the stewardesses recalled, 'but one and all refused at first to budge. On Mr Andrews's advice we put on our lifebelts. They felt rather funny at first, but helped to keep us warm when we were in the boats.' Mrs Gold and Mrs Martin then retrieved lifebelts from lockers on a lower deck and showed the passengers how to put them on, and everyone remained calm during these proceedings.[46]

At approximately this same time, Mrs Jacques Futrelle was watching the evacuation proceedings that were unfolding on the boat deck. 'I stood right beside Captain Smith and the first officer as he ordered the first boat away – I mean the first boat officially sanctioned,' she remembered:

Captain Smith was very calm, almost paternal. 'Don't rush, now, ladies. Just take your time; there is nothing to be frightened about. Everything will be all right,' he kept reassuring them. But I knew from the look on his face that we were doomed.[47]

Despite the extraordinary situation that now existed on the *Titanic's* decks, Mrs Lucian Smith heard Captain Smith doing his best to reassure his passengers that all would be well. 'I heard him tell several people that when the *Republic* was struck, everyone was saved and that all on the *Titanic* would also be saved,' she remembered. 'I think that he was the means of keeping many men on the boat.'[48]

Marconi operators Jack Phillips and Harold Bride were still transmitting distress signals from the wireless cabin, but a serious problem was interfering with their communications with other vessels. 'The noise of escaping steam directly over our cabin caused a deal of trouble to Mr Phillips in reading the replies to our distress call,' Bride recalled later, 'and this I also reported to Capt. Smith, who by some means managed to get it abated.'[49]

★

It was roughly an hour after the collision occurred when Washington Dodge noticed fellow passengers John Jacob Astor and Major Archibald Butt standing together with Captain Smith. 'There was absolutely no excitement among them,' Mr Dodge observed. 'Captain Smith said there was no danger ... None of us [passengers] had the slightest realization that the ship had received its death wound.'[50]

Vera Dick agreed. 'Captain Smith and a man who was said to be the personal aide to the President of the United States were among the coolest men on board,' she wrote later.[51]

'On the deck there was a strange quiet,' Seaman Albert Horswill remembered. 'I realized the engines had been stopped. I heard the officers talking rapidly in undertones, but the passengers, even the women, were quiet. Captain Smith, barking orders in a muffled voice, looked worried.'[52]

John and Nelle Snyder were standing on the forward boat deck while crewmen were doing their best to fill lifeboat 7 with passengers. 'We got to the deck just as Captain Smith ordered the lifeboats lowered,' Nelle Snyder recalled. 'At his command to enter, many persons drew back and said they would rather stay on board.'[53]

'Somebody, I afterward heard it was Mr Ismay, called out that families should keep together in getting into the boats,' John Snyder remembered:

> The people were reluctant to get into the boats at first. Those in front stepped back. Some of them looked over the side of the vessel into the darkness of the night and were loth to trust themselves to the frail-looking boats swinging on the davits.[54]

Mr and Mrs Snyder decided to get into lifeboat 7 despite some alarming talk they overheard from fellow passengers who were declining to enter the boat. 'Everyone was talking about how the first lifeboat to be lowered from a ship in times of wrecks generally tips over,' John Snyder reported later.[55]

Meanwhile, Thomas Andrews concluded his quick visit to the stewardesses' cabins and returned to the boat deck, where he was now standing alertly while lifeboat 7 was being readied for lowering. 'I saw Mr Ismay standing with Mr Andrews when the first boat drew away,' Mrs Hoyt recalled, 'and he was trying to keep order.'[56]

Steward Henry Etches was helping to prepare lifeboat 7 for lowering and agreed about Ismay's behaviour. 'Mr Ismay was assisting with the falls,' Etches remembered:

> Mr Ismay, in the first place, was asking the gentlemen to kindly keep back, as it was ladies first in this boat; and they wanted to get the boat clear first … The gentlemen were lined up, those that were trying to assist, and Mr Ismay said, 'Kindly make a line here and allow the ladies to pass through'; and I think it was Mr Murdoch's voice that was calling out, 'Ladies, this way; is there any more ladies before this boat goes?'[57]

Dorothy Gibson was seated in lifeboat 7 as it hung in the davits. She could see Thomas Andrews assisting crewmen on deck and watched as he 'ran to and fro with a face of greenish paleness and declined to answer any of the questions hurled at him from the panic-stricken passengers crowding the rail'.[58]

Spencer Silverthorne was also standing near lifeboats 7 and 5 when he noticed Captain Smith's demeanour during the early stages of the evacuation. 'Captain Smith was cool at all times,' he noted, 'and devoted his efforts to directing the officers and crew in getting the passengers into the lifeboats.'[59]

Elmer Taylor was equally impressed with Captain Smith's behaviour. 'He was extremely cool,' Taylor remembered, 'but so was Mr Ismay. The latter acted as though he was accustomed to handling such a crisis each night and his calm demeanor struck my fancy. I believe he enabled me to keep my head.'[60]

'We saw Mr Ismay on the deck when he first came up,' Mr Taylor went on. 'He looked as if he had just tumbled out of bed, but he was as careful and energetic on getting the people quietly into the boats as any of the ship officers.'[61]

At 12.40 a.m. lifeboat 7 was lowered to the water – the very first lifeboat to leave the *Titanic*, and John Snyder and his wife Nelle were both seated safely in it as it slowly drew away from the liner's side.

'At the time we got away from the *Titanic* I did not see Captain Smith,' Mr Snyder said later, 'but I understand he was on the bridge.'[62]

6

12.40–1 A.M.

Quartermaster George Rowe was stationed all by himself on the aft docking bridge on the *Titanic*'s poop deck, and for some time he'd been listening to the roar of steam being vented from the safety valves atop the motionless ship's funnels. Now, however, he suddenly noticed that a lifeboat had just been launched from the *Titanic*'s starboard side:

> I reported it [via telephone] to the bridge, asked them if they knew there was a boat being lowered. They said they did and wondered who I was. I said I was the after quartermaster. They asked me if I knew where the distress rockets were. I said yes. They said bring them on the bridge.[1]

'I had sent in the meantime for some rockets,' Fourth Officer Boxhall remembered, 'and told the captain I had sent for some rockets, and told him I would send them off, and told him when I saw this light. He said, "Yes, carry on with it."'[2]

The light Boxhall referred to was the masthead lights and sidelight of a distant steamer that were visible in the blackness off *Titanic*'s port bow. 'I told the captain about this ship,' Boxhall recalled, 'and he was with me most of the time when we were signalling … I went over and started the Morse signal. He said, "Tell him to come at once, we are sinking."'[3]

Eventually Quartermaster George Rowe arrived on the *Titanic*'s bridge carrying the box of distress rockets he'd been asked to bring with him after leaving the aft docking bridge. As Rowe recalled:

> Captain Smith told me to fire one and fire one every five or six minutes … After about two or three minutes he said to me 'Can you Morse?' I said, 'Yes, a bit.' He said 'Call that light up, tell her we are the *Titanic* sinking, please get all your boats ready.'[4]

Captain Smith was paying close attention to the lights of the nearby steamer, and he joined Fourth Officer Boxhall in training his binoculars on the vessel to see if she was replying to the *Titanic*'s Morse signal. 'Captain Smith also looked,' Boxhall testified later, 'and he could not see any answer.'[5]

In the meantime, Third Officer Herbert Pitman was hard at work taking the canvas cover off lifeboat 5 even though he felt Captain Smith's order to do so was merely a precautionary measure. Suddenly a tall man sporting a moustache approached Pitman with the quiet, unsolicited comment that 'There is no time to waste'. Officer Pitman paid no attention to the stranger's advice and proceeded to swing lifeboat 5 out over the ship's side, but once it was ready for boarding, the same man returned and told Pitman he should load it immediately with women and children.

'I await the commander's orders,' Third Officer Pitman told the stranger.

'Very well,' the man replied.

'It then dawned on me that it might be Mr Ismay, judging by the description I had had given me,' Pitman testified later:

> So I went along to the bridge and saw Capt. Smith, and I told him that I thought it was Mr Ismay that wished me to get the boat away, with women and children in it. So he said, 'Go ahead; carry on.' I came along and brought in my boat. I stood on it and said, 'Come along, ladies.' There was a big crowd. Mr Ismay helped to get them along; assisted in every way.[6]

Presently Eleanor Cassebeer finished putting on warm clothing in her cabin and made her second trip up to the *Titanic*'s boat deck:

When I came on deck again I found that the deck had started to list in a very alarming manner ... I had already donned a life preserver which I found with some difficulty, and when I reached the deck I met Mr Andrews again and he took me by the arm and led me to the lifeboat. I could not hear just what he said to me at the time on account of the din, but I saw him motion to me to get into the boat [5], which was about to be swung over the rail 90 feet above the water. I asked him why he did not get in also, and he said: 'No, women and children first.'

Mrs Cassebeer also took special notice of Bruce Ismay's attempt to assist with the evacuation:

Right here I wish to say that Bruce Ismay was there also, helping to load the women and children into the boat ... He was dressed in pajamas and slippers with a coat thrown over his shoulders.[7]

An unnamed steward agreed with Mrs Cassebeer. 'I saw Mr Bruce Ismay run on deck in his pajamas,' he said. 'He rendered most valuable assistance, being cool and collected all the time.'[8]

Bruce Ismay and Thomas Andrews didn't have an easy time filling the lifeboats with passengers, however. 'Some of the women absolutely refused to leave their husbands' sides,' Mrs Cassebeer observed, 'and it almost became necessary for Mr Ismay and Mr Andrews to use force in making some of the men get into the boats with the womenfolk so that they might be saved.'[9]

Stewardess Sarah Stap was favourably impressed by Bruce Ismay's attempt to help evacuate the ship that night. 'He was on deck in his pajamas and a coat, vainly endeavoring to get the passengers into the boats,' she remembered. 'They [the crew] had the utmost difficulty in trying to persuade the people to get into the boats ... Mr Ismay ... worked might and main all the time, and I did not think he actually realized that the ship was sinking.'[10]

Mr and Mrs George Harder had their own experience with Bruce Ismay on the forward starboard boat deck. 'Once on deck,' Mr Harder remembered, 'I found that one boat had already put off, and then my wife and I got into the second [5] with about thirty others including Karl Behr. Mr Ismay helped us get into the boat, and he acted splendidly.'[11]

An unnamed male passenger who was standing near lifeboat 5 observed Ismay's polite manner as he helped to load the boat with passengers. He said later:

> Mr Ismay and a ship's officer stood by the boat and called for people to fill the boat ... Even at that time there were few on deck.
> 'Come,' said Mr Ismay, 'some of you people may as well start along.'
> 'Can my whole family go?' asked a woman near him.
> 'Certainly, madame,' interrupted the officer, 'there is no question of that. There is room for everyone.'
> Mr Ismay then helped that family in, and for a few moments they waited for enough to fill the boat. Mr Ismay handed up a child to the mother and smiled as she took the child in her arms.[12]

The family in question may have been Mr and Mrs Richard Beckwith and Miss Helen Newsom, who had arrived on the boat deck with Karl Behr after realising that the *Titanic* was listing. At first they found a few small groups of passengers who were talking together and wondering what had happened. Karl Behr wrote in later years:

> Shortly a tall civilian arrived who we recognized as Mr Ismay, the Chairman of the White Star Line ... He approached a group of passengers near us and told them they should get into the life boats. This was our first intimation that something serious may have occurred ... Ismay walked over to us and calmly told us that we should get into a second lifeboat [5] which was being filled ... It was swung over the side flush with the deck. No one in our group however was anxious to obey ... To our minds the idea of the *Titanic* sinking was preposterous ... No one therefore moved to obey Ismay as he walked off ...
> In a few minutes, Ismay noticed us still standing together ... He again walked over and with considerably more emphasis told us we must follow instructions and get into the lifeboat – we were the last passengers on the deck. I told Mrs Beckwith I thought we should do what he said, and she finally led the way to the boat. Stopping in front of Ismay, she asked if all her party could get into the same lifeboat and he replied, 'Of course Madam, every one of you.' ...

We got into the boat in which all were standing up … and there we hung for probably five minutes, during which time Ismay was apparently waiting for more people. An officer finally came up to him and said there were no more passengers on the boat deck. Ismay then told this officer to take charge of the boat, telling four or five more sailors to get in; he then said 'Lower away' and walked off.[13]

Helen Ostby and Anna Warren were two more first-class passengers who entered lifeboat 5, and a newspaper reporter later told his readers what Miss Ostby saw taking place on the boat deck at the time. 'The last she saw of Captain Smith of the *Titanic* he was on deck in charge of things,' the reporter wrote. 'Mr Ismay, when she saw him last, was clad in pajamas and helping women into the boats. She was told later that he put on evening clothes and was thus clad when he came aboard the *Carpathia*.'[14]

Steward Henry Etches was one of the crewmen who was busy preparing lifeboat 5 for lowering. He testified later:

There was Mr Murdoch, Mr Ismay, Mr Pitman, and a quartermaster [Olliver], two stewards, and myself there … Mr Murdoch stood there the whole time, giving orders … Mr Pitman assisted … and Mr Ismay was assisting with the falls … Mr Ismay, in the first place, was asking the gentlemen to kindly keep back, as it was ladies first in this boat; and they wanted to get the boat clear first … After getting all the women that were there they called out three times – Mr Ismay called out twice, I know, in a loud voice – 'Are there any more women before this boat goes,' and there was no answer. Mr Murdoch called out; and at that moment a female came up whom I did not recognize. Mr Ismay said: 'Come along; jump in.' She said: 'I am only a stewardess.' He said: 'Never mind, you are a woman, take your place.' That was the last woman I saw get into No. 5 boat.'[15]

The stewardess in question may have been Evelyn Marsden, who entered a lifeboat only after Bruce Ismay told her 'You are all women now', even though she thought that, as a crewmember, she should remain on board the stricken vessel.[16]

Samuel Goldenberg had already helped his wife Nella into lifeboat 5, but when she begged him to join the men who were already seated in the boat, he refused. The lifeboat then began lowering towards the ocean's surface. 'When I saw that he was not coming,' Mrs Goldenberg remembered, 'I called, "For God's sake say goodbye to me then," and suddenly Mr Ismay and one of the crewmen seized Mr Goldenberg and threw him over the side. He managed to catch the boat ropes, and I and others pulled him in.'[17]

'Most fortunately for us,' Karl Behr said later, 'when we left the ship everything was handled in perfect discipline, Mr Ismay launching our lifeboat in a most splendid fashion, with absolute coolness, making sure that all passengers were on board and that our crew was complete.'[18]

Bedroom Steward Alfred Crawford was on the starboard boat deck when he noticed Bruce Ismay hard at work there. 'I saw him lowering a boat on the starboard side too, and Mr Murdoch,' Crawford testified later. 'I think it was No. 5.'[19]

As lifeboat 5, in charge of Third Officer Pitman, began descending along the *Titanic*'s side, Fifth Officer Harold Lowe, who was in charge of the actual lowering process, turned and found Ismay standing at his elbow. Lowe testified later:

He was there ... and I distinctly remember seeing him alongside of me – that is, by my side – when the first detonator [distress rocket] went off ... It was because the flash of the detonator lit up the whole deck. I did not know who Mr Ismay was then, but I learned afterwards who he was, and he was standing alongside of me.[20]

A few moments later Mr Lowe found himself receiving some unsolicited help from Ismay, and he reacted rather harshly towards the White Star Line's chairman:

The occasion for using the [strong] language I did was because Mr Ismay was overanxious and he was getting a trifle excited ... He said, 'Lower away! Lower away! Lower away! Lower away!' ...

Because he was, in a way, interfering with my duties ... I told him, 'If you will get to hell out of that I shall be able to do something.' He did not make any reply. I said, 'Do you want me to lower away quickly?' I said, 'You will have me drown the whole lot of them.'

After being thoroughly chastised by Fifth Officer Lowe, Ismay walked away from where Lowe was working and stepped over to where lifeboat 3 was being prepared for lowering.[21] (Despite Ismay's excitement, Lowe still realised that the chairman of the White Star Line 'did everything in his power to help'.)[22]

It's possible barber Augustus Weikman was one of the witnesses to Fifth Officer Lowe's brief altercation with Bruce Ismay:

> I saw Mr Ismay at the rail, directing and helping the men … One of them did not recognize him and said: 'What are you interfering for? You get back out of the way.' Another seaman warned the first man that he was speaking to the head of the Line. 'I don't care who he is: he's got to get back or go overboard. We can't be bothered with him and his orders now,' was the reply. Mr Ismay stuck to his place and continued giving orders and directing the men.[23]

Steward Edenser Wheelton was definitely present when Fifth Officer Lowe spoke harshly to Ismay, and it might have been Wheelton who eventually revealed Ismay's identity to Lowe after the *Carpathia* picked up the survivors. 'Mr Lowe told Mr Ismay to get to hell out of it, because I was the steward who stood back of Mr Lowe,' Wheelton testified later.[24]

'Two officers were supervising the loading of the boats,' Eleanor Cassebeer remembered:

> The first was tall and young and the second was short and was sporting a mustache. Both of them were waving to the women to step into the boats, but few of them were willing to take that risk, so a few men had to get in first before the women could follow. Mr Ismay was there, and constantly repeating the officer's orders as soon as they were given, which gave way to an argument between the two men.[25]

Charlotte Collyer recalled:

> There were two more lifeboats at that part of the deck … A man in plain clothes was fussing about them and screaming out instructions. I saw Fifth Officer Lowe order him away. I did not recognize him, but

from what I have read in the newspapers it must have been Mr J. Bruce Ismay, the managing director of the line.[26]

Steward Alfred Crawford later testified to having seen Bruce Ismay and an officer he identified as being First Officer Murdoch both helping to get passengers into lifeboat 5:

They were calling out and assisting all the women into the boat ... Mr Ismay stopped Mr Murdoch from lowering the boat a bit because the after end was getting hung up. Mr Murdoch called out to the aft man that was lowering the fall to lower away all the time, that he would beat him, and they lowered the boat to the water ... I was over there assisting Mr Ismay to clear the falls after they were lowering it.[27]

Lifeboat 5 was lowered away at about 12.43 a.m.

★

Meanwhile, Vera Dick and her husband Albert were still standing on the starboard boat deck after Mrs Dick had earlier resisted Captain Smith's urging to enter lifeboat 7. Mrs Dick wrote later:

As a matter of fact ... there were women older and more nervous than I, and I thought they should have the first chance. I realized the danger, but I am young and felt equal to the situation.

Capt. Smith, or maybe it was Mr Moore – I don't know which – finally insisted that I leave, 'This is no place for a woman, and you will have to go in the next boat,' they told me. I then allowed myself to be put off the *Titanic*, although I would like to have stayed until the last. I could have jumped overboard as some of the men did.

Albert and Vera Dick finally obeyed Captain Smith's instructions and took their places in lifeboat 3.[28]

Afterwards, Vera Dick recalled that Captain Smith had been doing his best to reassure his passengers during the entire evacuation process. 'We had been assured by the captain that she could not sink,' Mrs Dick recalled.[29]

In addition to seeing Captain Smith, Vera Dick also got a good view of Thomas Andrews' activities while the first lifeboats were being loaded with passengers. 'I can never forget Mr Andrews,' she said later. 'Quietly he went around helping everyone, calming any alarm. Indeed, there was no panic whatever that we saw or heard.'[30]

Chief Pantry Steward Wilfred Seward was another person who took a seat in lifeboat 3. 'As we left the ship,' he recalled:

I could see many of the men passengers walking about the decks smoking, and apparently little concerned about its safety. I could hear the band playing. It was rumored that the *Olympic* was near at hand and would take off everyone in safety. I noticed Mr Ismay on the ship, and he was busy taking care of women and children and placing them in boats.[31]

Bathroom Steward Samuel Rule likewise saw Ismay helping women to board lifeboat 3: 'Mr Ismay was seeing them into No. 3 boat ... He had his slippers and a light overcoat on and no hat ... He was just the same as any of the crew; he was doing all he could to assist to get the boats out.'[32]

From where he was sitting in lifeboat 3, Albert Dick could see that Thomas Andrews was fully occupied during this portion of the evacuation. 'The last that I saw of Mr Andrews,' he recalled, 'he was standing by the side of the navigating officer, apparently engrossed in the question of how many more women could be squeezed into the boats that remained. As a matter of fact, there could have been at least ten or twelve added to the complement of the boats that did get away.'[33]

Lifeboat 3 was finally lowered away at 12.55 a.m.

★

After lifeboat 3 left the ship, Thomas Andrews apparently hurried back down to the lower decks to ensure that the evacuation of passengers there was proceeding according to plan. After Dr William O'Loughlin told her 'Child, things are very bad,' Stewardess Mary Sloan grabbed her lifebelt and stepped from her cabin into the alleyway to begin alerting her passengers of the urgent situation:

I went round my rooms to see if my passengers were all up and to see if they had lifebelts on. Poor Mr Andrews came along, I read in his face all I wanted to know. He saw me knocking at some of the passengers' doors, he said 'that was right,' also told me to see that they had lifebelts on and to get one for myself and go on deck. He was a brave man.[34]

Mary Sloan was so impressed by Thomas Andrews' conduct during the evacuation that she later repeated her impressions of the gallant man to whoever would listen. She told a reporter:

Mr Andrews realized from the first the gravity of the accident, and I saw by his face soon after the collision how serious he knew it to be …But he worked nobly and like a true hero, going round the vessel to see that all the women had lifebelts before they went on deck to take their places in the boats. He thought of everyone except himself.[35]

She later wrote that Thomas Andrews looked as if he were 'heartbroken', and that he assured her the accident was 'very serious'. After asking her to keep the bad news to herself for fear of panic, Mr Andrews hurried away to continue the work of warning and rescue. 'He was here, there and everywhere … looking after everybody, telling the women to put on lifebelts, telling the stewardesses to hurry the women up to the boats, all about everywhere, thinking of everyone but himself.'[36]

Despite the excitement of what was taking place, Mary Sloan even noticed how Mr Andrews was dressed. 'He had his cap off,' she recalled, 'and was running about the ship in his ordinary clothes, just in his usual way.'[37]

Stewardess Annie Robinson was likewise doing her best to help her own passengers when she again encountered Thomas Andrews below decks. 'Tell them to put on warm clothing, see that everyone has a lifebelt and get them all up to the boat deck,' Andrews instructed the stewardess.

Fifteen minutes later Andrews again encountered Annie Robinson and told her, 'Open up all the spare rooms, take out all lifebelts and spare blankets and distribute them.' Miss Robinson did as she was instructed and accompanied a number of passengers up to the boat deck, but when she returned below decks to retrieve more lifebelts, Andrews asked her whether all the ladies had left their rooms. She answered, 'Yes, but would make sure.'

'Go round again,' Andrews told the stewardess. 'Did I not tell you to put on your lifebelt. Surely you have one?'

'Yes,' she replied, 'but I thought it mean to wear it.'

'Never mind that,' Andrews urged her. 'Now, if you value your life, put on your coat and belt, then walk round the deck and let the passengers see you.'

'He left me then,' Miss Robinson wrote later, 'and that was the last I saw of what I consider a true hero and one of whom his country has cause to be proud.'[38]

During his ongoing efforts to help the victualling staff rouse their passengers on B deck, Thomas Andrews urged cashier Ruth Bowker to don her own lifebelt and go up on deck. When Miss Bowker asked if anything serious had occurred, Mr Andrews replied very candidly, 'Oh yes: she is going down.'[39]

After helping to launch lifeboat 5 from the boat deck, Saloon Steward Edenser Wheelton was ordered to go down to the ship's storeroom. 'The way I went to the storeroom was down B deck, along B deck,' he recalled. 'As I went along B deck I met Mr Andrews, the builder, who was opening the rooms and looking in to see if there was anyone in, and closing the doors again.'[40]

★

In the meantime, Fourth Officer Boxhall continued to send Morse signals and fire distress rockets to attract the attention of the nearby steamer that could be seen north of the *Titanic*: 'I was sending rockets off and watching this steamer … Between the time of sending the rockets off and watching the steamer approach us I was making myself generally useful round the port side of the deck.'[41]

Unfortunately, the nearby steamer seemed to be paying no attention to the *Titanic's* distress signals. 'I cannot say I saw any reply,' Boxhall said later. 'Some people say she replied to our rockets and our signals, but I did not see them.'[42]

It was shortly after 12.49 a.m. that Harold Bride left the Marconi cabin and told Captain Smith that senior operator Jack Phillips had just established contact with the *Carpathia*, after which Smith accompanied Bride back to the wireless cabin. 'He asked Mr Phillips what other ships he was in communication with,' Bride remembered. 'He interrupted Mr Phillips when Mr Phillips was establishing communication with the *Olympic*, so he was told the *Olympic* was there.'

In his head, Captain Smith roughly calculated the *Carpathia*'s distance from the *Titanic*,[43] and it was probably at this point that he asked Jack Phillips a pointed question. 'What are you sending?' Smith asked the senior operator.

'C.Q.D.,' Phillips replied, referring to the standard wireless distress call. Harold Bride would remember:

The humor of the situation appealed to me ... and I cut in with a little remark that made us all laugh, including the captain. 'Send S.O.S.,' I said, 'it's the new call, and it may be your last chance to send it.' Phillips, with a laugh, changed the signal to S.O.S. ... The captain told us we had been struck amidships, or just aft of amid-ships.[44]

After discussing the *Carpathia* and *Olympic*, Captain Smith recalled operator Phillips' earlier wireless contact with the *Frankfurt*. 'He asked us where the *Frankfurt* was,' Bride remembered, 'but we told him we could not tell him.'[45]

At that point Captain Smith left the Marconi cabin, and Jack Phillips continued to send out distress calls to all vessels within range of his instrument's spark.[46] It was 12.57 a.m. when Phillips sent an SOS message to the *Titanic*'s elder sister *Olympic*.[47]

Saloon Steward William Burke was assisting a group of seamen on the starboard boat deck when Captain Smith approached and ordered:

the sailors that were working with me to go aft and assist about the last boat which I thought was going to be launched on that side. The sailors ran down there to assist at this boat, and I did not go. I went to the port side from there. I assisted with No. 8 boat.[48]

After leaving their cabin and ascending to the boat deck, first-class passengers Fred and Marion Kenyon were unconcernedly walking around on A deck. Marion Kenyon remembered:

We separated ourselves [from the crowd] and we walked along the outer deck and leaned against the staircase that went up to the top deck where the captain's cabin is, and Captain Smith evidently saw us down there. He said, 'Is that you, Kenyon? And he says, 'Yes, we're just waiting around.' 'Well, come on up on deck,' and we went on up on deck and talked with Captain Smith.

And after a while – Captain Smith didn't stay very long with us; he kept going into the little cabin and conversing and telephoning, but he came back and he said, 'Mr Kenyon, I want to speak with you,' and my husband left me and went and spoke with Captain Smith and came back and said, 'Captain Smith said he'd feel a lot better if all the women would go on the little boats and stay around. He'd feel better if we did,' and I started my old song, 'I won't leave you.' When Captain Smith went to the edge of the boat and he whistled, and a boat [8] came up, and he and my husband lifted – helped me over into it, and I sat in the middle of two men on the front of the boat.[49]

She would later tell *New York Press*:

Captain Smith would not allow my husband in the boat and I said I would not go without him, but finally I was forced to go. There were but twenty-eight persons in the boat, which was built for fifty-six.[50]

Second Saloon Steward William Burke was one of the crewmen who was preparing lifeboat 8 for lowering. 'An officer sent me for a lamp,' he remembered:

and as I was going forward there was a man coming with two or three lamps in his hand. I went back again, and this No. 8 boat was there, all swung out, and there were about 35 ladies in it. I jumped in the boat. The captain asked me was the plug in the boat, and I answered, "Yes, sir.' 'All right,' he said, 'Any more ladies?' [51]

Marie Young, who was also in lifeboat 8, remembered:

The captain was beside us and from a hamper nearby he threw a huge loaf of bread into the boat. To a group of waiting seamen and stewards we heard the question put, 'Can you row?' No sailor had any station assigned him for any boat, and this 'scratch' crew had known no boat drills. Eagerly, four men entered our boat as oarsmen.[52]

Emil and Tillie Taussig, as well as their daughter Ruth, witnessed the 'scratch' crew enter lifeboat 8. Tillie Taussig remembered:

When we came on deck, Captain Smith was preparing the eighth boat to be let down ... There was only one seaman in sight, but a number of stewards had rushed up between crowding men and women. The captain turned to the stewards and asked them if they knew how to row. They answered 'Yes' hastily, and four of them were allowed to jump in.

Only twenty women were near the boat, and these were put in. My daughter Ruth was among the first, but I said that I wouldn't go if my husband did not accompany me. There was room for fourteen more after the last woman had found her place, and they all pleaded to let the men take the empty seats. But the captain said that he would not allow it. I was frantic. There was that boat, ready to be lowered into the water and only half full.[53]

Emma Bucknell remembered:

I was put in the second lifeboat from the bow and I think it was Captain Smith himself who put me in the boat ... 'It is only a matter of precaution,' explained the captain, 'and there is really no danger.' It was lifeboat 8 and it was manned by four men, a steward and three ordinary seamen ... Wives and husbands were separated when the women were placed in our boat. A few of the men grew seemingly desperate, and Captain Smith, who was standing by, cried out 'Behave yourselves like men! Look at all the women. See how splendid they are! Can't you behave like men!' Then Captain Smith himself picked up a big basket of bread and handed it across to me in the lifeboat. That was all the provisions I saw.[54]

Dr Alice Leader and Mrs Joel Swift arrived on the boat deck after some-one near their cabin warned them of danger:

> When we reached the boat deck we saw Captain Smith standing there quietly giving orders to the men as they lowered the lifeboats. We watched one go down with passengers and noticed that there were no men in it – that is, none except seamen.

Shortly afterwards, they got into lifeboat 8:

> There were twenty-two persons, including three seamen and a stew-ard, aboard our boat and as we were suspended over the water far below, Captain Smith tucked a loaf of bread in the bow where there were two casks of water. That was all the provisions we had.[55]

Mrs Swift agreed:

> The boats were provisioned and in ours we had two barrels of water and some bread. The captain, poor, dear, brave man, threw in another loaf as we pulled away. I am sorry to say that I sat with my foot on that loaf for some time. As we went, the captain told us to pull for a light that was far, far away from the *Titanic*.
>
> I think it must have been a fishing smack, and I believe now that the captain realized that the vessel was sinking and told us to row away as fast as we could in order to get away from the suction should the boat go down.[56]

Emma Bucknell later described hearing Captain Smith issuing orders after she'd taken her seat in lifeboat 8. '"There is a light out there," said Captain Smith, to the man in charge of our lifeboat, which contained thirty-five persons. "Take the women to it and hurry back as speedily as possible."'[57]

Saloon Steward Alfred Crawford was one of the crewmen who were working at lifeboat 8:

> Captain Smith came to the boat and asked how many men were in the boat … There were two sailors. He told me to get into the boat.

He gave us instructions to pull to a light that he saw and then land the ladies and return back to the ship again. Captain Smith could see the light quite plain, as he pointed in the direction that we were to make for. He pointed in the direction of the two lights, and said: 'Pull for that vessel; land your people and return to the ship.' Those were Captain Smith's words [to us].[58]

'There were no more [passengers] there,' Steward William Burke recalled, 'and [Captain Smith] lowered away ... He told me to row for the light, and land the passengers and return to the ship.'[59]

Marie Young heard the captain's command as well. 'Capt. Smith called to us to pull for a green light seen in the distance to unload passengers and return to the boat at once,' she related later.[60]

'Captain Smith stood shoulder to shoulder with me as I got into the life boat,' the Countess of Rothes remembered:

and the last words were to the able seaman – Tom Jones – 'Row straight for those ship lights over there; leave your passengers on board of her and return as soon as you can.' Captain Smith's whole attitude was one of great calmness and courage, and I am sure he thought that the ship – whose lights we could plainly see – would pick us up and that our lifeboats would be able to do double duty in ferrying passengers to the help that gleamed so near.[61]

Gladys Cherry agreed:

The captain gave us orders to row to a light he saw, and come back to the boat to get others ... We were only twenty-four women and three men, and we could have held 50. It was the stillest night possible, not a ripple on the water and the stars wonderful; that icy air and the stars I never want to see or feel again.[62]

Seaman Thomas Jones remembered:

I jumped in the boat ... The captain asked me was the plug in the boat, and I answered, 'Yes, sir.' 'All right,' he said, 'Any more ladies?' There was one lady came there and left her husband. She wanted her husband to go with her, but he backed away, and the captain shouted again – in fact, twice again – 'Any more ladies?' There were no more there, and he lowered away … [Captain Smith] told me to row for the light, and land the passengers and return to the ship.[63]

Captain Smith again addressed Mrs Kenyon seated in lifeboat 8:

He said 'Do you see that light in the northwest?' I said yes. He said, 'You tell the men to keep rowing towards that light.' Then I wondered, and my husband [on deck] turned abruptly, and he turned round – he wouldn't look at me – and the boat was lowered.[64]

Tillie Taussig remembered:

Then the orders came to lower … The men were pleading for permission to step in, and one came forward to take a place next to his wife. I heard a shot, and I am sure it was he that went down …

Then the boat [8] swung out from the deck … I was still with my husband, and [our daughter] Ruth had already disappeared below the deck. I gave a great cry – I remember calling out the name of my daughter – and two men tore me from my husband's side, lifted me, one by the head and one the feet, and dropped me over the deck into the lowering boat. I struck on the back of my head, but I had furs on and that fact probably saved me from greater injury. The horrible thing was that we had so much room left for the poor men who were snatched from our sides.[65]

Roberta Maioni was one of the lucky passengers who found a seat in lifeboat 8, and in later years she wrote an account of her experiences: 'An elderly officer, with tears streaming down his cheeks, helped us into one of the lifeboats … He was Captain Smith – the master of that ill-fated vessel. As the lifeboat began to descend, I heard him say, "Goodbye, remember you are British."'[66]

As lifeboat 8 gradually descended towards the ocean's surface, Steward Crawford could see Captain Smith taking an active part in the launching process. 'Captain Smith and the steward lowered the forward falls of the boat I was in,' Crawford observed. 'The captain, he came there; he came there and lowered the forward falls, he assisted in doing so.'[67]

'Slowly we dropped down, down and down, until the keel of our tiny craft struck the sea,' Dr Leader remembered, 'and the captain shouted to pull over to a red light in the distance, which was evidently a ship. "Come back again if you like," were his final words.'[68]

'When we put off from the boat,' Seaman Tom Jones remembered:

Captain Smith ordered me to proceed to the fishing smacks, whose lights we could see in the distance, and then to come back to the boats. But the fishing smacks paid no attention to us, probably because we used no rockets, and, then again, there was but one boat among the whole fleet of lifeboats that carried a blue light, the signal of distress.[69]

Lifeboat 8 left the *Titanic* at 1 a.m.

★

After lifeboat 8 was safely in the water, Steward Crawford thought he saw Captain Smith stepping aft along the boat deck to check on how things were going at lifeboat 10 in the aft quad of port lifeboats.[70]

'Captain Smith did all any man could do under the circumstances,' an unnamed female survivor said later, 'and when the boat that I was in pulled away from the side of the ship he was quietly giving orders as though he were in harbor.'[71]

THE EYEWITNESSES

A Portrait Gallery

Elizabeth Allen. (Author's collection)

Harry Anderson. (Courtesy of Philip Gowan)

John Jacob Astor. (Author's collection)

Madeleine Astor. (Author's collection)

Fred Barrett. (Courtesy of Philip Gowan)

Karl Behr. (*Illustrated London News*)

Joseph Bell. (Author's collection)

Dickinson Bishop. (Courtesy of Philip Gowan)

Helen Bishop. (Author's collection)

Joseph Boxhall. (National Archives)

Harold Bride. (Author's collection)

Caroline Brown. (Author's collection)

Edward Brown. (Author's collection)

Kate Buss. (Author's collection)

Archibald Butt. (Author's collection)

Helen Candee. (*Washington Post*)

Eleanor Cassebeer. (Courtesy of Mike Poirier)

Gladys Cherry. (Author's collection)

John Collins. (Courtesy of Philip Gowan)

Edward Dorkings. (Courtesy of Philip Gowan)

Lucy Duff Gordon. (*Illustrated London News*)

Henry Etches. (Author's collection)

Elizabeth Eustis. (*Daily Graphic*)

Cecil Fitzpatrick. (Author's collection)

Antoinette Flegenheim. (Courtesy of Gerhard Schmidt-Grillmeier)

Laura Francatelli. (Courtesy of Philip Gowan)

Jacques Futrelle. (Author's collection)

May Futrelle. (Author's collection)

Dorothy Gibson. (Courtesy of Philip Gowan)

Katherine Gold. (Courtesy of Dr Paul Lee)

Archibald Gracie. (Author's collection)

John Hart. (Author's collection)

Samuel Hemming. (Author's collection)

Charles Hendrickson. (Author's collection)

Robert Hichens. (*Edinburgh Evening News*)

Fred Hoyt. (Courtesy of Philip Gowan)

Carlos Hurd. (*St Louis Post Dispatch*)

Violet Jessop. (Courtesy of Margaret and Mary Meehan and John Maxtone-Graham)

James Johnston. (*Liverpool Echo*)

Charles Judd. (*Reading Standard*)

Frederick Kenyon. (Author's collection)

Marion Kenyon. (Courtesy of Don Lynch)

Emilie Kreuchen. (Courtesy of Phil Gowan)

Hugh McElroy. (Author's collection)

Charles Mackay. (Courtesy of Mike Poirier)

Pierre Maréchal. (Author's collection)

Annie Martin. (Author's collection)

Paul Maugé. (Courtesy of Olivier Mendez)

Isaac Maynard. (Author's collection)

William Mellors. (Courtesy of Philip Gowan)

William Murdoch. (Author's collection)

William O'Loughlin. (Author's collection)

Alfred Olliver. (Author's collection)

Alfred Omont. (Courtesy of Olivier Mendez)

Helen Ostby. (Courtesy of Philip Gowan)

Alma Pålsson. (Courtesy of Lars-Inge Glad)

Jack Phillips. (Author's collection)

Herbert Pitman. (Author's collection)

John Poigndestre. (*Jersey Illustrated Weekly*, courtesy of Dr Paul Lee)

George Rheims. (Author's collection)

Annie Robinson. (Author's collection)

Countess of Rothes. (*Daily Graphic*)

Harry Senior. (Courtesy of Gavin Bell)

Spencer Silverthorne.
(Courtesy of Philip Gowan)

Mary Sloan. (*Sphere*)

William Sloper. (*Daily Graphic*)

Mary Eloise Smith. (*Daily Sketch*)

John Stewart. (Association Française du *Titanic*)

Gunnar Tenglin. (Author's collection)

Jack Thayer. (Courtesy of Olivier Mendez)

Alfred Theissinger. (Courtesy of Malte Fiebing-Petersen)

William Törnqvist.
(Courtesy of Peter Engberg)

Anna Warren. (Courtesy of
John Lamoreau)

Augustus Weikman.
(Author's collection)

August Wennerström.
(Author's collection)

Edenser Wheelton. (Courtesy
of Philip Gowan)

Eleanor Widener. (Author's
collection)

George Widener. (Author's
collection)

Charles Williams. (*Illustrated
London News*)

7

1–1.30 A.M.

Down on B deck, cashier Ruth Bowker had followed Thomas Andrews' earlier instructions and donned her lifebelt inside her own cabin before going up to the boat deck. 'Miss Bowker was told to get into a boat on the port side by Captain Smith himself,' a newspaper reporter wrote later. 'She was reluctant to do so, until dragged in by one of the sailors. The discipline and coolness of the captain and officers, who must have known well the awful danger, was admirable. The boat was launched with difficulty.'[1]

Steward Henry Etches was another member of the victualling crew who encountered Thomas Andrews down on B deck. Etches remembered:

He stopped me ... I was going along B deck, and he asked had I waked all my passengers ... Mr Andrews then told me to come down on C deck with him, and we went down the pantry staircase together. Going down he told me to be sure and make the passengers open their doors, and to tell them the life belts were on top of the wardrobes and on top of the racks, and to assist them in every way I could to get them on, which I endeavored to do ... We walked along C deck together. The purser [Hugh McElroy] was standing outside of his office, in a large group of ladies. The purser was asking them to do as he asked them, and to go back in their rooms and not to frighten themselves, but, as a preliminary caution, to put the lifebelts on, and the stewards would give them every attention. Mr Andrews said: 'That is exactly what I have been trying to get them to do' … On C deck … I threw the life belts down, and then threw some of them into the corridor. Mr Andrews said to be sure there were no lifebelts left … and, with that, he walked down the staircase to go on lower D deck. That is the last I saw of Mr Andrews.[2]

Down on E deck, barber Augustus Weikman 'met Mr Andrews, the builder, and he was giving instructions to get the steerage passengers on deck'.[3] When Stewardess Annie Robinson encountered Andrews again on that same deck, he instructed her to put on her lifebelt and to advise her passengers to leave E deck.[4]

Meanwhile, up on the starboard boat deck, Fireman Charles Hendrickson saw preparations being made to launch lifeboat 1. '[I] heard the captain say they were to get all the women and children into the boats first,' Hendrickson remembered. 'Then the captain walked along and gave his orders to the officers, whoever were there; they were walking up and down to see if they were being carried out.'[5]

It was at about this time that lookout George Symons got his last glimpse of Captain Smith: 'The last I saw of him he was on the bridge … That was just before I went away in boat No. 1.'[6]

Earlier, Captain Smith had ordered Quartermaster Walter Wynn to help another quartermaster get emergency lifeboats 1 and 2 ready for lowering.[7] Seaman Frank Evans was now beginning the actual process of lowering lifeboat 1 when he saw Captain Smith approaching. 'He came to the starboard action boat that I was lowering,' Evans testified later. 'He passed some remark to a tall military gentleman there with white spats on [Bruce Ismay?], but what it was I could not say, as I was attending to the fall; it was a tall military-looking gentleman who was giving orders as to lowering away forward or aft or both together.'[8]

Fireman Hendrickson and Seaman Albert Horswill had both been ordered to help man lifeboat 1. 'As we were being lowered,' Horswill remembered, 'I heard Captain Smith shout to me: "Pull away as fast as you can!" I never heard his voice again.'[9]

While lifeboat 1 was being lowered towards the ocean's surface, Bathroom Steward Samuel Rule could see Ismay standing nearby. 'He was standing by [the empty davits that had launched] No. 3,' Rule testified later.[10]

Lifeboat 1 was launched at 1.05 a.m.

★

Meanwhile, on the opposite side of the ship, lifeboat 6 had been uncovered before being lowered level with the port boat deck. Arthur Peuchen remembered:

> I was standing near by the second officer and the captain was standing there as well, at that time. The captain said – I do not know whether it was the captain or the second officer said – 'We will have to get these masts out of these boats, and also the sail.' He said, 'You might give us a hand,' and I jumped in the boat, and we got a knife and cut the lashings of the mast, which is a very heavy mast, and also the sail, and moved it out of the boat, saying it would not be required. Then there was a cry, as soon as that part was done, that they were ready to put the women in; so the women came forward one by one. A great many women came with their husbands.[11]

First-class passengers Helen Candee and Hugh Woolner were standing nearby watching crewmen preparing lifeboat 6 for lowering.

'The captain was close by at that time,' Woolner remembered:

> He sort of ordered the people in. He said, 'Come along, madam,' and that sort of thing. There was a certain amount of reluctance on the part of the women to go in, and then some officer said, 'It is a matter of precaution,' and then they came forward rather more freely.[12]

Mrs Candee remembered:

> The captain, speaking to my two men, indicating me said, 'Take this lady and put her in that boat [6],' ... Each man took an arm. We were half way to the lonely boat when the captain's voice again called, 'Hey, you two, come away from that boat! No men are allowed near the lifeboats.' At the implication, the two men dropped me as if I had been a leper. I was left to walk alone to the boat which hung beside the deck, touching it for a very little space.

… Mighty oars lay length-wise, forming almost a deck … I stepped on this perilous platform which rolled and unbalanced me. I took a falling jump to the bottom. To arise was almost impossible as I had hurt my leg. While I struggled, the captain came near and seeing me down called, 'Get up, get up and help these women to get in.' 'I can't, Captain, I have hurt my ankle.' He went away in disgust. I managed to arise and balance on a thwart.[13]

'We waited to see that boat filled,' Hugh Woolner recalled with satisfaction. 'It was not filled, but a great many people got into it.'[14]

Cashier Ruth Bowker was unwilling to get into lifeboat 6 even though she was told to do so by Captain Smith himself. In fact, she was so reluctant to enter the boat that finally a crewman dragged her into it against her will.[15]

Martha Stone also happened to be standing close to lifeboat 6 when she decided it was time for her to make a decision:

I saw there was room in the boat they were lowering, and I said to my maid 'Let us go now,' The man in the boat gave me his hand, but the boat swung out so far he had to let go of my hand to catch a rope, and I fell in. Before I could get up he was calling for a knife to cut something. The captain came and stood in front of us saying 'Women and children first.' Many men were standing near but not one moved, only those assisting their wives. The captain asked the man in charge of the boat how many men he had. He answered, 'Two of us.' Then the Captain said 'All right. Lower the boat, row out and all keep together.'[16]

Colonel Archibald Gracie later repeated what Helen Candee told him regarding the occurrences that took place at lifeboat 6: 'Just before her boat was lowered away a man's voice said: "Captain, we have no seaman." Captain Smith then seized a boy by the arm and said, "Here's one." The boy went into the boat as ordered by the captain, but afterwards he was found to be disabled. She does not think he was an Italian.'[17]

Mary Smith and her husband Lucian were also standing beside lifeboat 6. Mary Smith remembered:

They kept calling for one more lady to fill it and my husband insisted that I get in it, my friend having gotten in. I refused unless he would go with me.

In the meantime, Capt. Smith was standing with a megaphone on deck. I approached him and told him I was alone, and asked if my husband might be allowed to go in the boat with me. He ignored me personally, but shouted again through his megaphone, 'Women and children first.'[18]

In a newspaper interview, Mary Smith said, 'I turned to Captain Smith, who was standing by the port rail, and asked him to allow my husband to go with me. He said: "No, madam; under no circumstances will any man be permitted to leave this boat."'[19] 'Good boy,' Lucian Smith exclaimed as he gave the *Titanic*'s master a hearty pat on the back.[20]

'My husband said, "Never mind, captain, about that; I will see that she gets in the boat,"' Mrs Smith remembered:

He then said, 'I never expected to ask you to obey, but this is one time you must; it is only a matter of form to have women and children first. The boat is thoroughly equipped, and everyone on her will be saved.' I asked him if that was absolutely honest, and he said, 'Yes.' I felt some better then, because I had absolute confidence in what he said. He kissed me goodbye and placed me in the lifeboat with the assistance of an officer.[21]

Meanwhile, Captain Smith continued to reassure all passengers who were standing in the vicinity of lifeboat 6. 'He kept repeating "The *Titanic* cannot possibly sink for twenty-four hours,"' Mrs Smith recalled, '"and the *Olympic* will pass this way at 2 o'clock, so everyone is safe."'[22]

Finally, at 1.10 a.m., as lifeboat 6 began its slow descent towards the ocean's surface, Lucian Smith called out one final word of advice to his departing wife. 'As the boat was being lowered,' she recalled, 'he yelled from the deck, "Keep your hands in your pockets; it is very cold weather."'[23]

Then, as a sudden afterthought, Mr Smith exclaimed to his wife, 'Oh, I forgot that watch I bought for your father. I will be right back.' She never saw her husband again.[24]

Lifeboat 6 had descended only part-way to the water when Quartermaster Robert Hichens, who was in charge of the boat, shouted up to the crewmen on deck that he had only one man in the boat to assist him in navigating the small craft. Second Officer Lightoller heard the appeal for assistance and said, 'We will have to have some more seamen here.'

First-class passenger Arthur Peuchen overheard Lightoller's comment and turned to the second officer. 'Can I be of any assistance?' he asked. 'I am a yachtsman, and can handle a boat with an average man.'

'Why, yes,' Lightoller replied. 'I will order you to the boat in preference to a sailor.'

Captain Smith was standing nearby and overheard this exchange. 'You had better go down below and break a window and get in through a window, into the boat,' he advised Major Peuchen, who later remembered:

> That was his suggestion and I said I did not think it was feasible, and I said I could get in the boat if I could get hold of a rope. However, we got hold of a loose rope in some way that was hanging from the davit, near the block anyway, and by getting hold of it I swung myself off the ship, and lowered myself into the boat ... I imagine it was opposite the C deck at the time.[25]

Rose Amélie Icard was very favourably impressed with Captain Smith's behaviour while he was working at lifeboat 6. 'I can still see him, a handsome old man with a white beard,' she wrote later. 'It is him who helped me get in the lifeboat.'[26]

Peuchen was likewise impressed by Captain Smith's devoted attention to his duty. 'He was doing everything in his power to get women in these boats, and to see that they were lowered properly,' he remembered. 'I thought he was doing his duty in regard to the lowering of the boats.'[27]

From his own vantage point, Fireman William Major was favourably impressed with Ismay as well as with Captain Smith. 'Captain Smith and Mr Ismay ... were aft when the ship began to go down by the head,' Major recalled. 'Captain Smith was acting calmly, but doing a lot of work, and Mr Ismay was giving orders just like an officer.'[28]

Unfortunately, not everyone had taken advantage of the opportunity to leave the *Titanic* in lifeboat 6. Mrs Jacques Futrelle was one such person who stepped away from the boat at the last minute. 'The captain and Mr Wilde, the chief officer, launched the first boat, No. 6,' she recalled:

> Just to look at those men I knew we were doomed. They knew they had to die. Wilde had the look of death in his eye. The captain was very different from the first officer. He treated us as nice children. We were ordered into the boat. I hung back and slid out of the group, having some idea that I could help my husband's chances of getting into a boat if I stayed with him.[29]

After lifeboat 6 reached the ocean's surface, Margaret Brown looked up from her seat in the boat and got one final glimpse of Captain Smith. Archibald Gracie later repeated what Mrs Brown related to him:

> When the sea was reached, smooth as glass, she looked up and saw the benign, resigned countenance, the venerable white hair and the Chesterfieldian bearing of the beloved Captain Smith with whom she had crossed twice before, and only three months previous on the *Olympic*. He peered down upon those in the boat, like a solicitous father, and directed them to row to the light in the distance – all boats keeping together.[30]

From her own seat in lifeboat 6, Helen Candee heard the *Titanic*'s master issue one final command to the occupants of her lifeboat. 'The captain's voice again shouted emphatically, "All boats row away from the ship … All boats keep together."'[31]

Martha Stone remembered:

> As soon as we were in the [water], Captain Smith called to the sailors to get away. One of the two men in the boat turned to the women seated at the oars and said excitedly, 'You must row for your lives. If we are not half a mile away in twenty minutes, we will be sucked down with the ship.'[32]

It was while Second Officer Lightoller had been working at lifeboat 6 that he suddenly realised the *Titanic* had developed a list to port:

> I may say that my notice was called to this list – I perhaps might not have noticed it; it was not very great – by Mr Wilde calling out 'All passengers over to the starboard side'. That was an endeavor to give her a righting movement, and it was then I noticed that the ship had a list. It would have been far more noticeable on the starboard side than on the port.[33]

In any case, it was after Second Officer Lightoller finished launching lifeboat 6 that Chief Officer Henry Wilde came across from the vessel's starboard side to ask him if he knew where the ship's firearms were kept:

> I told the Chief Officer, 'Yes, I know where they are ... Come along and I'll get them for you,' and into the First Officer's cabin we went – the Chief, Murdoch, the Captain and myself – where I hauled them out, still in all their pristine newness and grease. I was going out when the Chief shoved one of the revolvers into my hands, with a handful of ammunition, and said, 'Here you are, you may need it.' On the impulse, I just slipped it into my pocket, along with the cartridges, and returned to the boats.[34]

'The captain was armed as he stood on the bridge, some of the survivors report,' a later newspaper advised its readers. 'Several say they saw him holding his pistol ready for use, but nobody was found today who saw him use it.'[35]

One of the few survivor accounts claiming that Captain Smith wielded a revolver during the evacuation process allegedly came from Lucy Duff Gordon, who reportedly said that the *Titanic*'s master was wielding a revolver while her own lifeboat (1) was pulling away from the *Titanic* after 1.05 a.m. 'A few men crowded into the last lifeboat,' she was quoted as saying, 'but were turned out by Captain Smith, who held a revolver. Several persons were knocked down before order was restored.'[36]

Edith Chibnall, who left the *Titanic* in lifeboat 6 at 1.10 a.m., was another passenger who reportedly made similar observations about

Captain Smith. At no time, it was stated by both Mrs Chibnall and her daughter, was there any panic among the first- and second-cabin passengers. There was a panic, however, among the third-class passengers, and it was necessary for Captain Smith to drive them away from the lifeboats at the point of a revolver.[37]

A third such account reportedly came from steerage passenger Bertha Mulvihill, who left the *Titanic* later in lifeboat 15 at 1.41 a.m. and would later allegedly claim:

> Some of the Italian men from way down in the steerage were screaming and fighting to get into the lifeboats ... Captain Smith stood at the head of the passageway. He had a gun in his hand. 'Boys,' he said, 'you've got to do your duty here. It's the women and the children first, and I'll shoot the first man who jumps into a boat.'
>
> But this didn't seem to have much effect on them, for they still cried and fought to get into the boats. But the captain – Oh, he was a good captain and a brave man – stood guard and wouldn't let any men get in before the women.[38]

Earlier during the evacuation process Renée Harris had seen Captain Smith conferring with one of her fellow first-class passengers, but it was only later that she observed the actual results of that conversation. 'When the order to man the boats came, the captain whispered something to Major [Archibald] Butt,' she recalled:

> The two of them had become friends. The major immediately became as one in supreme command. You would have thought he was at a White House reception. A dozen or more women [later] became hysterical all at once, as something connected with a lifeboat went wrong. Major Butt stepped over to them and said: 'Really, you must not act like that; we are all going to see you through this thing.' He helped the sailors rearrange the rope or chain that had gone wrong and lifted some of the women in with a touch of gallantry. Not only was there a complete lack of any fear in his manner, but there was the action of an aristocrat.[39]

Washington Dodge made a similar observation about the calm demeanour of John Jacob Astor. 'Astor was courageous,' he said. 'He assisted Captain Smith and Major Archibald Butt in allaying the panic and in assisting the women and children into the boats. Major Butt was calm and collected throughout everything.'[40]

Near the aft end of the port boat deck, Mary Compton and her daughter Sara were standing near lifeboat 14 when they were approached by Captain Smith, who handed each of them a lifebelt. 'They will keep you warm if you do not have to use them,' he said cheerily.

'Then the crew began clearing the boats and putting the women into them,' Mrs Compton remembered. 'My daughter and I were lifted in the boat commanded by the fifth officer.'[41]

'Men were not allowed to get into the lifeboats,' second-class passenger Edith Brown recalled, 'and Captain Smith told my mother and I to get into lifeboat number 14. My poor father had to stay behind on deck.'[42]

Lifeboat 14 was launched at 1.25 a.m.

★

Meanwhile, over on the starboard boat deck, Seaman George McGough was one of the people who was seated in lifeboat 9. When that boat finally began lowering towards the ocean's surface, McGough heard Captain Smith say, 'Don't mind me, men. Save your own lives. God bless you!'[43]

Saloon Steward William Ward got his last glimpse of Bruce Ismay from his own seat in lifeboat 9, and he noted that Ismay was not giving orders to anyone at that time. 'He was on deck when our boat left,' Ward testified later. '... I heard him say, "Steady, boys," or something like that – it was some expression like that – when he was standing talking to Mr [Hugh] McElroy [the purser].'[44]

It was during the launching of lifeboat 9 that Steward Edenser Wheelton got his own last glimpse of Ismay on the *Titanic*. 'The last I saw of him was when we sent No. 9 away,' Wheelton testified later. '... He stood there at the falls ... He helped the women and children into the boat, sir, and told the men to make way.'[45]

Lifeboat 9 left the *Titanic* at 1.30 a.m.

★

Emma Schabert and her brother Philipp Mock were still standing on the starboard boat deck as lifeboat 9 began pulling away from the ship's side. 'The great Mr Ismay [had] tried to make me enter the last boat on the upper deck,' Schabert wrote later. 'When I refused and it had gone, he said: "You made a great mistake not to get into that boat." I answered: "It does not matter. I prefer staying with my brother."'[46]

Meanwhile, over on the aft port boat deck, lifeboat 12 was launched at roughly the same time as lifeboat 9. As the boat was pulling away from the *Titanic*'s side, Lillian Bentham was later said to have heard Captain Smith reply to someone's question by exclaiming, 'It's neck or nothing now – every man for himself.'[47]

8

1.30–2 A.M.

By 1.30 a.m., Thomas Andrews had got his message of danger across to the *Titanic*'s victualling staff and to the passengers they were attending. By now most of the stewards and stewardesses had finished rousing their passengers and were now headed towards the upper decks along with their charges.

'After seeing that all the passengers we could find had their lifebelts, we went back to dress,' Stewardess Katherine Gold recalled, 'but it was then about half-past one, and Mr Andrews of the firm of Harland & Wolff, came and hurried us.' Mrs Gold and Mrs Martin finished dressing themselves, and Mrs Gold hurried up on deck just in time to join Stewardess Annie Robinson in boarding lifeboat 11, which had been lowered from the boat deck and was now hanging suspended just outside the railing at the aft end of A deck.[1]

Bruce Ismay had come down to A deck as well, and Stewardess Annie Martin was very impressed by his gallantry during the loading of lifeboat 11. 'He put two of our girls into a boat, when they wanted to stand back and make room for passengers,' Mrs Martin recalled. '"But we are only stewardesses, sir," they said. "You are women, anyhow," was Mr Ismay's reply.'[2]

Stewardess Hypatia McLaren may have been one of the two stewardesses who were assisted into lifeboat 11 by Ismay. 'We are not passengers,' Mrs McLaren told Ismay. 'We are members of the crew.'

'It doesn't matter,' Mr Ismay replied. 'You are women, and I wish you to get in.'[3]

Katherine Gold was apparently the second stewardess who was assisted into lifeboat 11 by Ismay even though she was reluctant to take a seat in the boat.

'Get in, stewardess,' Ismay told her.

'I am one of the crew and should stand by the ship,' Mrs Gold replied.

'But you are a woman, and must get in the boat,' Ismay countered.

It was only at the insistence of Ismay and the other men that Gold finally relented and entered lifeboat 11. 'I was not a bit afraid, somehow,' she said later. 'I was quite cool. There was really nothing in it.'[4]

At one point Ismay ascended from A deck to the boat deck, where first-class passenger Edith Rosenbaum was standing with no unlaunched lifeboats in sight. She remembered:

Just then I happened to turn around and I caught sight of a man standing in one of the doors. He was calling out and asking if all the women were being cared for. As he caught sight of me he motioned to me and I approached him … This man was Mr Ismay, who seized my arm and cried, 'Woman, what are you doing here? All women should be off the boat!' He thrust me down the passageway to A deck, where I found myself between two lines of men. I was picked up by two of them, carried to the side of the lifeboat [11], and thrust over into it head first …

I screamed as I lurched into the craft, and at the same time lost both my slippers … I remonstrated against going out in the lifeboat, and some of the men assisted me back to the deck again, where I retrieved my slippers. I had scarcely recovered from this frightful experience when one of the men hastened to my side. It happened that he was an acquaintance I had made in Cherbourg, Mr [Philipp] Mock, a miniature painter. He persuaded me to enter the lifeboat, and facilitated matters by allowing me to step upon his knee, gaining the lifeboat with less difficulty than the first time. The boat was not filled, and there were no other women in sight. As it swung out on the davits and lowered to the water, Mr Mock jumped in after me.[5]

Philipp Mock and his sister Emma Schabert had been standing on the boat deck for some time after Mrs Schabert had refused Ismay's earlier advice to enter lifeboat 9. 'Meanwhile the boat was sinking lower,' Schabert wrote later:

> Then someone said there was a boat [11] on the lower [A] deck and we went down to find it nearly crowded. There were just a few women left on deck, so I risked it and went in, and after the other women were put in then there was room for one man, and Boy [Philipp] was allowed to enter. The officers had pistols to shoot any man who entered without permission.[6]

As lifeboat 11 began its slow descent towards the ocean's surface, Edith Rosenbaum got a last glimpse of Ismay as he continued his self-imposed mission to help evacuate the ship's passengers. 'I last saw him calling out, "Any more women? If so, all off now!"' she recalled later.

Meanwhile, up on the boat deck Able Seaman Robert Hopkins was helping to man the davits that were lowering lifeboat 11, but suddenly the lifeboat's falls became tangled. As Hopkins bent over the ropes to unsnarl them, Captain Smith stepped up to him and slapped him heartily on the shoulder.

'What's the matter here, my lad?' asked the *Titanic*'s master.

Presently Seaman Hopkins was able to straighten out the tangled ropes, and lifeboat 11 reached the ocean's surface safely at 1.35 a.m.[7]

★

From her seat in lifeboat 11, Marie Jerwan heard a fellow occupant of her boat complain about Captain Smith. 'The sailor who rowed our boat told me that he had followed the sea for forty years,' Miss Jerwan said later, 'and had never been in any kind of an accident before, except on the *Olympic* when she rammed the *Hawke*.'

'That was under the same captain,' the crewman grumbled, 'and now I'm having my second experience under him.'[8]

Thomas Andrews appears to have gone up to the boat deck at about the same time Mrs Gold and Mrs Martin headed up to board lifeboat 11, but – unlike the two stewardesses – he seems to have sought a few brief moments of solitude in order to gather his thoughts and prepare for the inevitable. Shortly before getting into lifeboat 15, Steward John Stewart saw Mr Andrews standing all alone in the first-class smoking room, his arms folded over his breast and his lifebelt lying on a nearby table.

'Aren't you going to have a try for it, Mr Andrews?' Stewart asked the shipbuilder, but Andrews didn't move or reply and 'just stood like one stunned'.[9]

Captain Smith was standing in the vicinity of lifeboat 15 when Stewardess Emma Bliss stepped into the boat. 'I was given a baby to look after,' she recalled. 'I put my lifejacket on the child. The captain told me it would be mine to look after if we didn't find the mother, but she was on the *Carpathia* when we were rescued.'[10]

Steerage passenger Luigi Finoli may have been standing near lifeboat 15 as well:

While standing on the deck awaiting my turn, the captain looked around and saw me ... 'In here,' he cried, 'and man this boat. You are a big, strong fellow and can pull an oar.' Before I could make ready to jump in, I was thrown into the bottom of the boat among a number of scantily clad women.[11]

Saloon Steward Percy Keen, who took his own place in lifeboat 15, was very impressed by Bruce Ismay's conduct during the overall evacuation:

All through the anxious times Mr Bruce Ismay set an example which stirred the crew to great exertions ... He was wonderfully calm, and went from boat to boat assisting in the lowering of them and in placing women and children in them. Once he was not recognized by the officer in charge, who ordered him away, but it was generally felt among the crew that he had struggled hard, and in no way deserved the unkind things said of him [later] in the American press. Once I heard Mr Ismay say, 'Don't forget you are English.' This was just before the last boat [15] was sent away.[12]

Samuel Rule agreed with Mr Keen:

I saw Mr Ismay on the deck working like a n***** ...We loaded [lifeboat 15] down to the gunwales, and we could pull just about half a stroke. When we were being lowered away we nearly came down on

No. 13 boat, which was in some difficulty in consequences of coming in front of an aperture through which water was being pumped. We shouted to the men above, 'Hold on,' and they did. I tell you, there were cool heads above, although they knew the last boats were leaving them.[13]

Lifeboat 15 left the *Titanic* at about 1.41 a.m.

★

After the departure of lifeboat 15, Bruce Ismay quickly walked forward along the boat deck until he found himself in the vicinity of the bridge, where Fourth Officer Boxhall had just finished firing a distress rocket and was returning the firing lanyard to the chartroom. Glancing up, Boxhall saw Bruce Ismay standing alone beside the wheelhouse door.

'He asked me why I did not get the people in the boat [2] and get away,' Boxhall testified later. 'I told him the boat's crew were ready, and the boat was ready to be put away when the captain's order was given.'

Apparently satisfied with the fourth officer's reply, Ismay walked away from Boxhall without saying anything further and let him get on with his work.[14]

Stewardess Mary Sloan was standing on the forward boat deck when Thomas Andrews also made an appearance there:

[The] last time I saw and heard him [he] ... was helping to get the women and children into the boats, imploring them not to hesitate, but to go when asked as there was no time to be lost.

'Ladies, you must get in at once,' Andrews insisted. 'There is not a minute to lose. You cannot pick and choose your boat. Don't hesitate. Get in, get in!'

Miss Sloan hesitated, because (as author Shan Bullock put it) 'all her friends were staying behind and she felt it was mean to go'. However, Thomas Andrews again called out, 'Don't hesitate! There's not a moment to lose. Get on!'

'I was still standing when I saw Captain Smith getting excited,' Miss Sloan remembered. 'Passengers would not have noticed, I did. I knew then we were soon going, the distress rockets were then going every minute, so I thought if anyone asked me again to go I should do so, there was then a big crush from behind me. At last they realized their danger, so I was pushed into the boat.'[15]

After entering lifeboat 2, Miss Sloan got one last glimpse of Thomas Andrews. 'He was near Captain Smith,' the stewardess recalled. 'I remember the captain was calling something about a megaphone.'[16]

All during the evacuation process Fourth Officer Boxhall had been firing periodic distress rockets trying to attract the attention of the nearby steamer whose lights could be seen in the darkness off *Titanic*'s port bow.

'I never knew how many I had fired,' Boxhall said later:

I knew very well that there were some in the box. The box holds a dozen, and when I told the captain, I said, 'There are still some in there, sir, but I don't know how many I fired.' I didn't see any reply [from the nearby ship.] Some of the passengers that were on the bridge said that they did see a reply.

Boxhall went on:

We also called up this ship as she grew closer with a Morse Lamp, a very powerful Morse Lamp that we had … And then eventually she turned away and showed her stern light, and about that time the captain came across the bridge and said, 'Mr Boxhall, you go away in that boat,' pointing to the port emergency boat number 2. And he said, 'Now hurry up, Mr Wilde is waiting to lower it.' So I said, 'You see that white light over there, sir?' pointing it out to him. He said, 'Yes.' I said, 'That is the stern light of that ship.'[17]

Prior to Captain Smith's conversation with Fourth Officer Boxhall, first-class passenger Mahala Douglas had been standing on the forward boat deck near Smith and emergency lifeboat 2. 'No one seemed excited,' Mrs Douglas remembered:

Finally, as we stood by a collapsible boat lying on the deck and an emergency boat swinging from the davits was being filled, it was decided I should go. Mr Boxhall was trying to get the boat off, and called to the captain on the bridge, 'There's a boat coming up over there.' The captain said, 'I want a megaphone.' Just before we got into the boat the captain called, 'How many of the crew are in that boat? Get out of there, every man of you'; and I can see a solid row of men, from bow to stern, crawl over on to the deck. We women then got in.[18]

It's possible Elizabeth Allen was another passenger who heard Captain Smith's outburst directed at the men who had seated themselves in lifeboat 2.

As we stood there we saw a line of men file by and get into the boat – some 16 or 18 stokers … An officer came along and shouted to them, 'Get out, you damned cowards; I'd like to see every one of you overboard.' They all got out and the officer said, 'Women and children into this boat,' and we got in.[19]

Miss Allen had already taken special note of Captain Smith and Bruce Ismay earlier during the evacuation. 'Capt. Smith and Mr Ismay were on one side of the boat part of the time and then on the other,' she said later.[20]

Steward James Johnstone was assigned to man lifeboat 2 with Fourth Officer Boxhall and, just like Boxhall, he could see the lights of another steamer off in the distance. 'The captain told the officer [Boxhall] to pull for that light and come back again,' Johnstone remembered.[21]

'It was while waiting in the boat [2] that I saw Ismay,' Elizabeth Allen remembered:

He was standing beside the boat near us when a stewardess started to get in. She saw him and, according to the English custom, she gave way to her superior. He did not take the seat, however, and ushered her into the boat with the statement, 'Women first, if you please.' He was a gentleman all the way through, and all that I heard and saw of him the night of the accident was that he played the part of a gallant gentleman in doing his part to carry out the law of the sea – women and children first. Our boat was next to the last, and when we left he was helping a little child into the last boat and there seemed to be few women in the vicinity.[22]

Charlotte Appleton agreed with Miss Allen's assessment of Bruce Ismay: 'Mr Ismay did everything possible to get the women and children off the *Titanic*.'[23]

Despite his occasional successes in convincing ladies to enter the earlier lifeboats, Ismay was now having difficulty persuading women to get into lifeboat 2. Saloon Steward James Johnstone recalled:

> Mr Ismay tried to walk round and get a lot of women to come to our boat ... I saw [bedroom stewards] driving [women], and I saw Mr Ismay try to drive a few, and he had a pair of slippers on and his dust coat, and he was trying to get the women, and they would not go in for him into our boat ... I saw Mr Ismay trying to get them into our boat, and he took them to the starboard side; he went to the starboard side with them ... he took them round there to the other side abaft the second funnel, I think ... because they would not come into ours, and he tried to get them to the other side to go into another boat ... he was doing as much as any other Englishman could do.[24]

Lifeboat 2 left the *Titanic* at 1.45 a.m. under the command of Fourth Officer Boxhall. After pulling away from the ship's side, however, Boxhall could hear someone on the ship calling down to him with further instructions. He later testified:

> I heard somebody singing out from the ship, I do not know who it was, with a megaphone, for some of the boats to come back again ... and to the best of my recollection they said 'Come round the starboard side [to the open gangway doors],' so I pulled round the starboard side to the stern and had a little difficulty in getting round there.[25]

Mrs Edward Robert was one of the passengers in lifeboat 2, and she heard the same instruction megaphoned to the occupants of her boat. 'There was room for about two or three more persons in the boat, and Captain Smith called for the boat to come back,' she wrote later. 'The officer ordered the boat turned, but as they started back they saw the stern of the *Titanic* rising in the air, and didn't dare to go near for fear it was going to sink.'[26]

Second Officer Charles Lightoller was currently hard at work at lifeboat 10, and he later agreed that the man issuing these supplementary orders to Fourth Officer Boxhall was undoubtedly Captain Smith himself. 'I heard the Commander two or three times hail through the megaphone to bring the boats alongside,' he testified later, 'and I presumed he was alluding to the gangway doors, giving orders to the boats to go to the gangway doors.'[27]

First-class passenger Peter Daly corroborated Second Officer Lightoller's statement about Captain Smith, and a newspaper reporter later relayed Daly's memory of the incident to his readers:

'Bring those boats back; they are only half filled!' yelled Capt. Smith of the *Titanic*, according to Peter D. Daly of Lima, Peru, one of the first cabin survivors.

'Many boats,' says Mr Daly, 'did get away half filled. How many of them obeyed Capt. Smith's order I do not know, but I do know that he rushed to the rail as the boats were leaving and shouted for them to come back for more passengers.'[28]

The *Titanic* was now listing heavily to port with her bows lying low in the water, and presently Captain Smith found a brief opportunity to visit the Marconi cabin once again.

'The captain also came in and told us she was sinking fast and could not last longer than half an hour,' Harold Bride remembered. 'Mr Phillips then went outside to see how things were progressing, and meanwhile I established communication with the *Baltic*, telling him we were in urgent need of assistance.'[29] (This message may have been one that *Baltic*'s Marconi operator recorded in his wireless logbook at 1.47 a.m. *Titanic* time: 'Engine room getting flooded.')[30]

It was apparently very late during the evacuation when steerage passenger William Törnquist took a seat in a lifeboat while fellow American Line employee William Cahoon Johnson continued to help women and children to enter the same boat. Törnquist called for Johnson to join him in the lifeboat, but just then Captain Smith hurried past the boat. Smith had befriended William Johnson earlier in the voyage, and when he noticed the young man standing beside the lifeboat he stopped and placed his hand on Johnson's shoulder.

'Jump in, kid,' urged the *Titanic*'s master. 'You might as well have a chance.'

'Nothing doing,' William Johnson replied. 'I'll wait until the women and children are all off and the other officers go.'

As Captain Smith turned away, he said, 'You're made of the right goods, kid, but it is too bad to waste them.'[31]

Robert Daniel was another passenger who saw the *Titanic*'s master very late during the evacuation. 'Captain Smith was the biggest hero I ever saw,' Daniel said later. 'He stood on the bridge and shouted through a megaphone, trying to make himself heard … He was still shouting when I last saw him.'[32]

An unnamed fireman was apparently standing nearby during this same time period. 'Captain Smith could have saved himself if he liked,' he told a reporter later. 'He could have jumped into the water and been rescued as others were, but up to the last he walked up and down the deck, giving orders through a megaphone to those trying to save their lives.'[33]

Second-class passenger Mary Davis left the *Titanic* in one of the last lifeboats, but later she said she could still hear Captain Smith actively supervising the evacuation. A newspaper reporter said later:

> She heard the captain giving his orders and his final one was that the boat was fast going and every man for himself! Even with this order, she stated that the captain still stayed aboard helping off passengers and paying no attention to his own welfare. She said that he … was recognized by all as a brave man.[34]

It must have been at about this same time that first-class passengers Martha Stephenson and Elizabeth Eustis were following Marian Thayer and her maid up a narrow iron stairway leading to the forward boat deck near the *Titanic*'s bridge. Mrs Stephenson recalled:

> At the top of the stairs we found Captain Smith looking much worried, and anxiously waiting to get down [to A deck] after we got up. The ship listed heavily to port just then … Shortly after that the order came from the head dining saloon steward to go down to the A deck, when Mrs Thayer remarked, 'Tell us where to go and we will follow. You ordered us up here and now you are taking us back,' and he said 'Follow me.'

Along with the other passengers, Mrs Stephenson returned to A deck and approached lifeboat 4, which was hanging suspended just outside the ship's now-open glass windows.[35] Captain Smith, who was standing nearby, firmly ordered all the women and children to jump into the lifeboat, but nobody made a move to obey his instruction. Finally, Smith walked over to Nellie Hocking, grasped her arm and forced her to enter the lifeboat.[36] After this precedent was set, Mrs Stephenson and her companions boarded lifeboat 4 as well.[37]

Mr and Mrs Arthur Ryerson, their two daughters and one son were also standing near lifeboat 4 when Mr Ryerson turned and spoke earnestly to his wife. Emily Ryerson remembered:

> My husband said, 'When they say women and children, you must go,' and I said, 'Why do I have to go on that boat,' and he said, 'You must obey the captain's orders, and I will get in somehow.' They said only women and children; but after we got stuck some men swarmed in that were not sailors. The captain called 'How many women have you' and someone said 'twenty-four' and he said 'That is enough' and after we stuck, someone said something about a knife, but we never used it, and during that wait some men got into the boat.[38]

Second-class passenger Anna Hämäläinen and her infant son Wiljo were seated in lifeboat 4 while crewmen were making final preparations to lower the boat:

> As the last boat, the one in which I and my baby were placed, was about to be lowered … Captain Smith walked over and asked another officer who the men of the crew who were to man the oars were. The names were called off to him, one by one.
>
> 'It is well,' he said quietly. 'They are good men and will do all they can.' And then to the oarsmen who sat, with white drawn faces looking up at him, he said, 'Men, these women and children are in your hands. Do your very best by them. Take good care of them.'
>
> When the boat was lowered, and even as we struck the water, I heard the captain's low, calm voice above the other noises. 'It's every man for himself now, friends,' he said, as calmly as though he were

bidding an acquaintance good morning. 'Each man look out for himself. The last boat's gone.'[39]

★

Lifeboat 4, the last full-sized lifeboat on the *Titanic*, was lowered away at 1.50 a.m., but its occupants soon realised that Captain Smith wasn't quite finished with them. 'We started to row,' Ida Hippach remembered. 'I knew the ship was sinking fast because I saw the portholes were near the water. We heard someone cry in an appealing voice to us to come back and get more passengers, but we did not dare to.'[40]

Lifeboat 10 also left the *Titanic* at 1.50 a.m. but, sometime before it did so, steerage passenger Nellie O'Dwyer had seen Captain Smith supervising the overall evacuation.

'The captain treated everyone alike whether they were from the first cabin or the steerage,' she remembered. 'He acted angry only towards the men that were rushing forward. He kept us from the panic, so he did.'[41]

It was late during the evacuation that Thomas Andrews was observed on the boat deck 'throwing deck chairs overboard to the unfortunates' who he knew would soon find themselves floundering in the freezing ocean. Soon afterwards, Mr Andrews was seen 'bareheaded and carrying a lifebelt, on his way to the bridge perhaps to bid the captain goodbye'.[42]

It may have been at this approximate time that a male passenger who happened to be walking past Captain Smith on the boat deck addressed a brief question to him as he did so.

'Aren't you going to save yourself, Captain?' the man asked.

'You look out for yourself,' replied the *Titanic*'s master.[43]

Wireless operators Jack Phillips and Harold Bride were still hard at work in the Marconi cabin, and Phillips had just noted that his transmissions were growing weaker when Captain Smith made a momentary appearance there.

'The captain came and told us our engine rooms were taking water, and that the dynamos might not last much longer,' Harold Bride remembered. 'We sent that word to the *Carpathia*.' At 1.57 a.m. Phillips tapped out the final wireless message that the rescue ship ever received from the dying White Star liner: 'Engine room full up to the boilers.'[44]

After Fourth Officer Boxhall left the *Titanic* in lifeboat 2, Captain Smith had continued to provide supervision to Quartermaster George Rowe, who for the past hour had been helping to fire distress rockets in an attempt to attract the attention of the ship whose lights could still be seen in the distance. Rowe wrote later:

> I kept calling her up [with the Morse lamp] in between the rocket firing, but we never got a reply though we could see his white light quite plain …
>
> After a while I said to Capt. Smith there is a [new] light on the starboard quarter; he looked through the glasses and told me he thought it must be a planet then he lent me his glasses to see for myself. Then [he] said the *Carpathia* is not so far away. During this time they were turning out the starboard Engelhardt raft [collapsible C] under the direction of Chief Off[icer] Wilde.[45]

Emily Goldsmith and her little son Frankie were two third-class passengers who were lucky enough to find seats in collapsible C, but the overall loading process of the lifeboat did not go smoothly, as she remembered:

> The officers stood with drawn revolvers, which they used once or twice. Except when some of the foreign steerage passengers attempted to rush the boats, there was little excitement. Several of these men forced their way to the upper deck and jumped into our lifeboat, but the officers were firm and drove them back. One of the men on our boat [First Officer Murdoch] pointed his revolver at them and then fired three shots in the air. That brought them to their senses, and as they evidently preferred a chance [of life by staying] with the *Titanic* to certain death by shooting if they remained in the lifeboat, they scrambled back on the deck. Four Chinamen refused to get out, but crept down among the women and remained there. The officer did not dare fire at them for fear of hitting the women … In our lifeboat there were about thirty women, five men and the four Chinamen.[46]

First-class passenger Hugh Woolner confirmed Mrs Goldsmith's description of the attempt to remove unwilling passengers from collapsible C:

> There was a sort of scramble on the starboard side [of the ship] ... and I looked around and I saw two flashes of a pistol in the air ... they were up in the air, at that sort of an angle. I heard Mr Murdoch shouting out, 'Get out of this, clear out of this,' and that sort of thing, to a lot of men who were swarming into a boat on that side ... We went across there because we heard a certain kind of shouting going on, and just as we got around the corner I saw these two flashes of the pistol, and [Mauritz Bjornström-Steffanson] and I went up to help to clear that boat of the men who were climbing in, because there was a bunch of women – I think Italians and foreigners – who were standing on the outside of the crowd, unable to make their way toward the side of the boat ... So we helped the officer to pull these men out, by their legs and anything we could get hold of ... I should think five or six [men]. But they were really flying before Mr Murdoch from inside of the boat at the time.[47]

After First Officer Murdoch and his helpers had ejected as many men from collapsible C as they could, the crowd of unruly passengers surrounding the boat seems to have left the area and gone elsewhere in search of a less hazardous means of rescue. Presently the forward starboard boat deck around collapsible C was almost deserted except for a group of stokers who were standing nearby.[48]

Quartermaster Arthur Bright knew that collapsible D was almost ready for lowering on the *Titanic*'s port side, but he now found himself standing on the starboard side near collapsible C, where Bruce Ismay apparently arrived a few moments before. 'I saw him standing there,' Bright testified later, 'and that was the only two boats left.'[49]

Ismay did not remain idle for long, because he soon began taking an active role in filling collapsible C with passengers. 'He was calling out for the women and children first,' Saloon Steward Edward Brown remembered. 'He helped to get them into that boat and he went into it himself to receive the women and children.'[50]

Presently, most of the passengers who'd been in the immediate vicinity of collapsible C had now found seats in the lifeboat,[51] at which point

Chief Officer Henry Wilde judged that the boat was almost ready to be lowered away.

'The chief officer, Wilde, wanted a sailor [at collapsible C],' Quartermaster George Rowe testified later:

> I asked Capt. Smith if I should fire any more [rockets], and he said 'No; get into that boat.' I went to the boat. Women and children were being passed in. I assisted six, three women and three children. The order was then given to lower the boat. The chief officer wanted to know if there were more women and children. There were none in the vicinity. Two gentlemen passengers got in; the boat was then lowered.[52]

The two gentlemen passengers in question were William Carter and Bruce Ismay. Ismay said he saw no sign of Captain Smith at the time he entered collapsible C, and he denied that Smith or anyone else urged him to get into the boat.

'I was not warned by Capt. Smith to seek safety in a lifeboat,' Ismay told a reporter later. 'I took to the boat of my own accord when it appeared to me the *Titanic* was in danger. The last I saw of Captain Smith [previous to that time] he was on the bridge.'[53]

Ismay later testified about this same matter at the US Senate *Titanic* inquiry:

> [I got into collapsible C] because there was room in the boat. She was being lowered away. I felt the ship was going down, and I got into the boat ... I should think there were about 40 women in it, and some children. There was a child in arms. I think they were all third-class passengers, so far as I could see ... I never saw the captain ... The ship had quite a list to port. Consequently this canvas boat, this collapsible boat, was getting hung up on the outside of the ship, and she had to rub right along her, and we had to try to shove her out, and we had to get the women to help to shove to get her clear of the ship. The ship had listed over that way ... We found four Chinamen stowed away under the thwarts after we got away. I think they were Filipinos, perhaps. There were four of them.[54]

One newspaper interview with William Carter supported Ismay's statement that he and Carter had entered collapsible C without receiving an invitation or order to do so:

> There were no women on the deck when that boat was launched ... We were the very last to leave the deck and we entered the lifeboat because there were no women to enter it. The deck was deserted when the boat was launched, and Mr Ismay and myself decided that we might as well enter the boat and pull away from the wreck.[55]

Even though William Carter's above interview is identical to Ismay's own version of events, a separate interview with Carter raises the question of whether or not Ismay may indeed have been invited to enter the boat before it was lowered:

> The women that were in the boat were from the steerage with their children. I guess there were about 40 of them. Mr Ismay and myself and several of the officers walked up and down the deck crying 'Are then any more women here.' We called for several minutes and got no answer. One of the officers then declared that if we wanted to we could get into the boat if we took the place of seamen. He gave us this privilege because we are among the first-class passengers. Mr Ismay called again, and after we got no reply we got into the lifeboat.[56]

Barber Augustus Weikman agreed with William Carter's second statement, affirming that Ismay did indeed receive an invitation to enter collapsible C.

'Mr Ismay ... got in along with Mr Carter, because there were no women in the vicinity of the boat,' Weikman testified. 'He was ordered into the boat by the officer in charge. I think that Mr Ismay was justified in getting in that boat at that time.'[57]

'When the first collapsible boat [C] went, there were no more women there to get in the boat and it was practically full then,' Saloon Steward Edward Brown observed. Quartermaster George Rowe agreed with Brown. 'There were no more passengers in the vicinity to get in,' he said.[58]

An unnamed trimmer who was standing near 'the last but one collapsible boat' (collapsible C) said that:

There were some men in it [earlier], and the chief officer ordered all the men out ... When the boat was about six feet down I jumped down into it, and heard the captain say 'Stand-by to pick up survivors.' We had 49 men and children in the boat, and could not take anyone else.[59]

Collapsible C left the *Titanic*'s starboard side at about 2 a.m., but a *Titanic* crewman who was standing on deck beside passenger Edward Dorkings is said to have taken special notice of Ismay's departure from the ship, remarking to Dorkings, 'Well, there goes the boss. There's only sixteen in the boat, but they won't let anybody else get in.'

Dorkings asked the sailor who he meant by 'the boss'.

'Don't you know Ismay?' the man replied. 'He's head of the line, and by God, if he's going, so am I!' Dorkings later said that the sailor in question helped crew the next lifeboat (which, if true, would have been collapsible D.)[60]

An unnamed fireman who was one of the crewmen who were manning collapsible C when it left the *Titanic* said later:

I was ordered into the last lifeboat but one. When we were lowered into the water and I sat down to row, I felt somebody under the thwart. I looked to see what it was, and I found two Chinamen there. I can tell you I wasn't pleased, but I did not like to throw them overboard, and I let them stay where they were.[61]

Eventually Bruce Ismay himself noticed the four Chinese men who had successfully resisted all efforts to eject them from collapsible C. Turning to William Carter, Ismay remarked that it was a shame the Chinese were being saved when so many 'fine, valuable men' were being left behind on the sinking *Titanic*.[62]

9

2–2.20 A.M.

Jane Hoyt and her husband Fred were standing on the port boat deck near the *Titanic*'s bridge watching collapsible D being prepared for lowering. 'Mr Hoyt went over and talked to Captain Smith a moment, remarking on the seriousness of the situation,' she remembered:

> He [Smith] replied that it was 'terrible'. Captain Smith was then at his post issuing orders here and there, but there was a general din and it is not likely the orders were heard a great distance. The last collapsible lifeboat was getting in readiness to be lowered by the davits when Mr Hoyt told me I would have to get in.[1]

Meanwhile, Mr and Mrs Henry Harris found themselves approaching collapsible D from the opposite side of the ship. 'We crossed to the port side, passing through the bridge where the captain was standing with Major Archibald Butt and the little doctor [O'Loughlin],' Renée Harris remembered in later years.[2] 'The doctor stopped me to speak with me, as the day before he had attended me in the breaking of my arm when I slipped down the stairs.'[3]

Perhaps understandably, not everyone on the bridge was pleased to see Renée Harris. She recalled:

The captain looked amazed when he saw me. 'My God, woman. Why aren't you in a lifeboat?'

I kept repeating, 'I won't leave my husband. I won't leave my husband.'

The little doctor said, 'Isn't she a brick?'

To which the captain replied: 'She's a little fool – she's handicapping her husband's chances to save himself.'

'Can he be saved,' I asked, 'if I go?'

'Yes,' he answered: 'there are plenty of rafts on the stern and the men can make for them if you women give them a chance.'

'Come along, Mrs Straus,' I said. 'We must make it easier for our men.'

Mr [Isidor] Straus spoke for the first time. 'We've been together all these years, and when we must go we will go together. You are very young, my dear. Life still holds much for you. Don't wait for my wife.'

I had had no time to protest. I was picked up and I felt myself being tossed into the nowhere. I heard a voice saying, 'Catch my wife. Be careful – she has a broken arm.' I was thrown a distance of perhaps three feet, and found myself in a boat being lowered from the bridge deck.[4]

It was apparently from her seat in the already-launched lifeboat 4 that steerage passenger Leah Aks saw Captain Smith superintending the loading of collapsible D. She remembered:

With our boat but a short distance from the *Titanic*, I could see the big steamer distinctly as she went down, and the scenes are too horrifying to relate … I saw Captain Smith step into the last boat, but he immediately stepped back on the ship. Then he stepped back into the life boat again, but turned, and as he saw the water going over his ship stepped back on the deck.[5]

It's possible that steerage passenger Bridget Bradley was standing on the boat deck near collapsible D, because a later newspaper report said she 'was among the occupants of the last lifeboat, which set off from the ill-fated ship, and she did not board it until Captain Smith had forced those in it to make room for herself and perhaps a dozen or more frightened women'.[6] Here is the way Miss Bradley described her experience in her own words:

> Just as the last lifeboat, the one with Mr Ismay in it, was launched over the side, one of the officers shouted 'There's more room in that boat [over on the ship's port side?]', and I and eleven other women were crowded into it. This was after 1 o'clock. I don't know how much, but it was after one. The lifeboat was manned by enough men to care for it properly, and immediately on touching the water the men rowed with all their strength to get away from the ship, so that, if it did go down, we would not be caught in the suction.[7]

Collapsible D left the *Titanic*'s side at 2.05 a.m. and was the last lifeboat to be launched from the ship's davits. There remained only collapsibles A and B, and crewmen worked frantically to get those two lifeboats off the roof of the officers' quarters and down onto the boat deck where they could be moved to the davits.

In the meantime, an unnamed first-class saloon steward who was apparently standing on the forward boat deck was favourably impressed by the conduct of Thomas Andrews and Captain Smith during the overall evacuation process:

> If you ask me who were the real heroes of the disaster, I should certainly say Colonel Gracie, the best American there. Then there was Mr Andrews, one of the designers of the ship, who was here, there and everywhere, helping always, and never troubling about his own life. He did not even put on a lifebelt, nor, of course, did Captain Smith. Murdoch was splendid, too, but I fear it is true he shot himself, but not, however, till the very end, when he had done everything he could for others.[8]

Lamp trimmer Samuel Hemming was working on the two collapsible lifeboats stowed on the roof of the officers' quarters, but when he climbed back down onto the boat deck at about 2.05 a.m. he noticed the *Titanic*'s strong list to port. 'The last time I saw the captain, sir, was just as I was coming down off the house,' Hemming testified later:

The captain was there, and he sung out: 'Everyone over to the starboard side, to keep the ship up as long as possible.' Hemming could see one or two hundred men who were clustered on the port boat deck, and he realized Captain Smith was trying to shift the *Titanic*'s center of gravity and bring the vessel back on an even keel. Hemming noticed that the *Titanic*'s master was standing all by himself at the time he issued this order.[9]

Trimmer James McGann was another who had been very impressed with Captain Smith's behaviour throughout the entire evacuation.

'How did he act on the bridge while I was there?' he later replied to a questioner. 'Always directing the lowering of the boats himself, and he was always shouting "Women and children first."'[10]

After watching his wife being lowered in collapsible D at 2.05 a.m., Fred Hoyt realised it was time for him to start thinking about his own precarious situation. Hurrying below to his stateroom, Hoyt stripped down to his lighter underclothing in preparation for a probable swim in the icy sea. He then returned to the bridge where Captain Smith was still on duty, and the two friends briefly exchanged views on the morning's inevitable outcome.

'But I feel like taking a drink before I take the plunge, don't you, captain?' asked Hoyt, and Captain Smith agreed that this sounded like a good idea. 'The captain's room was on the bridge deck, the highest part of the superstructure,' Hoyt recalled. 'I went in to get a drink of water. The captain was perfectly calm. As I filled my glass he took a drink, too. He knew there was no hope.'

Captain Smith finally turned to Mr Hoyt and advised him, 'You will have to jump and you had better do it soon.'

'Yes, I know it,' Hoyt replied, 'but I won't take the plunge from this deck, but will go to one of the lower decks.'

'That will be better,' Captain Smith agreed. 'Go down on A deck and see if you cannot get into a boat.'

'I left the captain's room,' Fred Hoyt recalled, 'and when I got below they pushed off the collapsible boat in which Mrs Hoyt had been placed. There were then twenty persons in it. Just as the boat left the side I jumped into the ocean.'[11] (Mr Hoyt was soon picked up by collapsible D and was thereby reunited with his wife.)

Trimmer Eustace Snow was standing on the forward boat deck when he and his mates were issued new orders from Captain Smith concerning the two unlaunched collapsible lifeboats A and B that were stowed on the roof of the officers' quarters. Smith seems to have realised there wouldn't be enough time for the two boats to be launched properly from the forward davits. 'The Captain from Chart Room called out for firemen to launch two boats from top of chart house,' Eustace Snow remembered:

I helped launch the starboard collapsible boat [off the roof], but she stove her bow in when she fell on the boat deck ... There were no women or children about, and I heard the Captain shout 'Wait till the boat [takes?] the water, then every man for himself.' I did not see the captain again.[12]

The earlier flooding of the forward steerage quarters had prevented third-class passenger Victor Sunderland from retrieving his lifebelt from his cabin, and he now found himself on the forward boat deck trying to find someone to help him. After a nearby officer was unable to tell him where he could obtain a lifebelt, the steerage passenger approached Captain Smith with the same question.

'I don't know where you can get one now,' the *Titanic*'s master replied. 'I have given mine away.'

'He was a brave man,' Sunderland remembered. 'He seemed to be everywhere, always trying to get the women and children off.'[13]

Although we don't know where he heard the following information, Sidney Collett (who had already left the *Titanic* in lifeboat 9) later suggested that Captain Smith's thoughts now turned to those crewmen who might still be working below decks: 'For three minutes, Captain Smith sounded what is called the "three minutes bell", warning all below decks that their lives were in danger. Even then few believed that the ship would sink.'[14]

Meanwhile, wireless operators Jack Phillips and Harold Bride were still transmitting distress messages in the *Titanic*'s Marconi room, and they had just received messages from the *Frankfurt* and *Carpathia* when Captain Smith stopped by the wireless cabin one final time. 'Men, you have done your full duty. You can do no more,' Smith told the two young men. 'Abandon your cabin. Now, it's every man for himself. You look out for yourselves. I release you. That's the way of it at this kind of time. Every man for himself.'[15]

'I looked out,' Bride remembered later. 'The boat deck was [almost] awash. Phillips clung on, sending and sending. He clung on for about ten minutes, or maybe fifteen minutes, after the captain released him.'[16]

Several hearsay accounts of unknown reliability purport to describe Captain Smith's last few minutes on board the doomed *Titanic*. A British newspaper reporter later wrote:

> One of the [crew] men survivors, I am told, went to Captain Smith just before the ship sank and begged him to put on a lifebelt and swim to one of the boats. The captain shook his head, said 'Nothing doing, my lad,' and waved the man away.[17]

Second-class passenger Kate Buss heard a second-hand story about Captain Smith's final activities on board the *Titanic*:

> From a raft survivor, I heard that Capt. Smith made a wonderful address urging the men to be British & lined them up for the Lord's Prayer & then said when the right moment came he would order 'Every man for himself' to stay & sink with the boat or jump overboard as they thought best & warning them against wreckage.[18]

Fireman Charles Judd was one of the many hundreds of people who were left stranded on the *Titanic* after collapsible D left the ship. 'A lot of us [had] worked like mad getting people off, mostly women and children,' he remembered, 'and with my own eyes I saw an officer [whose name he knew] shoot two or three first-class passengers. He was frenzied, and Captain Smith was very pale too.' In desperation, Judd made his way to one of the two unlaunched collapsible lifeboats (apparently collapsible A) and joined fellow crewmen in their futile attempt to launch that boat.[19]

'I saw four or five women when we were trying to get the boat [collapsible A] away,' Saloon Steward Edward Brown remembered. 'I suppose it took us about 10 or 12 minutes to get the other boat down [from the roof of the officers' quarters.]'[20]

From where he was working to get collapsible A off the roof of the officers' quarters and across the boat deck to the starboard davits, Steward Edward Brown saw Captain Smith walk past him just a few moments before the end came. Brown recalled that Smith had 'a megaphone in his hand, and he spoke to us ... He said, "Well, boys, do your best for the women and children, and look out for yourselves,"' and then walked onto the bridge.[21]

Steward Fred Ray believed that Captain Smith's personal steward, James Paintin, was last seen on the *Titanic's* bridge, standing beside the captain.[22]

Mess Steward Cecil Fitzpatrick was making his way along the *Titanic's* port boat deck with the apparent intention of crossing over to the starboard side, where crewmen were doing their best to drag collapsible A over to the davits. Fitzpatrick remembered:

I was passing through the bridge when I saw Capt. Smith speaking to Mr Andrews, the designer of the *Titanic* ... I stopped to listen. I was still confident that the ship was unsinkable, but when I heard Capt. Smith say: 'We cannot stay any longer: she is going!' I fainted against the starboard side of the bridge entrance. After some minutes I recovered sufficiently to realize that unless I got into a boat or swam for it, there would be no chance of being saved. I then went to launch one of the collapsible boats [A] which had been eased down off the top decks on the starboard side. We found, when we tried to swing her in the davits that she was wedged between the winch of the davits and the spar ... Just before I went overboard, I saw the captain and Mr Andrews rush past me.[23]

'There was a great friend of mine – a steward named [Edward] Brown – was saved after being in the water some hours,' Saloon Steward Alexander Littlejohn recalled later. 'He told me he was washed off the bridge as the forward funnel dipped and that the captain was on the bridge at the time and said to the other stewards around him, "Do what you can for yourselves, boys."'[24]

During later discussions with his mates, Fireman Thomas Threlfall was told that Captain Smith ordered all deck chairs and other buoyant items to be thrown overboard for the benefit of swimmers, after which Smith gave the order 'Every man for himself'.[25]

Shortly before, greaser Alfred White had left the light engine room below decks and climbed up through the fourth funnel to the boat deck, and he now found himself standing near Captain Smith. He remembered:

> By that time all the boats had left the ship, and yet everyone in the engine room was at his post ... I was near the captain and heard him say, 'Well, boys. I guess it's every man for himself now.' I slipped down some loose boat falls and dropped into the water. There was a boat not far away which later picked me up.[26]

Fireman James McGann and Captain Smith were standing close to one of the unlaunched collapsible boats that were now lying on the boat deck near the *Titanic*'s bridge. McGann remembered:

> I was standing beside him. ... He gave one look all around, his face firm and his lips hard set. He looked as if he might be trying to keep back the tears as he thought of the doomed ship. I felt mightily like crying myself as I looked at him. Suddenly he shouted: 'Well, boys, you've done your duty and done it well. I ask no more of you. I release you. You know the rule of the sea. It's every man for himself now, and God bless you.'[27]

An unnamed steward reportedly said that 'Captain Smith's last words [to the crew] were not "Be British," although by sentiment they might have been; they were, "I'm finished. Look after yourselves."'[28] Captain Smith then walked onto the bridge.[29]

First-class passenger William Mellors was standing nearby as the *Titanic*'s bridge sank closer and closer to the ocean's surface:

> I was not far from where Captain Smith stood on the bridge, giving full orders to his men ... The brave old seaman was crying, but he had stuck heroically to the last. He did not shoot himself. He jumped from the bridge when he had done all he could. I heard his final instructions to his crew, and recall that his last words were: 'You have done your duty, boys. Now every man for himself.'[30]

Meanwhile, amidships on the *Titanic*'s boat deck, an unnamed crewman was making his way towards the vessel's stern and later described a haunting experience that a newspaper reporter paraphrased for his readers:

> There was one man on the *Titanic* who related a wonderful story of the ship's final agony who is still alive. Retreating from the crawling water as it advanced along the sagging decks, it drove him back foot by foot as it advanced, and every foot led him up a steeper incline as she settled by the head.
>
> And, as he retreated, he saw something that almost broke his big heart. Up on the middle of the bridge deck, now deserted by all but them, there stood two women, hand in hand, silently, not weeping, not even afraid, it would appear, just waiting for the end. Up and up the gentle, cat-like little waves crawled, whispering along the deck quietly, relentlessly, swallowing everything as they came, while the women stood and watched and waited. The *Titanic* bowed her head, accepting her doom, and the waves licked up over D deck, C deck, and B deck. Soon the forward end of A deck was awash and the water tickled the foot of the bridge. Up and up and up, and there was no help. The last boat was rowing away for its life from the ship's death agony.
>
> And that is the end of the story. Who were they, how they got there, why they missed a boat, no one knows. They went down with the ship without a whimper or a cry, side by side at the end.[31]

Meanwhile, on the forward boat deck, Richard Williams and his father Duane stepped out of the *Titanic*'s gymnasium onto the boat deck and looked around them. The end was very near. 'The boat was now only about two or three decks above the water,' Richard wrote in later years:

> The situation was getting serious. Quite automatically we started up – we happened to be forward; presently we found ourselves on the captain's bridge – only two other people were there, Captain Smith and a quartermaster – I believe, who presently wandered away. We spoke to the captain for a few minutes. The ship seemed to give a slight lurch; I turned towards the bow. I saw nothing but water with just a mast sticking out of it. I don't remember the shock of the cold

water, I only remember thinking 'suction' and my efforts to swim in the direction of the starboard rail to get away from the ship. Before I had swam more than ten feet, I felt the deck come up under me and I found we were high and dry. My father was not more than 12 or 15 feet from me. I heard the crack of a revolver shot from the direction where I had left Captain Smith; I did not look around.[32]

From his own vantage point on the forward boat deck, steerage passenger August Wennerström could see everything that was happening near the *Titanic's* bridge right before his world fell apart. He and Captain Smith were standing near each other when they both noticed steerage passenger Alma Pålsson standing nearby with her four small children. Wennerström later described how Smith took personal charge of one of the children and then told Mrs Pålsson that there was no way to be saved. Mr Wennerström recalled that the grief of the mother and children was heart-rending.[33]

'She had, if I remember right, four small children, and had not got them dressed in time to get them in the lifeboat,' Mr Wennerström wrote in a first-hand account in later years:

We helped her with the children and I carried one of them. We met Captain Smith, he picked up one of her children, but said that our time was coming, and before he finished the words one of the boilers in the engine room exploded and threw us all apart. This was the last I saw of the captain and the last I saw of the woman and her children from Chicago.[34]

The 'boiler explosion' was undoubtedly the chaotic moment when the forward end of *Titanic's* boat deck began to plunge beneath the ocean's surface. That plunge was coupled with the collapse of the ship's forward funnel, a horrific event that resulted in Richard Williams' father, Duane, being crushed to death before he could get clear of the falling mountain of metal.

Fireman Charles Judd was standing near August Wennerström and later described what happened to the unlaunched collapsible A when the *Titanic's* bridge submerged. 'The water was getting higher and higher,' Judd remembered, 'and a wave caught her and flung her up in the davits.'[35]

Fellow fireman John Thompson said later:

Captain Smith was within five feet of me at the time our lifeboat [one of the unlaunched collapsibles] went over the side, with nobody between us. He was swept away with the rush of water. He had two lifebelts on, one on his stomach and another over his neck and chest. As he went overboard, he shouted 'Every man for himself.' That was the last I saw of him.[36]

Fireman James McGann was also standing near Captain Smith at the crucial moment, and he later corroborated August Wennerström's first-hand account describing how Smith attempted to save the life of a small child that night:

He held the little girl under one arm ... As he jumped into the sea and endeavored to reach the nearest lifeboat with the child, I took the other child into my arms as I was swept from the bridge deck. When I was plunged into the cold water I was compelled to release my hold on the child and I am satisfied that the same thing happened to Capt. Smith.

... I had gone to the bridge deck to assist in lowering a collapsible boat. The water was then coming over the bridge, and we were unable to launch the boat properly. It was overturned and was used as a life raft. Some thirty or more of us, mostly firemen, clinging to it. Capt. Smith looked as though he was trying to keep back the tears as he thought of the doomed ship.

He turned to the men lowering the boat and shouted, 'Well, boys, it's every man for himself.' He then took one of the children standing by him on the bridge and jumped into the sea. He endeavored to reach the overturned boat, but did not succeed. That was the last I saw of Capt. Smith.[37]

A week after granting the above interview, Fireman McGann gave a second interview in which he repeated his statement about Captain Smith's final moments:

Then he took one of the two little children who were on the bridge beside him. They were both crying. He held the child, I think it was a little girl, under his right arm and jumped into the sea. All of us jumped. I jumped right after the captain, but I grabbed the remaining child before I did so. When I struck water, the cold was so great that I had to let go my hold of the kiddie.[38]

Wireless operator Harold Bride happened to glance towards the *Titanic*'s bridge at the same time Captain Smith plunged into the sea.

'The last I saw of the captain of the *Titanic*, he went overboard from the bridge about, I should think, three minutes before I left it myself,' Bride said later. The wireless operator didn't notice whether Smith was wearing a lifebelt at the time, but he was positive the captain wasn't wearing one during his earlier visits to the Marconi cabin.[39]

Robert Daniel had just made his own escape from the *Titanic* and later claimed to reporters that he had seen Captain Smith go into the water as well.

'After I had jumped I turned around and saw Captain Smith jump into the water with a lifebelt around his waist,' Daniel claimed. 'His head struck a life raft near the side of the ship, and I believe he was stunned, but I do not know what became of him after that.'[40]

Cecil Fitzpatrick had seen Captain Smith and Thomas Andrews rush past him towards the bridge a few minutes earlier, and right before jumping into the sea he glanced in that same direction to see if the two men were still there.

'When I looked again they were gone,' Fitzpatrick remembered, 'and I did not see them again. I suppose they went overboard.'[41]

Cecil Fitzpatrick had run out of time to think about Captain Smith and Thomas Andrews, but – just like William Mellors – he suddenly felt the *Titanic*'s submerging bridge deck rise underneath him again after its first brief submergence beneath the ocean's surface. Fitzpatrick said later:

The next thing I remember was the ship suddenly dipping, and the waves rushing up and engulfing me ... After ten seconds the *Titanic* again righted herself, but then I saw that everyone who a minute before had been attempting to lower away [the last two collapsibles], except myself had been swept into the fo'castle head. I saved myself by clinging on to the davit winch.

I looked down the fo'castle and saw the most horrible, heart-rending scenes I have ever witnessed … there were women and children and firemen and stewards all fighting, praying, shrieking for help in their death struggles. I got on the other side of the winch which was towards the after-part of the vessel, and levered myself up on to the deck. Then I went to the edge of the ship and jumped into the icy water. In order to escape the suction which I surmised would be caused by the sinking of the gigantic liner, I struck out for very life. I swam from the ship as the for'a'd was sinking. I did not feel any suction.[42]

★

After going overboard from the *Titanic*'s bridge Thomas Andrews disappears from the realm of recorded human history, but a number of survivor interviews hint at what happened to Captain Edward J. Smith after he, James McGann and August Wennerström all leapt overboard while carrying (apparently) three of Alma Pålsson's four children.

Fireman Harry Senior's memory of Captain Smith's final moments seemingly supports August Wennerström's personal first-hand memoir describing Smith's attempt to save one of the Pålsson children. From where he was swimming in the icy water, Senior could see Captain Smith struggling towards the overturned collapsible B with a small child clasped in his arms; the *Titanic*'s master eventually reached the collapsible and handed the child up to several men who were already sheltering on the capsized boat's bottom.[43]

'The captain was swimming close alongside me,' Senior remembered, 'and he, too, had a baby in his arms. I saw him swim to one of the boats and hand the baby to someone, and the last I saw of him he was heading back towards the ship.'[44]

Harry Senior later gave a few more details to a different reporter:

Captain Smith was dragged on the upturned boat … He had on a lifebuoy and a life preserver. He clung there a moment and then he slid off again. For a second time he was dragged from the icy water. Then he took off his life preserver, tossed the lifebuoy on the inky waters and slipped into the water again with the words: 'I will follow the ship.'[45]

'I do know that one of the circular life rings from the bridge was there when we got off in the morning,' Jack Thayer wrote later after surviving the sinking on collapsible B. 'It may be that Captain Smith was on board with us for a while.'[46]

James McGann was also swimming in the water after the *Titanic*'s bridge submerged, and, after abandoning the lifeless body of the second Pålsson child, he succeeded in reaching collapsible B and clambered up onto the bottom of the capsized craft.

'I looked around for the captain after I got to the overturned boat, but he was nowhere in sight,' McGann recalled later. 'I don't think he wanted to live after seeing how things were. Dead bodies were all around floating in the water when he jumped, and I think it broke his heart.'[47]

Archibald Gracie was another man who sheltered on collapsible B, and he later wrote about Captain Smith's fate:

After we had left the danger zone in the vicinity of the wreck, conversation between us first developed, and I heard the men aft of me discussing the fate of the captain ...

At least two of them, according to their statements made at the time, had seen him on this craft of ours shortly after it was floated from the ship ... Still another witness, the entrée cook of the *Titanic*, J. Maynard, who was on our boat, corroborates what I heard said at the time about the inability of the captain to keep his hold on the boat.[48]

The man Gracie referred to was Isaac Maynard, a cook on the *Titanic*, who gave a reporter his own version of how Captain Smith met his end:

I saw the captain standing on the bridge ... He was fully dressed and had his cap on. When the water rushed over the top deck, the remaining boats were carried away. Another rush of water washed me overboard, and as I went I clung on to one of the upturned boats. There were some six other men clinging to the woodwork when we were in the water. I saw Captain Smith washed from the bridge, and afterwards saw him swimming in the water. He was still fully dressed, with his peak cap on his head. One of the men clinging to the raft tried to save him by reaching out a hand, but he would not let him, and called out 'Look after yourselves, boys.' I do not know what became of the captain, for I could not see him at the time, but I suppose he sank.[49]

In a lengthy post-disaster account, *Carpathia* passenger Carlos Hurd wrote that: 'It is also related that when a cook [Isaac Maynard?] later sought to pull him [Captain Smith] aboard a lifeboat he exclaimed "Let me go," and jerking away, went down.'[50]

Although Isaac Maynard did not mention the incident in his own newspaper interview, a period British newspaper labelled Maynard as being the man on collapsible B who took a dying child from Captain Smith's arms.[51]

Hugh Woolner was saved in collapsible D, which remained close to the *Titanic* until the very end:

The boat was then almost flush with the water ... I looked toward the vessel and saw Captain Smith assisting a little girl on a raft. The next I knew the *Titanic* had plunged to the bottom. There were moans and groans and cries from where she sank for what seemed like several minutes. Then all was quiet.[52]

Another sighting of Captain Smith was described to a reporter by Fireman Frederick Harris, who apparently climbed into the swamped lifeboat collapsible A before later being transferred to lifeboat 14. The newspaper reporter wrote:

Fredk. Harris, of Gosport, said when the last boat had gone and it was realized that the vessel was going to sink, there was wild confusion, and deck chairs and anything that would float were seized by the men as they jumped overboard ... He saw the captain jump into the water and swim to a child, which he placed on a raft.[53]

Another newspaper reporter described Harris' story as follows:

He saw the captain jump into the water and grasp a child, which he placed on one of the rafts, of which there were all too few. He did not see the captain afterwards. He thought the first officer, Mr Murdoch, shot himself. He himself got onto a small raft, but was afterwards taken into a boat. He was half dead with the cold.[54]

Leading Fireman Fred Barrett (who was saved in lifeboat 13) later told a newspaper reporter about stories fellow crewmen were telling about Captain Smith's final moments: 'There are men here who saw Captain Smith swimming in the water with a child under his arm after the ship sank. He gave the child to the boat and then swam away. He refused to get into the boat himself.'[55]

An unnamed crewman corroborated Fred Barrett's statement:

I heard from one of the last men to leave the ship that the last seen of Capt. Smith was when he swam up to one of the boats with a baby in his arms …

He handed the child to one of the occupants of the boat, but the poor mite died soon afterwards. Efforts were made to get the captain into the boat, but he refused assistance, and swam back to where the *Titanic* sank and was never seen again in the darkness.[56]

Second-class passenger Elizabeth Nye spoke with one of the men who sheltered on the overturned collapsible B, and her slightly inaccurate rendition of the man's story was later paraphrased by a newspaper reporter:

Survivors say the captain did everything possible to save the lives of those committed to his care, and that his last act was to leap from the deck to place a young girl on a raft. He then swam back after refusing to endanger the lives of others by overburdening the frail craft to which they were clinging.

Mrs Elizabeth Nye, who belongs to the Salvation Army and is a friend of Miss Eva Booth, said that she had this account from one of those who was on the raft. The girl whom the captain saved died half an hour later, and all except two – a young man and a young woman who were on the raft – died from exposure.

Other passengers say the captain was seen swimming not far from where the *Titanic* went down. He wore oilskins, which weighed him down, and he seemed so exhausted that he could barely keep afloat.[57]

It has already been mentioned that Fireman Harry Senior was one of the men on collapsible B who saw Smith swimming towards that boat with a small child in his arms. Senior also described how he himself attempted to save the life of yet another child (possibly another of Mrs Pålsson's children) when the *Titanic*'s forward boat deck began to submerge:

> I saw an Italian [sic] woman holding two babies … I took one of them and made the woman jump overboard with the baby, while I did the same with the other. When I came to the surface the baby in my arms was dead. I saw the woman strike out in good style, but a boiler burst [i.e., the forward funnel collapsed] on the *Titanic* and started a big wave. When the woman saw that wave, she gave up. Then, as the child was dead, I let it sink, too.[58]

In a second interview, Harry Senior expanded on his own attempt to save the child in question:

> After all the boats had gone … I was standing at the foot of the bridge, when I heard the captain say, 'Everyone for himself now.' The ship was then far down by the head, and it was not easy to stand on the deck. Close beside me, holding on to the rail, was an Italian woman with two children. I could not understand what she said to me, but she looked piteously at me, and pointed to one of the children; she had the other in her arms. I took the child, and signed to the mother to jump into the sea with the other. We went over the side together, and I never saw the woman again. I tried to swim away from the ship. After a while I noticed the child I had was not moving, and I saw it was dead. The cold water had killed it, I suppose. It was icy cold, and I felt almost paralyzed by it. I let the child go after I had carried it about an hour. Shortly afterwards I scrambled on to an upturned collapsible boat, and towards morning I was picked up by a boat.[59]

In a third interview, Harry Senior posed the unanswerable question of why the 'Italian' woman whose child he attempted to save had somehow failed to get into a lifeboat:

As far as I know, that woman was on the deck all the while the last few boats were being launched and while Mr Ismay and others were calling for more women ... There were other women there, too, but they were most of them afraid to move, and Mr Ismay and the others didn't call very long.[60]

It's significant to note that, after arriving back in England two weeks after the *Titanic* disaster, Harry Senior repeated the identical story he'd told in America, describing his first-hand observations of Captain Smith's final moments:

As I was swimming to the boat [collapsible B], I saw the captain in the water ... He was swimming with a baby in his arms, raising it out of the water as he swam on his back. He swam to a boat, put the baby in, and then swam back to the ship. I also had picked up a baby, but it died from the cold before I could reach the boat.[61]

Harry Senior also made a heartfelt declaration about whether or not Captain Smith had taken his own life, as was occasionally rumoured in post-disaster newspaper articles.

'No, Captain Smith never shot himself,' Senior insisted. '*I saw* what he did. He went down with that ship. I'll stake my life on that.'[62]

Ever since the disaster, it has often been claimed that the story of Smith's attempt to save the life of a small child was just silly nonsense created by sensation-hungry newspaper reporters, but a letter written on board the *Carpathia* by survivor Elizabeth Nye proves this notion to be false. The letter in question was written on 16 April 1912 while the rescue ship was still at sea, and in that letter Miss Nye told her parents:

Just before the ship went down the captain, the same Captain Smith of the twin ship *Olympic*, jumped into the sea and picked up a little girl who was hanging to the ship, and put her on the raft. They pulled him on, too, but he would not stay. He said 'Good-bye boys, I must go with the ship.' He swam back through the icy waters and died at his post.[63]

Carpathia passenger Fred Beachler told a similar story after talking with several *Titanic* survivors while the rescue ship was still at sea. 'I also learn on the same reliable authority, verified by others, that Captain Smith of the *Titanic* was in the water with a child in his arms, which he succeeded in placing in one of the boats,' he said. 'He was begged to come on board himself, but refused and turned back as though to aid others, and was not seen again.'[64]

Carpathia passenger Jose Mardones heard a similar story from another *Titanic* survivor while on board the rescue ship, because he later told a reporter that an English passenger told him Captain Smith was washed from the bridge and saved a woman and a child by putting them into lifeboats; Smith then refused to be saved himself.[65]

Even though Elizabeth Nye and Fred Beachler were not actual eyewitnesses to Captain Smith's actions, their comments prove beyond all shadow of a doubt that Smith's attempt to save a small child was being discussed on board the *Carpathia* long before New York newspaper reporters had the opportunity to speak with the *Titanic*'s survivors.

In short, there seems to be little doubt that Captain Smith succeeded in reaching collapsible B, because numerous additional survivor accounts describe Smith doing that very thing even though they make no mention of him carrying a child.[66]

As we've already seen, the survivor stories about Captain Smith attempting to save a child support August Wennerström's first-hand primary source account describing how – with his own eyes – he saw Smith pick up one of Alma Pålsson's children a few seconds before the *Titanic*'s bridge submerged. James McGann likewise saw Captain Smith pick up a child before the bridge submerged, and Harry Senior confirmed that Smith was still carrying a child in his arms when he swam up to the overturned collapsible B. Fred Barrett heard this same story from the lips of fellow crew survivors, as did survivors Charles Williams and Elizabeth Nye as well as *Carpathia* passenger Carlos Hurd. In other words, the story of Captain Smith's futile attempt to rescue the Pålsson child was current among survivors while the *Carpathia* was still at sea and was definitely not an invention of overzealous newspaper reporters after the rescue ship reached New York.

It should also be pointed out that the story of a *Titanic* crewman attempting to save the life of a child during the sinking isn't unique to Captain Smith alone, because *identical* lifesaving attempts were made by James McGann, Harry Senior, August Wennerström and an unnamed steward, all of whom attempted to save small children when the *Titanic* went down. In order to make our discussion more complete, we'll quote two additional accounts, the first being a primary source account by John Collins, the assistant cook, who told the US Senate *Titanic* inquiry about his own attempt to save the life of yet another child:

> I ran … to the port side on the saloon deck with another steward and a woman and two children, and the steward had one of the children in his arms and the woman was crying. I took the child off of the woman and made for one of the boats. Then the word came around … there was a collapsible boat getting launched on the starboard side and that all women and children were to make for it. So me and another steward and the two children and the woman came around … the starboard side … We saw the collapsible boat taken off of the saloon deck, and then the sailors and the firemen that were forward seen the ship's bow in the water and seen that she was intending to sink her bow. They shouted out for all they were worth we were to go aft … and we were just turning around and making for the stern end when the wave washed us off the deck – washed us clear of it – and the child was washed out of my arms; and the wreckage and the people that was around me, they kept me down for at least two or three minutes under the water.[67]

Our final account comes from steerage passenger Carl Jonsson, who apparently found refuge on collapsible A and whose own first-hand experiences were later paraphrased by a newspaper reporter:

> Johanson [sic] made no attempt to get into a lifeboat and stuck to the ship almost until the time the boat took the final plunge. Before he jumped overboard Johanson picked up a little girl who had been left motherless, and for a time held on to her, but while swimming toward the raft he was obliged to let go of the baby. He said to him that [this event] was the most heart-rending of the whole disaster.[68]

If four ordinary *Titanic* crewmen and two *Titanic* passengers all went into the water clasping other people's small children in their arms, the present author can see no viable reason for anyone to ridicule the possibility that Captain Smith did the very same thing – especially since August Wennerström *personally* wrote about *seeing* Smith pick up a child right before the *Titanic*'s bridge submerged. Indeed, the only difference between the first six humanitarian lifesaving attempts and Captain Smith's own is that – whereas the other six men eventually released the dead children from their grasp – Captain Smith managed to carry the Pålsson child all the way to collapsible B without realising that the youngster was either dying or already dead.

One final word about Captain Smith's attempt to save the life of an innocent child that night.

Aside from August Wennerström's first-hand account of Captain Smith and the Pålsson child, the only other primary source we have that describes Smith's actual departure from the *Titanic* is that of wireless operator Harold Bride, whose affidavit to the Marconi Company included his statement: 'I noticed Captain Smith dive from the bridge into the sea.' (At the Senate inquiry itself, Bride testified that 'The last I saw of the Captain he went overboard from the bridge, sir. He jumped overboard from the bridge when we were launching the collapsible lifeboat.')

Sceptics of the Smith/Pålsson story will point out that Bride said nothing about seeing Smith carrying a child when he jumped overboard, but at this point we recall the old scientific maxim that 'Absence of evidence is not the same thing as evidence of absence'. In other words, it's possible Harold Bride simply neglected to mention seeing a child in Smith's arms, or he might not have noticed what Smith was attempting to accomplish during his last moments of life – especially since Bride was standing some distance behind Smith, who was apparently turned away from the wireless operator as well.

In a similar vein, a number of survivors related that they never heard the *Titanic*'s band playing during the sinking, but it would be unwise for a researcher to use such stories as a basis for insisting that the band therefore did not play *at all* while the *Titanic* was sinking. After all, which option is more likely to be true – that dozens of eyewitnesses somehow *imagined* hearing the band play, or that a few remaining eyewitnesses were simply too preoccupied to pay attention to such things? Once again, 'absence of evidence is not the same thing as evidence of absence'.

Newspaper interviews exist in which survivors claimed to have seen Captain Smith swim up to collapsible B with no mention of his carrying a child, but (as we've demonstrated in this book) other newspaper survivor interviews claim that Smith handed a child up to the occupants of the boat. In short, newspaper stories alone cannot solve the mystery of which version of the Smith story is true. Unless a new primary source comes to light in which an eyewitness specifies that he saw Captain Smith swim up to collapsible B with empty arms, Harold Bride's testimony about Smith jumping overboard cannot disprove the veracity of August Wennerström's typewritten eyewitness account describing how he and Captain Smith attempted to rescue two of the Pålsson children. With that being the case, the present author will go on record by expressing the opinion that Captain Smith may well have attempted to save a youngster that night and may well have handed the dead or dying child up to the occupants of collapsible B before refusing the opportunity to save his own life.[69]

Be that as it may, Captain Smith's widow believed the story was true and was immensely proud of the way her late husband was said to have met his end on the *Titanic*.

'Did you ever hear of dear Ted saving the child?' Eleanor Smith wrote to Frank Hancock on 6 June 1912. 'It is quite true and so like him.'[70]

Captain Smith's friend, Mr J. E. Hodder Williams, believed the story was true as well:

We crossed with him on many ships and in many companies, through seas fair and foul … and to us he was, and will ever be, the perfect sea captain. In the little tea parties in his private state-room we learned to know the genial-warm-hearted family man; his face would light as he recounted the little intimacies of his life ashore, as he told of his wife and the troubles she had with the dogs he loved, of his little girl and her delight with the presents he brought her and the parties he had planned for her. You have read that just before he sank to the deeps he rescued a baby. That was 'our' Captain Smith, and surely that was his last message to his own 'Babs' and her mother.[71]

★

The *Titanic* was no more, and survivor Violet Jessop was eloquent in describing her heartbreak at not seeing the familiar faces of Captain Smith, Thomas Andrews and hundreds of other friends and fellow crewmembers as the rescue ship *Carpathia* left the disaster site and began steaming back to New York:

> Then started the saddest search it has ever been my lot to witness. Alas, so few were reunited. We also looked without success for so many with whom we had ties of friendship. For our dear Tommy Andrews, for the good doctor, for the boys that made life aboard easier for us, for good friends in all departments. But they were all among the missing when the roll was called.[72]

Captain Smith and Thomas Andrews were dead, but Bruce Ismay survived the sinking of the *Titanic* in collapsible C and was one of the 712 passengers and crewmen who were picked up by the *Carpathia* on the morning of 15 April 1912. These three men had each dealt in their own individual ways with the knowledge that the *Titanic* was sinking, and their individual reputations were also destined to differ in the ensuing years ...

10

PUBLIC PERCEPTION OF CAPTAIN SMITH

The beginning of this book discussed the high regard in which Captain Edward J. Smith was held prior to the *Titanic* disaster. Although this high regard continued after his death, it was nevertheless tempered based on several poor decisions Smith made during the hours his ship was approaching the icefield on the night of 14 April 1912.

As has already been mentioned, a standard form letter advocating safe and prudent navigation practices was issued to Captain Smith by the White Star Line:

> Dear Sir,
>
> In placing the steamer [*Titanic*] temporarily under your command, we desire to direct your attention to the company's regulations for the safe and efficient navigation of its vessels and also to impress upon you in the most forcible manner, the paramount and vital importance of exercising the utmost caution in the navigation of the ships and that the safety of the passengers and crew weighs with us above and before all other considerations.
>
> You are to dismiss all idea of competitive passages with other vessels, and to concentrate your attention upon a cautious, prudent and ever watchful system of navigation which shall lose time or suffer any other temporary inconvenience rather than incur the slightest risk which can be avoided …

Although there's little doubt that the *Titanic* was attempting to beat the maiden voyage crossing time of her elder sister *Olympic*, it appears that

Captain Smith's actual overriding concern on the evening of 14 April was to get his vessel clear of the approaching icefield as quickly as possible. We know from several survivors that Smith was planning to increase the *Titanic*'s speed that evening based on the ice reports he'd been receiving with great regularity, and we know from his friend Henry Martyn Hart that it was Smith's standard operating procedure to increase his vessel's speed whenever ice was in the vicinity.

'I sailed home in the *Britannic*, with Captain Edward Smith, with whom I became very friendly,' Mr Hart wrote in his autobiography:

> One day, standing on the bridge, we were in the neighborhood of ice, and I asked him what his custom was in such water. He said, 'I go as fast as I can, for by so doing I shorten the time of danger, and if we are so unfortunate as to strike a berg, it would only be a matter of three minutes difference in going down, between low speed and high speed.' He had evidently held to his custom when he captained the *Titanic*.[1]

It has often been claimed that the *Titanic*'s engines would never have been run at their topmost speed utilising all twenty-nine boilers (as opposed to running them at 'full speed' using fewer boilers) during the maiden voyage, because brand-new engines are supposedly always broken in gradually. (This argument is sometimes put forward to 'prove' that the *Titanic* was not attempting to beat the *Olympic*'s maiden voyage crossing time.) However, this claim overlooks the fact that the *Titanic*'s engines had *already* been run at their topmost speed during her delivery trip from Belfast to Southampton and that the vessel had achieved a speed of 23.25 knots at that time.[2] (Another speed trial for the *Titanic* was scheduled to take place on either 15 or 16 April, during which her five as-yet-unlit single-ended boilers would have been used.)

At any rate, on the night of 14 April 1912 the *Titanic* was employing all twenty-four of her main boilers and was running at 22.5 knots, a decision that Captain Smith intended to serve two functions: (1) to enable him to utilise his standard operating procedure of getting his vessel clear of the ice danger as quickly as possible, and (2) to enable the *Titanic* to decisively better the *Olympic*'s maiden voyage crossing time by arriving in New York on Tuesday night instead of Wednesday morning.

The captain of every ship is ultimately responsible for the safety of his vessel as well as for each of his own navigational decisions – even if similar decisions were made routinely by other captains on board other ships (e.g., running a ship at high speed, day or night, until a specific danger became visible ahead of the vessel). To increase a ship's speed on a calm, black, moonless night in the presence of anticipated icebergs was not a prudent thing to do, because the lookouts' unlimited visibility in viewing the stars overhead was a far different thing from having unlimited visibility along the dark waterline in the blackness directly ahead of the *Titanic*.

In truth (and based on the distance at which the fatal iceberg was first detected), visibility of unilluminated objects ahead of the *Titanic* was apparently limited to slightly less than two ships' lengths – i.e., less than 600 yards. Considering the distance the *Titanic* would have covered during the time it took for the lookouts to actually comprehend the danger and warn the bridge (plus the additional distance the ship would have covered while the bridge officers reacted to the warning and assessed the situation for themselves before issuing a new steering order), it would seem that – considering her 22.5-knot speed – there was little hope of the *Titanic* avoiding *anything* that might have lain directly in her path during that pitch-black night.

In actuality, this is the same verdict that was arrived at by a court of law in 1913, at which time the judge presiding over the legal case of *Ryan vs. the Oceanic Steam Navigation Company* found *Titanic*'s officers to be guilty of negligence in running their ship at high speed under the conditions that prevailed on the night of 14 April 1912. According to the *London Times* of 26 June 1913:

> In the action for damages for negligence brought against the Oceanic Steam Navigation Company by a man whose son was lost in the *Titanic* disaster, the jury returned a verdict to the effect that the navigation of the vessel had not been negligent as regards keeping a good look-out, but that there had been negligence as regards speed.

Despite the harsh reality that excessive speed that night was the main cause of the disaster, post-sinking newspapers extolled the very real virtues of Captain Smith based on his excellent pre-disaster reputation as well as his undeniable heroism during the evacuation of the *Titanic*. Chapter 1 has already detailed many examples of these glowing assessments of Smith's character and abilities, but we'll now examine several additional post-disaster assessments of his actions as they pertained specifically to the loss of the *Titanic*.

★

On 18 April 1912 (the same day the *Carpathia* arrived back in New York with the *Titanic*'s survivors), Captain Smith's widow sent a poignant letter to the newspapers expressing her heartbreak over the tragedy:

> To my poor fellow-sufferers: My heart overflows with grief for you all and is laden with sorrow that you are weighed down with this terrible burden that has been thrust upon us. May God be with us and comfort us all.
>
> Yours in deep sympathy,
> Eleanor Smith[3]

★

After arriving in New York, the *Carpathia*'s Captain Arthur Rostron offered his own assessment of Captain Smith's abilities: 'Smith was one of the coolest, bravest and most careful commanders I have ever known. His seamanship was of the highest order. Too high a tribute cannot be paid to him by anybody who knew him.'[4]

Mrs Ann O'Donnell, a friend of Captain Smith's since childhood, said the following:

> He always expected to go down with his ship, and I know he tried to do all in his power to save the lives of as many passengers as possible. While he was supervising the taking off of the women and children, I know there was never a thought for himself. His family has been bereft of a loving husband and father, and I know his thoughts at the last moments were for them.[5]

Survivor Lawrence Beesley wrote the following comments following the *Titanic* disaster:

I do not wish to seem to take away any responsibility that should be laid on Captain Smith, but as he is not here to defend himself, let us all see that no undeserved censure be meted out to him. He took the risk which many other Captains have taken. What the chances were in taking the risk no man can say, but in his case the awful thing happened that should never have happened. In the case of all other Captains who have taken a similar risk it did not happen. If he is to be blamed it seems they are all equally blamable for the disaster, for he took the same risk as they did – no more or no less. Remember how the fastest boats are timed to run: 'Leave New York Wednesday, dine in London the following Monday,' and it is done.

Now there must be times when fog and icebergs are dangerous factors, but do the vessels slow down much? My information is that they do not, but if I am wrong, then it will be very easy to give particulars that such and such a boat on a certain date was so many hours or days late because of reduced speed through fog and icebergs. Extracts from ships' logs can be cited, &c. The following was told me by an experienced traveler:

We left Southampton by a boat timed to do the journey to New York in seven days. From the moment of leaving Queenstown to docking at New York there was fog except for the brief space of half an hour, and they did the journey in some hours over the seven days.

If such experiences are uncommon, and if the best boats do not take risks, then let us hear that it is so, and the public will rejoice to know. It will not be so in the future, I am convinced, but for the sake of Captain Smith it seems important to know what the custom has been, for if he has taken a risk many take, the responsibility for such loss of life is fixed on a common system, to which many owners and Captains have agreed, perhaps unconsciously. If he took an uncommon and extraordinary risk, then it seems he is largely to blame.[6]

After the US Senate *Titanic* inquiry concluded, Senator William Alden Smith's own assessment of Captain Smith's pre-collision decisions was very similar to survivor Carrie Chaffee's negative opinion of Bruce Ismay, an opinion we'll be examining presently:

> Captain Smith knew the sea and his clear eye and steady hand had often guided his ship through dangerous paths. For 40 years storms sought in vain to vex him or menace his craft. But once before in all his honorable career was his pride humbled or his vessel maimed. Each new advancing type of ship built by his company was handed over to him as a reward for faithful services and as an evidence of confidence in his skill. Strong of limb, intent of purpose, pure in character, dauntless as a sailor should be, he walked the deck of this majestic structure as master of her keel.
>
> *Titanic* though she was, his indifference to danger was one of the direct and contributing causes of this unnecessary tragedy, while his own willingness to die was the expiating evidence of his fitness to live. Those of us who knew him well – not in anger, but in sorrow – file one specific charge against him, overconfidence and neglect to heed the oft-repeated warnings of his friends; but, in his horrible dismay, when his brain was afire with honest retribution, we can still see, in his manly bearing and his tender solicitude for the safety of women and little children, some traces of his lofty spirit when dark clouds lowered all about him and angry elements stripped him of his command. His devotion to his craft, even as it writhed and twisted and struggled for mastery over its foe, calmed the fears of many of the stricken multitude who hung upon his words, lending dignity to a parting scene as inspiring as it is beautiful to remember.
>
> The mystery of his indifference to danger, when other and pretentious vessels doubled their lookout or stopped their engines, finds no reasonable hypothesis in conjecture or speculation; science in shipbuilding was supposed to have attained perfection and to have spoken her last word; mastery of the ocean had at last been achieved; but overconfidence seems to have dulled the faculties usually so alert. With the atmosphere literally charged with warning signals and wireless messages registering their last appeal, the stokers in the engine room fed their fires with fresh fuel, registering in that dangerous place her fastest speed.[7]

At the end of the day, however, we are left with the cautionary words that the White Star Line issued to Captain Edward J. Smith as part of its Standard Sailing Order to all of the company's shipmasters:

> You are to dismiss all idea of competitive passages with other vessels, and to concentrate your attention upon a cautious, prudent and ever watchful system of navigation which shall lose time or suffer any other temporary inconvenience rather than incur the slightest risk which can be avoided …
>
> We request your cooperation in achieving those satisfactory results which can only be obtained by unremitting care and prudence at all times, whether in the presence of danger or when by its absence you may be lured into a false sense of security; where there is least apparent peril the greatest danger often exists, a well-founded truism which cannot be too prominently borne in mind.

11

PUBLIC PERCEPTION OF THOMAS ANDREWS

Thomas Andrews was one person whose post-disaster reputation tremendously augmented and enhanced the sterling reputation he'd already attained before travelling on the *Titanic*'s maiden voyage. Personable, likeable and highly competent at his job of shipbuilding, Andrews' actions during the *Titanic*'s evacuation ignored his own safety and were devoted solely to ensuring that as many passengers as possible would leave the ship in lifeboats and thereby survive the sinking.

At any rate, let's examine a number of written accounts that highlight the tremendous honour Thomas Andrews brought to his own name by his selfless attempts to help others while the *Titanic* was dying.

★

After the disaster, Lord Pirrie wrote a letter to his sister, Mrs Thomas Andrews Sr, regarding the death of her son:

> A finer fellow than Tommie never lived, and by his death – unselfishly beautiful to the last – we are bereft of the strong young life upon which such reliance had come to be placed by us elders who loved and needed him.[1]

In April 1912 Sir Horace Plunkett, an Irish Member of Parliament, wrote a letter to Thomas Andrews Sr:

Dublin, 19th April, 1912.

My Dear Andrews,

No act of friendship is so difficult as the letter of condolence upon the loss of one who is near and dear. Strive as we may to avoid vapid conventionality, we find ourselves drifting into reflections upon the course of nature, the cessation of suffering, the worse that might have been, and such offers of comfort to others which we are conscious would be of little help to ourselves. In writing to you and your wife on the sorrow of two worlds, which has fallen so heavily upon your home and family, I feel no such difficulty. There is no temptation to be conventional, but it is hard to express in words the very real consolation which will long be cherished by the wide circle of those now bitterly deploring the early death of one who was clearly marked out for a great career in the chief *doing* part of Irish life.

Of the worth of your son I need not speak to you – nothing I could say of his character or capacity could add to your pride in him. But you ought to know that we all feel how entirely to his own merits was due the extraordinary rapidity of his rise and the acknowledged certainty of his leadership in what Ulster stands for before the world. When I first saw him in the shipyard he was in a humble position, enjoying no advantage on account of your relationship to one of his employers. Even then, as on many subsequent occasions, I learned, or heard from my Irish fellow workers, that this splendid son of yours had the best kind of public spirit – that which made you and Sinclair save the Recess Committee at its crisis.

It may be that the story of your poor boy's death will never be told, but I seem to see it all. I have just come off the sister ship, whose captain was a personal friend, as was the old doctor who went with him to the *Titanic*. I have been often in the fog among the icebergs. I have heard, in over sixty voyages, many of those awful tales of the sea. I know enough to be aware that your son might easily have saved himself on grounds of public duty none could gainsay. What better witness could be found to tell the million who would want and had a right to know why the great ship failed, and how her successors could be made, as she was believed to be, unsinkable? None of his breed could listen to such promptings of the lower self when the call came to show to what height the real man in him could rise. I think of him displaying the very highest quality of courage – the true heroism – without any of the stimulants which the glamour and prize of battle supply – doing all he could for the women and children – and then going grimly and silently to his glorious grave.

So there is a bright side to the picture which you of his blood and his widow must try to share with his and your friends – with the thousands who will treasure his memory. It will help you in your bereavement, and that is why I intrude upon your sorrow with a longer letter than would suffice to tender to you and Mrs Andrews and to all your family circle a tribute of heartfelt sympathy.

Pray accept this as coming not only from myself but also from those intimately associated with me in the Irish work which brought me, among other blessings the friendship of men like yourself.

Believe me,
Yours always,
Horace Plunkett[2]

The day after the *Titanic*'s surviving crewmen arrived back in England, an unnamed newspaper correspondent visited the facilities where some of the survivors were being housed prior to their giving affidavits to Board of Trade investigators. The correspondent described his visit with the crewmen:

All spoke with enthusiasm of the gallantry of the ship's officers and of the men generally. In nearly every case mention was made of Mr Andrews, the *Titanic*'s designer, who seems to have been to every part of the ship during the first hours of suspense – even into the engine rooms – giving advice, warning and encouragement.[3]

On 3 May 1912 Bruce Ismay wrote a letter to Thomas Andrews' grieving wife:

Dear Mrs Andrews,

Forgive me for intruding upon your grief, but I feel I must send you a line to convey my most deep and sincere sympathy with you in the terrible loss you have suffered. It is impossible for me to express in words all I feel, or make you realize how truly sorry I am for your loss, or how my heart goes out to you. I knew your husband for many years, and had the highest regard for him, and looked upon him as a true friend.

No one who had the pleasure of knowing him could fail to realize and appreciate his numerous good qualities and he will be sadly missed in his profession. Nobody did more for the White Star Line, or was more loyal to its interests than your good husband, and I always placed the utmost reliance on his judgment.

If we miss him and feel his loss so keenly, what your feelings must be I cannot think. Words at such a time are useless, but I could not help writing to you to tell you how truly deeply I feel for you in your grief and sorrow.

Yours sincerely,
Bruce Ismay[4]

On 22 April 1912 Mr James Moore, of Belfast, received the following brief telegram from a *Titanic* survivor in New York in reference to Mr Andrews: 'Heroic unto death thinking only of safety others.'[5]

★

On 9 May 1912 Thomas Andrews Sr wrote a letter on black-bordered stationery to a Mr Hunter, a childhood friend of his late son Thomas Andrews Jr:

9 May, 1912

Dear Mr Hunter,

My wife, my daughter-in-law, myself & all our family thank you with all our hearts for your thoughtful sympathy with us in our great sorrow.

Our poor son died heroically; this, & the wide sympathy of our friends are our comfort.

Sympathy from one who knew him as well as you did is especially grateful.

Very sincerely yours,
Thomas Andrews[6]

On 16 January 1913 Thomas Andrews Sr sent a second black-bordered letter to Mr Hunter regarding a biography of his son that had just been written by author Shan Bullock:

16 Janry, 1913

Dear Mr Hunter,
I duly recd your letter of the 9th inst. I thank you very sincerely for it, & all your appreciation of our dear lost son.

You are quite right; Mr Shan Bullock had your letter to the Cheshire newspaper before him when he wrote the little book. We were all so pleased with it that we procured many copies & preserved them with others in Albums which the 'Press Cutting Fancy' prepared for us. If you will kindly come see us when you are next in Belfast I should like to show you one of these albums, & there will always be a bed & a welcome for you at Ardara. A line or a telephone message the day before you come will make sure that we will be at home.

Your estimation of him is high but he was worthy of it.

We see a good deal of his widow who lives at Conway, Dunmurry with her brother & with her very fine little girl, who is an especial pet with her grandparents.

I return your book with another, a presentation copy of which we had a few printed and bound.

It was very stupid in me neglecting to send you one before.
Kindest remembrances to you & yours,

Very sincerely yours,
Thomas Andrews[7]

12

PUBLIC PERCEPTION OF J. BRUCE ISMAY

As we've seen during our discussion of Bruce Ismay's activities during the *Titanic*'s maiden voyage, survivor Elisabeth Lines made it clear that Ismay was enthusiastic about the prospect of the *Titanic* beating the *Olympic*'s maiden voyage crossing time and arriving in New York on Tuesday night instead of Wednesday morning. However (and despite poorly researched claims to the contrary), there is currently zero evidence that Mr Ismay ever put actual *pressure* on Captain Smith to achieve that result. As will be seen presently, though, the suspicion that Ismay was guilty of doing that very thing was very strong in the minds of at least a few survivors of the *Titanic* disaster.

During the actual evacuation of the *Titanic*, we have shown that Ismay did everything in his power to assist passengers in boarding lifeboats and leaving the great vessel before she went down. Subsequent criticism was largely based on the fact that the White Star Line chairman got into a lifeboat himself at the last minute, thereby saving his own life while hundreds of his fellow passengers were left behind to perish when the ship went down.

Additional criticisms were heaped upon Ismay because erroneous newspaper articles claimed he occasionally acted in questionable ways that would have put *anyone* in a bad light if those stories were true.

In this chapter we shall examine some of these criticisms of Bruce Ismay and try to determine whether they have any merit.

Bruce Ismay: The Criticisms

One thing that cannot be denied is the fact that Bruce Ismay's life was changed forever from the very moment that the *Titanic* went down. This unfortunate situation was hinted at by survivor William Carter, who had joined Mr Ismay in boarding collapsible C.

'I looked around just as the *Titanic* went down, being attracted by the explosion,' he said later. 'Mr Ismay did not turn and look out, but instead was very quiet, pulling on the oars.'[1]

Not everyone felt charitable towards Bruce Ismay even though he had done his best to save the lives of as many passengers as possible after learning that the *Titanic* was truly sinking. One negative viewpoint was expressed by the widowed Mrs Herbert Chaffee, whose opinion about Ismay was expressed in a subsequent newspaper interview:

> 'Don't ask me what I think of him,' Mrs Chaffee cried through clenched teeth last night. 'I would not care to put my real thoughts in his connection into words. I can tell you this, however, that the utmost criminal negligence was responsible for the disaster. Mr Ismay and all the ship's officers were aware that we were passing through the ice fields. All of them talked about it at the tables. When several of the passengers begged that the ship's terrible speed be reduced, all we received in answer were smiles.'[2]

Survivor John Snyder agreed with Mrs Chaffee about the danger of steaming at high speed towards a known icefield in the dead of night:

> The *Titanic* accident was doubtless due to the desire of the ship-owner to make the port of New York a day ahead of schedule ... No censure is too severe for those men who knew the dangers in the path of the ship, yet insisted on full steam ahead.[3]

After the disaster, *Carpathia* passenger Mrs Charles M. Hutchison wrote the following about Bruce Ismay while the rescue ship was still at sea:

> Mr J. Bruce Ismay, president and manager of the White Star Line, was one of the passengers aboard [the *Titanic*], and he was saved. He

has not yet appeared on deck, and Mrs Smith and other rescued of the *Titanic* say he knows better than to risk his presence among his people. It is reported that he was asked on the other ship whether he was going to leave his ship, and he replied that he intended to save himself.[4]

Two hearsay accounts of unknown reliability were given to newspaper reporters by *Carpathia* crewmen who allegedly described Ismay's selfish behaviour after boarding the rescue ship. Our first account came from an unnamed *Carpathia* officer:

'Mr Ismay reached the *Carpathia* in about the tenth lifeboat,' said an officer. 'I didn't know who he was, but afterward heard the others of the crew discussing his desire to get something to eat the minute he put his foot on deck. The steward who waited on him, [John Harold] McGuire, from London, says Mr Ismay came dashing into the dining room, and throwing himself in a chair, said: "Hurry, for God's sake, and get me something to eat; I'm starved. I don't care what it costs or what it is; bring it to me."

'McGuire brought Mr Ismay a load of stuff and when he had finished it, he handed McGuire a two-dollar bill. "Your money is no good on this ship," McGuire told him. "Take it," insisted Mr Ismay, shoving the bill in McGuire's hand. "I am well able to afford it. I will see to it that the boys of the *Carpathia* are well rewarded for this night's work." This promise started McGuire making inquiries as to the identity of the man he had waited on. Then we learned that he was Mr Ismay. I did not see Mr Ismay after the first few hours. He must have kept to his cabin.'[5]

★

Our second hearsay account of the same incident was given by James William Barker, the *Carpathia*'s assistant storekeeper:

When Bruce Ismay was taken on board the first thing he did was to demand something to eat and went into the dining room for some breakfast. One of the stewards gave it to him, and he offered the man $2 as a tip. At first it was refused, but he insisted, saying that he was going to see to it that all of the 'boys' on the *Carpathia* would be rewarded generously. It was then that the steward learned that the hungry passenger was Mr Ismay.

After the first meal Mr Ismay kept to the stateroom which he was sharing with another passenger, and ate all of his meals there. I did not see him again in the restaurant. I did hear some talk among some of the women from the *Titanic* about his having been saved, but nothing that I can remember.[6]

Eleanor Danforth was a *Carpathia* passenger who gave a sarcastic description of the low profile Bruce Ismay kept on board the rescue ship: 'Mrs Astor I did not see. She went at once to a stateroom and did not come out at all. Nor did I see Mr Ismay. Nobody did. Nobody wanted to. He was busy arranging a committee meeting or something.'[7]

Carpathia passenger Fr Henry Burke later spoke with Fr J. W. Malone in New York regarding Bruce Ismay:

The reception J. Bruce Ismay, president of the company that owned the *Titanic*, got in the four days' run from the icefield into New York harbor was one that he will not forget till death, if he lives to be as old as the oldest man. The feeling against Mr Ismay was intense. We did not bother to inquire whether he jumped into the first lifeboat or the last, but it was enough to drive him out of his head if he knew the feeling against him.[8]

After the *Carpathia* reached New York, passenger Philip Mauro wrote a letter to his daughter Isabel: '[The *Carpathia*] docked about nine o'clock … Thursday evening. A dense crowd, filling the streets leading to the dock and estimated at 25,000 persons, awaited the arrival of the vessel in the hope of merely catching a glimpse of some of the survivors.'

Mauro's daughter Isabel and her husband Charles were waiting at the wharf when the *Carpathia* came in. They saw two of the *Titanic*'s lifeboats being rowed away to a separate location and saw and heard J. Bruce Ismay, president of the White Star Line, booed and hissed as he came off the *Carpathia* because he had allowed himself to be rescued.[9]

In later years Dr Árpád Lengyel (one of *Carpathia*'s doctors) wrote an account describing his experiences on the rescue ship:

The survivors included Bruce Ismay, president of the White Star Line. Because the survivors blamed him for the disaster, he shut himself up in his cabin for the whole voyage and in New York left our ship secretly, accompanied by detectives.[10]

In addition to being blamed for the disaster itself, Bruce Ismay was reviled because of the manner in which he allegedly left the *Titanic*. While still on board the *Carpathia*, survivor Charles Stengel was told that Ismay got into one of the first lifeboats to leave the *Titanic*.[11]

★

A more detailed (and more imaginative) newspaper interview with two unnamed *Titanic* crewmen undoubtedly did a great deal to help fan the flames of antipathy towards Bruce Ismay:

At this juncture the sailors described without apparent prejudice or bitterness how J. Bruce Ismay, chairman of the Board of Directors of the White Star Line, was the first to leave the *Titanic*.

'Ismay,' the sailors asserted, 'with his two daughters and a million-aire, Sir Cosmo Duff-Gordon, and the latter's family, got into the first accident or emergency boats, which are about twenty-eight feet long, and were always ready for lowering under the bridge. The boat in which Ismay and Sir Cosmo left was manned by seven seamen. There were seventeen persons in the boat.

'This boat pulled away from the ship a half hour before any of the lifeboats were put into the water.

'There were thirteen first-class passengers and five sailors in the emergency boat. Both boats were away from the ship within ten or fifteen minutes of the ship's crashing into the berg.'

Asked to explain how it was possible for two boats to be put over the ship's side into the water without being subjected to a rush on the part of the great ship's passengers, the *Titanic* seamen said: 'Ismay and those who left in the two emergency boats occupied cabins deluxe. The two boats were swinging from davits ready for lowering. We have no idea who notified Mr Ismay and his friends to make ready to leave the ship, but we do know that the boats in which they were got away first ...'

One man stands out in a most unenviable light amid the narratives of heroism and suffering attending the great *Titanic* sea tragedy. This man is J. Bruce Ismay, managing director of the White Star Line, who, according to accounts of survivors, made himself the exception to the rule of the sea, 'Women first,' in the struggle for life.

Some of these survivors say he jumped into the first lifeboat, others that he got into the third or fourth. However that may be, he is among the comparatively few men saved, and the manner of his escape aroused the wrath and criticism of many.[12]

[Note: Although Cosmo Duff Gordon, his wife and maid did leave the *Titanic* in the starboard emergency lifeboat (1) at 1.05 a.m., this was almost an hour before Ismay left the ship in collapsible C.]

★

Another imaginative newspaper account of Bruce Ismay's supposed departure from the *Titanic* came from survivor Charlotte Cardeza, who (with her son Thomas) left the ship in lifeboat 3 at 12.55 a.m. – more than an hour before Mr Ismay left the *Titanic* in collapsible C:

> According to Mrs W. J. Cardeza, of Philadelphia, after she had arrived at the Ritz-Carlton with Thomas D. M. Cardeza, J. Bruce Ismay was not only safely seated in a lifeboat before it was filled, but he also selected the crew that rowed the boat. According to Mrs Cardeza, Mr Ismay knew that Mr Cardeza was an expert oarsman and he beckoned him into his boat. Mr Cardeza manned an oar until the boat was picked up about two hours later.[13]

A completely different version of events was allegedly given to a reporter by Thomas Cardeza, who – instead of going into the water as this account claims – actually accompanied his mother into lifeboat 3 long before Madeleine Astor and Bruce Ismay left the ship in lifeboat 4 and collapsible C respectively:

> Mr Astor was with Mrs Astor. A crowd of women gathered around the nearest boat and was helped in by the men. There was not a man

passenger in the boat. The sailors manipulated the davit ropes and just as the boat was about to swing out into the water, one of the women cried out for a man to get in with them.

Mrs Astor was in the party. I saw Col. Astor kiss her goodbye. But she was not the one to call out. The woman who did, said: 'We must have one of you men to steer for us. You know something about the ocean, Mr Ismay. Won't you come with us? We will feel safer.'

'No, I will remain here, and not take the place of a woman,' Mr Cardeza quoted Mr Ismay as saying. The women urged him, however, he said, and some of the men joined in, requesting him to get into the boat. Mr Ismay, said Mr Cardeza, finally consented and got in. The boat was then launched and drew away.

'With several others, I caught a piece of the wreckage when the vessel sank,' [Mr Cardeza said.] 'We tried to paddle it with pieces of wood. I don't remember much that happened after we were thrown into the water, except that I was picked up by a [lifeboat].'[14]

After returning home to Canada, survivor Mary Fortune spoke with a newspaper reporter, who then paraphrased her story of how she and her daughters entered a lifeboat:

Before they left the ship a boat containing a number of men passengers was lowered on the starboard side. Among those in the boat was a gentleman who had distributed hymn books to the cabin passengers on Sunday. This gentleman had been pointed out to them as J. Bruce Ismay. The boat in which this man, supposed to be Ismay, left, was only partly filled. Mrs Fortune and her daughters left the *Titanic* on lifeboat No. 10, which was the sixth boat to be lowered.[15]

[Note: The Fortune family left the *Titanic* in lifeboat 10 at 1.50 a.m. – ten minutes before (and at the opposite end of the *Titanic* from) Bruce Ismay's location when he entered collapsible C at 2 a.m.]

★

During the days following the *Carpathia*'s return to New York, William Randolph Hearst's newspapers seemingly went out of their way to castigate Bruce Ismay's behaviour on board the *Titanic*. This stratagem was described in 1980 by Ernest St Clair, who in 1912 had been a waiter on the *Carpathia*:

> So to New York; which we reached four days later. To the tragic welcome. To the court of enquiry at the dock side. To the snarling of the yellow press at 'Brute' Ismay, as they dubbed the unfortunate Bruce Ismay, chairman of the White Star Line, owners of the *Titanic*. The American souvenir hunters besieged the *Carpathia*'s crew members when they went ashore.[16]

After the *Carpathia* arrived in New York, Norman Lynd, who was on the *New York Herald*'s staff of artists, wrote a letter to his father, Rev. Professor Lynd, in Belfast:

> I don't think that in the English journals they put in the things some of the papers do here. As you know, the fact that J. Bruce Ismay came safely to shore while a lot of his passengers were left to drown caused a lot of talk. Hearst's papers have been full of vituperation and abuse for him, printing his name in large type under his picture 'J. Brute Ismay'. They also had a cartoon of him in a lifeboat full of women, looking like a poor shivering coward. All of which is cheap and yellow, and appeals to the ignorant. The United States Government may not perhaps have the power to compel Ismay and the other British subjects to answer their subpoena; but as a large number of the victims were citizens, they wanted to have details, and they opened their investigation about twelve hours after the survivors got here.[17]

After the American Senate began its investigation into the sinking of the *Titanic*, at least one newspaper was unfavourably impressed with Bruce Ismay's testimony and published a list of subjects it felt he wasn't interested in knowing or talking about:

THINGS THAT ISMAY DID NOT OBSERVE
'I saw no passengers in sight when I entered the lifeboat.'
'I did not see what happened to the lifeboats.'
'I did not look to see after leaving the *Titanic* whether she broke in two.'

'I did not look to see if there was a panic.'
'After I left the bridge, I did not see the captain.'
'I saw nothing of any explosion.'
'I saw no struggle, no confusion.'
'I did not recognise any passengers on the *Titanic* as she sank.'
'I saw no women waiting when I entered the lifeboat.'[18]

A summary of things people found objectionable about Bruce Ismay's survival was published in Logan Marshall's 1912 book *Sinking of the Titanic & Great Sea Disasters*:

From the moment that Bruce Ismay's name was seen among those of the survivors of the *Titanic* he became the object of acrid attacks in every quarter where the subject of the disaster was discussed. Bitter criticism held that he should have been the last to leave the doomed vessel.

His critics insisted that as managing director of the White Star Line his responsibility was greater even than Captain Smith's, and while granting that his survival might still be explained, they condemned his apparent lack of heroism.

Even in England his survival was held to be the one great blot on an otherwise noble display of masculine courage.

A prominent official of the White Star Line shook his head meaningfully when asked what he thought of Ismay's escape with the women and children. The general feeling seemed to be that he should have stayed aboard the sinking vessel, looking out for those who were left, playing the man like Major Butt and many another and going down with the ship like Captain Smith.

He was also charged with urging a speed record and with ignoring information received with regard to icebergs.

The belief in England was that the captain of the *Carpathia* had acted under Ismay's influence in refusing to permit any account of the disaster to be transmitted previous to the arrival of the vessel in New York. Ismay's telegram making arrangements for the immediate deportation of the survivors among the *Titanic*'s crew was taken to be part of the same scheme to delay if not to prevent their stories of the wreck from being obtained in New York.

Another circumstance which created a damaging impression was Ismay's failure to give the names of the surviving crew, whose distraught families were entitled to as much consideration as those whose relatives occupied the most expensive suites on the *Titanic*. The anguish endured by the families of members of the crew was reported as indescribable, and Southampton was literally turned into a city of weeping and tragic pathos. The wives of two members of the crew died of shock and suspense.[19]

Two days after the disaster, legendary newspaperman Ben Hecht published a poem in which he contrasted the perceived difference in behaviour between Captain Smith and Bruce Ismay while the *Titanic* was sinking:

Master and Man.

The Captain stood where a Captain should,
For the law of the sea is grim;
The Owner romped ere his ship was swamped
And no law bothered him.

The Captain stood where the Captain should,
When Captain's boat goes down;
But the Owner led when the women fled,
For an Owner must not drown.

The Captain sank as a man of rank,
While the Owner turned away:
The Captain's rave was his bridge and, brave,
He earned his seaman's pay.

To hold your place in the ghastly face
Of Death on the sea at night,
Is a seaman's job, but to flee with the mob
Is an Owner's noble right.

B. M. Hecht[20]

Bruce Ismay: The Reality

We have already examined Bruce Ismay's heroic attempts to get as many passengers as possible into the *Titanic*'s lifeboats, and we have just seen the way inaccurate newspaper stories served to inflame public opinion against him after the *Carpathia* brought him and the other survivors to New York. In the following section we shall examine a different selection of eyewitness accounts, newspaper articles and personal letters that cast Mr Ismay in a far more favourable light.

★

In speaking with a newspaper reporter, survivor John Pillsbury Snyder had a specific observation to make about Bruce Ismay's conduct: 'The *Titanic* passengers had no criticism to make of Mr Ismay in the fact that he did not stick to the ship ... His conduct in directing the orderly lowering of the boats was praised by everyone as largely responsible for the saving of those who were saved.'[21]

Contrary to our earlier account alleging that Bruce Ismay's first act upon reaching the rescue ship was to demand breakfast, *Carpathia* passenger John R. Joyce had something different to say on that matter:

'How did Mr Ismay get out?' Mr Joyce was asked.

'Well,' said Mr Joyce, 'he got into a lifeboat. On the *Carpathia* he went to a stateroom without saying a word. There was some criticism regarding him on board the boat, but he was not severely censured. Survivors said that everybody could have been saved if there had been enough lifeboats.'[22]

After the rescue ship reached New York, a reporter related what an unnamed *Carpathia* steward told him about Ismay: 'Bruce Ismay went to his cabin immediately after boarding the *Carpathia* and stayed there until the ship made port.'[23]

Carpathia passenger Carlos Hurd made a similar observation about the way Ismay boarded the rescue vessel:

To another stateroom a tall, dark man had been conducted, his head bowed, anguish in his face. He was J. Bruce Ismay, head of the International Mercantile Marine and chief owner of the *Titanic* and her sister ship, the *Olympic*. He has made the maiden voyage on each of his company's great ships. He remained in his room in a physician's care during the voyage back to New York. Capt. Rostron, his only caller, was not admitted to see him till Tuesday evening.[24]

After arriving in New York, an unnamed *Carpathia* steward was asked if he saw Bruce Ismay on the rescue ship:

Oh, he was sick all the way back. All the boys said – I believe every one of them will tell you the same – Mr Ismay did everything he could – helping the ladies first and all that. I couldn't tell you a thing about him – I didn't see him at all, you know – but all the boys said that Mr Ismay did everything he could.[25]

After the *Carpathia* arrived in New York, D. W. McMillan spoke with a reporter about what his sister, survivor Georgette Madill, told him about Bruce Ismay's conduct on the *Titanic*:

She told me that Mr Ismay and Mr Astor were helping the passengers to get into the lifeboats until the last boat, and when no more women and children were around Mr Ismay got into the back of one. Shortly following that young Thayer jumped into the water. There was no disorder during the whole thing.[26]

★

After motoring from Devonshire to Fishguard on the evening of 15 April 1912, Mrs Bruce Ismay had received a telegram informing her of the *Titanic* disaster. With an effort she reached a telephone office, but was so overcome with emotion that for the next hour she remained in a state of collapse until news of her husband's safety came in a telegram.[27]

On 20 April 1912 it was pointed out in the press that J. Bruce Ismay did not land from the *Carpathia* with the other survivors of the *Titanic*'s wreck, but that P. A. S. Franklin, vice-president of the White Star Line, went on board, and he and Mr Ismay had a consultation that lasted until 11.15 p.m. The two men then came ashore and went to the captain's office on the pier, where Mr Ismay made this formal statement:

In the presence and under the shadow of a catastrophe so overwhelming my feelings are too deep for expression in words, I can only say that the White Star Line, its officers and employees will do everything humanly possible to alleviate the suffering and sorrow of the survivors and of the relatives and friends of those who have perished.

The *Titanic* was the last word in shipbuilding. Every regulation prescribed by the British Board of Trade had been strictly complied with; the master, officers and the crew were the most experienced and skillful in the British service.

I am informed that a committee of the United States Senate has been appointed to investigate the circumstances of the accident. I heartily welcome the most complete and exhaustive inquiry, and any aid that I or my associates or our builders or navigators can render is at the service of the public and the governments of both the United States and Great Britain. Under the circumstances I must respectfully defer making any further statement at this time.[28]

On 22 April 1912 Mr Ismay gave the American press a true account of the way he left the sinking *Titanic* in collapsible C:

As the boat was going over the side, Mr Carter, a passenger, and myself got in. At that time there was not a woman on the boat deck, nor any passenger of any class, so far as we could see or hear. The boat had between 35 and 40 in it, I should think, most of them women. There were, perhaps, four or five men, and it was afterward discovered that there were four Chinamen concealed under the thwarts in the bottom of the boat. The distance that the boat had to be lowered into the water was, I should estimate, about 20ft.

Mr Carter and I did not get into the boat until after they had begun to lower it away. When the boat reached the water, I helped row it, pushing the oar from me as I said. This is the explanation for the fact that my back was to the sinking steamer. The boat would have accommodated certainly six or more passengers in addition if there had been any on the boat deck to go. These facts can be sub-stantiated by Mr W. E. Carter, of Philadelphia, who got in at the same time I did and was rowing the boat with me. I hope I need not say that neither Mr Carter nor myself would for one moment have thought of getting into the boat if there had been any women there to go in it; nor should I have done so if I had thought that by remain-ing on the ship I could have been of the slightest further assistance.

It is impossible for me to answer every false statement, rumor or invention that has appeared in the newspapers. I am prepared to answer any question that may be asked by the committee of the senate, or any other responsible person. I shall, therefore, make no further statement of this kind, except to explain the messages that I sent from the *Carpathia*.[29]

In discussing the work of the US Senate *Titanic* investigation with the press, Bruce Ismay described the proceedings as 'brutally unfair':

'I have searched my mind with the deepest care. I am sure I did noth-ing I should not have done. My conscience is clear. I took a chance of escape when it came to me. I did not seek it. Every woman and child had been cared for before I left, and more, all the men within reach had been cared for before I took my turn.'

Mr Ismay has announced (says a Reuter message) that he has given instructions to all lines under the control of the International Mercantile Marine Company to equip all its steamers with sufficient lifeboats and rafts to carry all the passengers and crew, without regard to the regulations prescribed by the Government of any nation.[30]

On 22 April 1912, after seeing the rough treatment Bruce Ismay was receiving in the press and elsewhere, William Carter corroborated Ismay's description of how he and Carter had left the *Titanic*:

The statements which have been made by many persons regarding Mr Ismay's conduct are an injustice to him. While the lifeboat contain-ing myself and Ismay was moving away from the *Titanic*, Ismay rowed with two seamen and myself until we sighted the *Carpathia*.

The women that were in the boat were from the steerage, with their children. I guess there were about 40 of them.

Mr Ismay and myself and several of the officers walked up and down the deck crying, 'Are there any more women here?' We called for several minutes, and got no answer. One of the officers then declared that if we wanted to, we could get into the boat if we took the place of seamen. He gave us this preference because we were among the first-class passengers.

Mr Ismay called again, and receiving no reply, we got into the lifeboat. We took the oars and rowed with the two seamen. We were about a mile from the *Titanic* when she went down. It seemed to me that it was less than a half hour.

All the women were clad in thin clothes, while I was in my evening clothes, without a hat, and had on a pair of slippers. I looked around just as the *Titanic* went down, being attracted by the explosions. Mr Ismay did not turn and look, but instead was very quiet, pulling on the oars.

I desire to correct what has been said about him. He was perfectly cool and collected, and aided a great deal in keeping the women from the steerage quiet. I will probably be called before the senatorial investigating committee, and I can say that Mr Ismay only left the boat after he saw that there were no more women on the deck. He called, and so did I, and we found none.[31]

On 28 April 1912, 13-year-old Christine Elsie Stormont wrote the following letter to Bruce Ismay:

Dear Sir,
I wonder if I may send to you a little letter of loving thoughts, I wish with all my heart I could say something to comfort you.

I am only a little stranger a country lassie, a lonely one too because I have lately lost my mother and daddy, grieving for them, and I know, [although] I am only a queer girl, what pains in one's heart mean and awful loneliness, and I have been so glad many a time for even the dumb love of my big dog who follows me everywhere. I know that no one can really understand your sorrow at present but will you accept from me pure beautiful sympathetic love. Even tho I am no one but the helpless lonely girl, perhaps my loving sympathy may comfort you just as my big dog's dumb love comforts me often. It hurt me when I read you wished you had perished, God could never have let your life be spared had he not work for you to do. I have thought sometimes it would be easier to die and be with mother and daddy than live without their love, but we have not to wish for the easiest, have we, and your life is a useful one, not like mine where I am no real use to anyone.

I often wonder at God's plans, but he plans that is the best comfort. I know that it is better comfort than all the sympathy in the world.

Will you please take care of yourself and not look backwards. God spared you and I am very very grateful, and tho it makes it harder at present to live than to have died, God understands. There will be beautiful sunshine ahead for you.

Forgive me intruding, but if I could lessen your pains I would, tho I have never seen or known you. I am grateful that God spared you, and if my love can comfort you, you ask God to let it.

Your little friend,
Elsie Stormont[32]

On 21 May 1912 Miss Stormont wrote a response to Bruce Ismay's reply to her earlier letter:

Dear Sir,
It is kind of you to think of my sorrow among your own great trouble. Perhaps it may comfort you a wee bit to know that you have cheered me more than you will ever know.

If I have done the smallest service for you I am happy. I cannot feel things very well, but I do feel all I say very very honestly.

I have never thought you would see my letter, but I knew God would let my thoughts reach you. It hurts me to think of anyone suffering, but to suffer in one's soul is far worse than in one's body.

After Mother died, I was very ill and for a time was almost blind. I was grateful when I could see the sky and the sunset and all my beautiful friends again these are my friends just all nature. I never miss the sunset. It tells me such very beautiful comforting things. I was glad about your dog, how it would love and understand and be so glad to see you back. I just know all about it. I don't understand people but I do dogs and animals, and he'd never leave you and if he could have spoken would it not have been too sacred just? I know that dumb sympathy. When I used to cry, my big collie used to put his paws up round my waist and whine, but I'm braver now. I should be very lonely without these friends.

I hope you are a little better now and that soon you will feel quite strong. You won't be angry, but I think a lot because I am alone much in the woods, and I feel that all that has happened is just God's own mysterious workings. I don't call it an accident. I don't question God's doings, but I think it is everybody's duty to help and comfort and not probe into awful wounds by questions.

Please forgive me, for I am truly a very quiet lonely home-girl, but I can't help thinking.

I cried today and told my big doggie that you were sorry for us even in all your great trouble. Daddy has only been gone a little time. I pray for you every day and those you love.

In deepest respect,
Elsie Stormont

I showed your picture in the paper to my dog and I gave it some of my wild flowers.[33]

On 5 May 1912 survivor Elmer Taylor spoke with the press about his impression of Bruce Ismay during the sinking. He also (apparently) denied that Mr Ismay and Captain Smith had attended a late dinner party together on 14 April (a claim survivor Arthur Peuchen was making in his own newspaper interviews):

Ismay was unjustly criticized and abused for his actions regarding the *Titanic* wreck. We saw Mr Ismay on the deck when he first came up. He looked as if he had just tumbled out of bed, but he was as careful and energetic on getting the people quietly into the boats as any of the ship officers.

Mr Ismay did not leave the ship until the last of the collapsible boats was launched and then he got in because there were no other people there to go. He got in with a whole lot of women from the steerage, for their boat did not have enough men in it. I was surprised, after I saw his work on the night of the wreck, to see the way he was abused and criticized and I believed it was so unjust that I wrote Mr Ismay a personal letter, telling him I thought it was entirely undeserved.

I had known Mr Ismay personally for some time and am confident he does not deserve the censure generally given him.

Mr Taylor described some of the incidents of the wreck in a graphic manner:

We were rushing along at a high rate of speed when the ship struck ... but I don't know just how fast. I do not believe there was any dinner party on the ship such as has been reported. I saw no indication of it on the part of the ship's officers nor anything like it at any time during the trip.[34]

Bruce Ismay's private secretary, William Harrison, lost his life in the *Titanic* disaster, and on 11 May 1912 Harrison's widow, Anne Harrison, wrote a letter to Mr Ismay.

May 11th 1912

Dear Mr Ismay,

Thank you very much for your kind letter, we are heartbroken but asking God to give us strength to bear our trouble. My husband was such a loving man and Father. I have a little boy 13 nearly overcome with grief he has gone to a new school a Mr Taylor's in Freshfield, he has promised to look after him, and to try to comfort him. We have taken a small house here for a year, our old home was too painful to stay in. How my husband loved his work at the office, and you for your kindness to him – he was so proud of his position as Private help to you.

I hope you will be able to do something for us, we should love to keep our home, so that we can keep together although very lonely. My daughter is not a strong girl, and not able to do much. Forgive me writing you like this, but it is my next trouble how we are going to live. My husband was insured for £500 but no Will so I get a 3rd only.

I do hope you have got over your very terrible time. Again thanking you for your kind letter

I am Yours sincerely
Harrison[35]

On 22 May 1912 Harrison's son William wrote a letter to Bruce Ismay:

May 22nd, 1912

Dear Mr Ismay,
I am writing to ask you if Mother and I may come to see you some time this week or next. We called to-day but you were engaged.

Poor Mother is broken-hearted, indeed so are we all, we loved him so much. He was so good and kind.

Do forgive my asking you, but do be kind to Mother please. I myself don't mind working for my living if I can. Although my Father sheltered me so, and kept me at home doing nothing. But now he is gone it is my place to look after Mother and my little brother as best I can.

On Saturday we had sent to us the things found on Pa, what a sad little package it was too. A bunch of rusty keys, the little silver knife you gave to him, a little Diary of your engagements, a pocket-book of his own, and some money, a little gold stud. So we think he must have been in evening dress.

We are quite settled now in our new little home, I do so hope we shall be able to keep together.

Again asking you for your kindness and forgiveness in writing as I have,

I am Yours truly,
Willie Harrison[36]

On 30 May 1912 young William Harrison wrote a second letter to Bruce Ismay:

Dear Mr Ismay,

I can't really tell you how truly thankful we are to you, for your great kindness to us. You will never know how grateful we are, because we can never tell you. Although our sorrow is still as big, we are so relieved to know that we can live comfortably all together. Poor Mother is quite bright to-night, and looks more like herself. Tommy was so pleased with his things, and became quite excited, when we told him, from whom they came.

   Again thanking you very very much

I remain yours,
Very Sincerely,
William Harrison[37]

On 15 May 1912 the following article about Bruce Ismay was published in an Irish newspaper:

MR ISMAY'S *TITANIC* MEMORIAL
Pensions for Seafarers' Widows
£11,000 promised for the fund

Lord Derby has received the following letter from Mr Bruce Ismay:

'Dear Lord Derby, – The terrible disaster for the *Titanic* has brought prominently before my mind the fact that no permanent fund exists to assist the widows of those whose lives are lost while they are engaged upon active duty upon the mercantile vessels of this country.

   'The need for such fund is emphasized by some remarks made by your Lordship on the occasion of the Liverpool Bluecoat dinner. The Mercantile Marine Service Association have administered with entire satisfaction the Liverpool Seamen's Pension Fund and the Margaret Ismay Fund, which were established by my father and mother to provide pensions for Liverpool seamen and their widows, but neither of these funds covers the object I have in view.

   'If, under the administration of the same body, and on the outlines of the enclosed memorandum, a fund were initiated to meet the cases to which I refer I should be happy to contribute £10,000 and my wife £1,000 thereto.

'I need scarcely add that the sufferers from the *Titanic* disaster would be eligible equally with others to the benefits of the proposed fund, so far as this is necessary to supplement the public's generous assistance.

'Yours truly,
'Bruce Ismay.'

Mr Bruce Ismay's memorandum states that the object of the fund is to provide pensions for widows of those who lost their lives at sea while engaged upon active service in any capacity whatever upon a mercantile vessel registered in the United Kingdom.

No pension shall exceed £20 per annum, and it will be continued or discontinued at the absolute discretion of the committee.

The fund may be invested in the name of the mercantile Marine Service Association, who will have complete discretion in electing those who are to receive the pension and in fixing its amount from time to time.

Lord Derby has written to Mr Ismay gratefully accepting the offer, and thanking him and Mrs Ismay for their generosity.[38]

On 24 May 1912, survivor Lucile Carter wrote the following letter to Bruce Ismay:

Dear Mr Ismay,
I want to write you how glad I am that you are home safely and also how pleased we were to read of the great ovation you had in England when you landed for no one realized more than Billy and I did how much you had been through, and how wonderful you were through it all. The [word unreadable] we all got, and the dreadful things our own press is allowed to say in this country is certainly revolting. and makes us sometimes ashamed that we live here, but fortunately when they go to extremes, it is quickly over, and now it has completely died out, and no one even mentions it, and they are now criticizing something else. I am enclosing a letter to you which Billy received in behalf our chauffeur's widow [Mrs Charles Aldworth] he was with us. Would you send her name into the fund, it seems ridiculous to bother you about such a trifle, but I really don't exactly know how to keep

her here, there was quite a sum raised at our home, Rotherty Leicester, because the chauffeur was the only one lost from there, I hope you are well and that your nerves have not suffered. We are all quite well. I send you many kind wishes, and I hope to see you next winter when we go back to Melton to [hunt?].

Sincerely yours,
Lucile Carter

Mrs Thayer is very well, and the boy splendid, you will be pleased to hear.[39]

After Bruce Ismay finished testifying at the government *Titanic* inquiries, his son Thomas wrote him the following letter:

Dearest Father:
This is just a line to let you know how sorry I am that I did not see more of you today and to let you know that I quite realize what an ordeal you have had to go through and how deeply I feel for you. However, I very much hope that the worst is over now and that you will never again be misjudged and your words misinterpreted as they have been in the present inquiry. I hope you will be benefited by your stay at Dalnaspidal and not be worried by any anonymous communication.

I hope you will have fine weather and be able to get some fishing. Evelyn and I went to the cricket ground this afternoon. It rained a good deal, though. Some of the games were very close, being mostly finals. I hope you did not meet much rain on your run up to Carlisle and that you will not be recognized, as I know how you must hate to be before the public eye especially under the present trying circum-stances. I know this letter [is] very badly expressed but I hope you will realize that the spirit in which it is written is none the less sincere for that, with hopes that your stay in Scotland will be a complete rest, I will close.

I am,
Always your loving son,
Tom[40]

On 29 July 1912 Bruce Ismay received a letter from W. A. James regarding his new bride, survivor Evelyn Marsden:

Dear Sir,
I had wished to write to you before this but now I have to; for I wish to ask your influence on my behalf.

I was married on Wednesday last, 24 July, and to you I feel so unspeakably, undyingly grateful, for as she says, had it not been for you, she would not have been alive, and so my wife today – words, and words written are very cold, Sir – but do believe me, when I say how utterly grateful I am to you for saving her life. She was a stewardess, only a stewardess, but that made no difference to you, and so you saved her. And I am happy to have made her my wife as soon as I returned to England. She is Australian, a nurse qualified at the Adelaide General Hospital. I am wishful to take her back to Australia and make a home for her out there. And so I ask your favour, that you will allow me to work my passage out to Australia as Surgeon on one of your ships, and also that you will allow her to accompany me. I have saved enough money to pay her passage.

I called today at your London Office and I was instructed to call again on Wednesday. In the meantime, I am making my appeal to you.

Well Sir whether you grant it or not, I shall get to Australia somehow or other. I cannot tell you how I thank you. She never ceases to sing your praises, and so from two hearts there will daily come a prayer for 'Bruce Ismay'. This, as you said 'you are all women now', and she and I sincerely say 'Dieu vous [illegible word]'.

Yours ever gratefully,
W A James[41]

At one point after the *Titanic* tragedy, survivor Edith Rosenbaum penned a sympathetic letter to Bruce Ismay, who wrote the following reply:

You are one of the few people who have ever said anything kind about me or to me – God bless you.

Bruce Ismay[42]

★

Lord Mersey, who presided over the British Titanic Inquiry, said it was not the business of the court to inquire into attacks on the moral conduct of Joseph Bruce Ismay, but that silence on the part of the court might be misunderstood:

> The attack on J. Bruce Ismay resolved itself into the suggestion that, occupying the position of managing director of the line, some moral duty was imposed upon him to wait on board until the vessel foundered. I do not agree. Mr Ismay, after assisting many of the passengers, found the last boat on the starboard side of the *Titanic* actually being lowered. No other people were there at the time. There was room for him and he jumped in. Had he not done so he would merely have added one more life to the number lost.[43]

On 11 December 1912 the following article was published on the occasion of Bruce Ismay's fiftieth birthday:

> When the accounts are balanced it will probably be found that Mr Ismay merited neither the wholesale condemnation visited upon him by the American people, nor the whitewashing bestowed upon him by the British court of inquiry. Whether he was personally responsible for the speed that undoubtedly caused the wrecking of the giant vessel is something that can never be known. Fair play demands that he be considered innocent unless he can be proved guilty and he cannot be proved guilty. True, he saved his own life when women and children died; but how many men are certain that they would not do likewise under similar circumstances?
>
> It must be punishment enough for Bruce Ismay to know that there were millionaires and stokers, black and white, religious and atheist who were given the opportunity to drink from the cup of life, and calmly and stoically turned down an empty glass.
>
> If Mr Ismay profits from the experience through which he has passed, and sees to it that every possible safeguard is provided for the passengers on his lines, and it is only fair to say that he has shown a disposition to do so, he may be of more value to humanity as a living steamship director than he would have been as a dead hero.[44]

On 26 February 1912 (more than a month before the *Titanic* disaster), Bruce Ismay and Harold Sanderson agreed that, subject to approval by J. P. Morgan & Co., Ismay would retire as president of the International Mercantile Marine effective 30 June 1913, to be succeeded by Sanderson.[45]

Contrary to subsequent rumour, however, Mr Ismay did not become a hermit at that point in his life and did his best to make his survival of the *Titanic* disaster become a thing of benefit to other people. Historian Geoff Whitfield has said the following regarding this subject:

I knew the daughter of Ismay's valet, Richard Fry, many years ago. She says that Ismay was quite an insular man, but at the same time was exceptionally kind hearted. Fry was a similar build to Ismay, and he always passed his suits on to him – often unworn. He looked after Fry's widow until his own death, making sure that she was well provided for. She said that there was little gaiety in 'The Big House', which was what they termed the manor house in Mossely Hill.

On 19 October 1937 the following obituary was published in the *New York Times*:

J. BRUCE ISMAY, 74, TITANIC SURVIVOR

Ex-Head of White Star Line Who Retired After Sea
Tragedy Dies in London

LONDON, Oct. 18 – Joseph Bruce Ismay, former chairman of the White Star Line and a survivor of the *Titanic* disaster in 1912, died here last night. He was 74 years old.

Mr Ismay was a passenger on the White Star's great new liner when she set out for New York on her maiden voyage. When she struck an iceberg and went down, 1,635 persons, most of them men, perished.

A commission of inquiry, investigating the disaster, found there was no foundation to assertions that third-class passengers had been unfairly treated when the lifeboats were filled. The commission's report stated Mr Ismay was aboard the liner as an ordinary passenger and that he had no control over actions of the crew. The report described how he had helped many women, and children into the boats, remaining aboard the stricken vessel until no woman or children were visible on deck. Several women testified he had helped them.

However, Mr Ismay, who had been one of the outstanding figures in the shipping world, resigned as chairman of the White Star Line the year after the *Titanic* sinking. He retained a few directorships in shipping companies, but lived thereafter in semi-retirement except for a short period during the World War, when he was chairman of the War Risks Board.

He is survived by his widow, who was Miss Julia Florence Schieffelin of New York. They were married in 1888.

Mr Ismay was born in Liverpool in 1863. His father, the late Thomas Henry Ismay, had amassed a $40,000,000 fortune as head of the White Star Line, which the son inherited. He, too, became head of the steamship line after being educated at Elstree and Harrow and after spending five years apprenticed to the British mercantile service.

He donated $50,000 to the pension fund for widows of seamen on the *Titanic* shortly after the disaster, and in 1924 inaugurated the National Mercantile Marine fund with a gift of $125,000.

Mr Ismay died without making any further public statement on the *Titanic* or his conduct than that which he told the Senate committee and Lord Mersey's Board of Trade investigations.[46]

On 18 October 1937 the following brief article was published in a British newspaper:

Joseph Bruce Ismay died on Sunday and will be sadly missed by his family and friends. It is reported when a friend came to visit him the following Monday, a mirror of his was found, shattered into a million pieces. This is the second such story of a mirror within the Ismay household. The first was on the sinking of the *Titanic* in 1912 when the large mirror above the fireplace at his father's home suddenly dropped from the wall and broke beyond repair.[47]

Frank Bustard worked for the White Star Line and eventually became the Line's traffic manager, but in 1934 he left the company when it merged with the Cunard Line. The morning after Bruce Ismay passed away, Bustard went to his own office in Cockspur Street as was his usual custom.

On arrival he was amazed to find that a mirror that Bruce Ismay had given him many years before was shattered into a thousand pieces.[48]

Ismay's great-grandson, Malcolm Cheape, has expressed the opinion that he never recovered from the public reaction to the *Titanic* disaster:

> I suspect he suffered from post-traumatic stress when he arrived on the rescue ships and was certainly given morphine or some sort of medicine; I think that the fact that he was getting letters from strangers asking about what he knew about their relatives must have been very difficult in those first hours or days after the disaster, and longer term I think he must have looked back on it and wished he'd never been there.[49]

★

In conclusion, the present author believes that Bruce Ismay was an honourable man who probably would have done the right thing on board the *Titanic* under any specific set of given circumstances. If the last lifeboat to leave the *Titanic* had been crowded with passengers and more women were trying to get in, I believe Ismay would have remained on deck and given the last seat in the lifeboat to a woman.

In actuality, Ismay found himself standing beside collapsible C only after First Officer Murdoch chased unauthorised men out of that boat and after most of those people had already left the area in search of another means of rescue. Collapsible C still had several empty seats, though, and it was pointless for Ismay to remain standing on deck while the boat was lowered away with those empty seats unfilled. (After all, it's easy for critics to condemn someone's decisions from the safe comfort of their armchairs, but those same critics might feel differently if they suddenly found themselves standing on the *Titanic*'s slanting boat deck at two o'clock in the morning on 15 April 1912.)

On the other hand, the fact that Ismay later feigned ignorance on a number of crucial subjects at the *Titanic* inquiries is a different matter.

On 13 April 1912 Ismay expressed enthusiasm to Captain Smith about the prospect that the *Titanic* would beat the *Olympic*'s (maiden voyage) crossing time and reach New York on Tuesday night, yet he later denied that the *Titanic* was attempting to achieve that goal. Ismay also claimed to know of only a single instance when the *Olympic* had arrived in New York on Tuesday night, but it's a fact that the *Olympic* routinely achieved that very goal during the months leading up to the *Titanic* disaster. Ismay also knew that extra boilers were scheduled to be connected to the *Titanic*'s engines on the evening of 14 April, but – despite the fact that he told a number of passengers about the impending addition of these extra boilers – he later claimed to a court of inquiry that 'I had no knowledge at all of what was being done [in the boiler rooms]'.[50]

Although Bruce Ismay does not seem to have actually *pressured* Captain Smith to achieve an early arrival in New York, he later attempted to cast doubt on all evidence documenting the fact that the *Titanic* was out to achieve that very goal. Mr Ismay knew that the *Titanic*'s officers risked being deemed negligent in speeding their vessel towards a known icefield under the conditions that existed on the night of 14 April, and he was clearly doing his best to minimise the chances of the inquiries arriving at that conclusion.

Were Bruce Ismay's motives *understandable* when he denied that the *Titanic* was trying for a Tuesday night arrival in New York? Yes, his motives were perfectly understandable, because the financial well-being of the White Star Line could easily have been hanging in the balance if negligence on the part of the *Titanic*'s captain and officers could be demonstrated convincingly to the general public.

However, one must also ask if Ismay's motives for denying these facts were *ethical*? This is a completely different question, and is one that each reader must answer for themselves.

In any case, the present author feels that Joseph Bruce Ismay acted commendably and honourably during the evacuation of the *Titanic* and that he did nothing wrong when he finally left the sinking ship in collapsible C. On the other hand, Ismay's 'faulty' recollection of several crucial facts about the *Titanic*'s operation during her maiden voyage was less commendable and occurred only after he began undergoing close questioning at the two government inquiries. It was only at that point that Mr Ismay's memory about the ship's increasing speed and projected early arrival in New York gradually began to depart from the true historical record.

APPENDIX 1

HEARSAY ACCOUNTS OF CAPTAIN SMITH AND THE CHILD

In addition to the accounts we've already discussed, several hearsay accounts exist in which survivors allegedly described Captain Smith's futile attempt to save the Pålsson child as the *Titanic*'s bridge began to submerge. Unfortunately, these particular accounts cannot be taken as gospel due to the fact that the survivors in question were in no position to see Captain Smith with their own eyes after he went into the water. If these survivors did indeed tell newspaper reporters about Captain Smith's rescue attempt, they must have been describing things that were told to them by other survivors on board the *Carpathia*.

Account 1: Charles Williams
First-class passenger Charles Williams survived the disaster in lifeboat 14, and he later told his friend George Standing about Captain Smith's final moments (although Standing mistakenly assumed Williams was describing something he'd seen with his own eyes).

'[Williams] says he saw Captain Smith swimming around in the icy water with an infant in his arms and a lifebelt,' George Standing recalled.

> When the small boat went to his rescue, Captain Smith handed up the small child but refused to get in himself. He did ask what had become of First Officer Murdoch. We told him Murdoch had blown his brains out with a revolver. Then Captain Smith pushed himself away from

the lifeboat, threw his lifebelt from him and slowly sank from sight. He did not come to the surface again.[1]

Account 2: Charles Williams

Charles Williams allegedly gave the following story directly to a newspaper reporter even though he was saved in lifeboat 14:

'I was in a lifeboat after a two-hour swim,' said Charles Williams in the home of George E. Standing, racquet player, No. 84 Water avenue, White Plains, yesterday. Williams is coach of the Racquet Club of Harrow School, in Harrow, England. He came to this country partly to visit Standing.

'After I was dragged into the boat,' the Englishman continued, 'I saw Captain Smith die. I knew the captain well by sight and could not mistake him. Besides, others in the boat recognized him.

'He was swimming vigorously when we sighted him. In one of his arms was an infant. Smith wore a lifebelt, and he made good headway through the quiet sea. Our boat pulled toward him quickly, and in a minute or two we were near enough to take the baby from him. He smiled as he passed the youngster over the side, but when two or three of us tried to draw him into the boat he refused to take our hands.'

'"Where is Murdoch?" he asked of one of the crew who was pulling an oar in our boat.

'"Blown out his brains, sir," answered the seaman.

'Captain Smith said nothing more. An awful look came over his face, and for a moment he stared at the sailor. Then he pushed himself away from the boat, tore off his life vest and went under. We stood by awhile in the hope of rescuing him even against his will if he came to the surface, but we saw nothing more of him. After what seemed many hours we were picked up by the *Carpathia*.'[2]

Again, the only problem with Mr Williams' account is that he was saved in lifeboat 14, not on collapsible B.

Account 3: Albert Horswill

Seaman Albert Horswill apparently repeated a hearsay story regarding Captain Smith's attempt to save a small child. However, since Horswill left the ship in lifeboat 1, the reporter was mistaken in attributing this sighting to Horswill himself.

'Asked if he saw anything of the [*Titanic*'s] master,' wrote the reporter, 'Horswell [Albert Horswill] said he saw Captain Smith swimming about with the dead body of a child in his arms.'[3] According to a different newspaper, Horswill 'said he saw Captain Smith in the water, swimming, with a baby in his arms, towards a raft. The captain afterwards disappeared.'[4]

Account 4: Sidney Collett

Sidney Collett is supposed to have related the following account to a newspaper reporter. However, since Collett left the *Titanic* in lifeboat 9, he was in no position to see Captain Smith after the latter went into the water:

In the water near us we recognized Captain Smith battling against the waves. Floating on a piece of wreckage was a baby. We saw Captain Smith swim to the little one, lift up the child and place it in a nearby lifeboat. Then he swam back. We could see him battling desperately in the water and then we saw him no more. He died like a hero.[5]

Account 5: Anna Hämäläinen

Second-class passenger Anna Hämäläinen left the *Titanic* in lifeboat 4 at 1.50 a.m. and later granted an interview to a newspaper reporter:

When the boat [4] was lowered and even as we struck the water, I heard the captain's low, calm voice above the other noises.

'It's every man for himself now, friends,' he said, as calmly as though he were bidding an acquaintance good morning. 'Each man look out for himself. The last boat's gone.'

And then while I was looking up, that man of men, whose courage seemed to be exceeded only by his kindness of heart and sense of duty, walked to the rail and threw himself into the sea. It is not true, as some of the survivors have said, that Captain Smith had a child in his arms when he leaped. He plunged to his death alone. It seemed as though the end were just a matter of that duty to which he had adhered so religiously all during that terrible ordeal when he saw hundreds, whose lives had been in his hands a few minutes before, facing certain death.

No one can blame Captain Smith for the end he chose. He had done everything a human being in his position could do, and when there was no more chance to save his passengers and crew he went to his death calmly and deliberately.[6]

This account deserves our special attention, because it suggests that Mrs Hämäläinen looked up at Captain Smith while lifeboat 4 was float-ing right beside the *Titanic*, and that she had a close-up view of Smith jumping overboard – supposedly without a child in his arms. Although earlier portions of Mrs Hämäläinen's newspaper interview sound per-fectly believable, her account of Captain Smith's death occurring just as lifeboat 4 touched the water can't be taken at face value, because we've already examined plenty of reliable survivor accounts describ-ing Smith's activities on board the *Titanic* long after lifeboat 4 left the ship at 1.50 a.m. As tempting as it might be to researchers, we cannot accept Mrs Hämäläinen's newspaper story of Captain Smith's death as being reliable while simultaneously dismissing August Wennerström's first-hand, typewritten account describing Captain Smith holding a child in his arms right before the *Titanic*'s bridge submerged.

Account 6: Thomas Whiteley
Another puzzling account comes from Steward Thomas Whiteley, whose account (as relayed through the pen of a newspaper reporter) contains glaring inconsistencies:

> 'When I saw the captain he was in the water trying to place a baby in one of the lifeboats crowded with people,' Whiteley said. 'Some women tried to drag him in the boat, but he pulled away from them and said, "Save yourselves. Let me go."
> 'I saw him go under and he never came up.'[7]

Even though Thomas Whiteley was saved on collapsible B and was in the right place at the right time to see what happened to Captain Smith, the present author is puzzled by Whiteley's reference to 'women' trying to pull Captain Smith into 'one of the lifeboats' instead of alluding to crewmen trying to pull Smith onto the overturned collapsible B. We can only surmise that the newspaper reporter's interview was hurried and that he added a few extra details to Whiteley's story in order to fill in a few 'informational gaps'. Nevertheless, the interview's obvious inaccuracies force us to class it alongside Mrs Hämäläinen's puzzling account and those accounts from other people who were relaying second-hand stories instead of describing their own eyewitness observations.

Account 7: Unnamed Seaman
After the *Carpathia* arrived in New York, Rev. Philip J. Magrath of the Catholic Seamen's Mission, No. 422 West Street, interviewed a surviving *Titanic* seaman:

> One of the last boats to leave was in charge of Faley [Steward William Foley] and McCarthy [Seaman William McCarthy], seamen, who called for assistance to help man the boat after they had put off. Their cries were answered by 'Sam' Jennings [Samuel Hemming], a lamp trimmer, who jumped into the sea and swam to the boat. Into the boat had been placed Mrs Astor, who was unaccompanied.
>
> As the last boat left the wreck the men manning it called for Mr Murdoch, chief officer, and the captain to jump into it. 'Look out for yourselves and your charges,' was the answer they received. Murdoch was seen making his way to the bridge, and in a few seconds a shot was heard. We can only guess at what happened.
>
> Some distance from where the bridge had sunk the crew of a lifeboat came upon Captain Smith struggling in the midst of the wreckage with a child on his shoulder. The lifeboat made its way toward him and took the child aboard, but the captain sank out of sight.[8]

The unnamed seaman telling this story apparently believed that a lifeboat physically approached Captain Smith and that its occupants took the dying child from his arms. In truth, collapsible B was overturned and was incapable of being moved by its occupants, which makes it clear that this crewman was relaying a hearsay account and that he didn't see the events in question with his own eyes.

Account 8: George Hogg

Lookout George Alfred Hogg spoke with a newspaper reporter, who relayed the account to his readers as follows:

> 'I was on a raft that was right alongside the boat when it broke in half and went down,' said A. C. Hogg, a fireman.
>
> 'We pulled the skipper on with us from out of the water, but he just went over the other side and started to swim back to the *Titanic*. Someone said that he had a baby in his arms, but I didn't see it. That must have been before we pulled him out.'[9]

Two things make it clear that this was a hearsay account that can't be taken as gospel:

(1) George Hogg was a lookout, not a fireman
(2) Hogg was saved in lifeboat 7 instead of being one of the occupants of the overturned collapsible B.

Account 9: George Hogg

George Hogg spoke with a second reporter in more detail and apparently told the same false story he'd given to the earlier newspaper:

> 'I was one of the last to leave the *Titanic*,' said G. A. Hogg, able seaman, in the American Seaman's Friend Society's building, No. 507 West Street. He is one of 150 survivors of the *Titanic*'s crew who are being housed in that institution.
>
> 'I was standing on the deck, looking to see if there were any passengers that I could help into the preservers, when a big wave washed over my head and carried me over the side. I threw up my hands and prayed as soon as the wave hit me, and I landed on a raft carrying thirty-five persons. As I struck the raft I rolled over the edge, but I managed to catch hold and someone shouted: "Hold on, Charlie, don't give up." I did hold on and someone dragged me on the raft.
>
> 'The next moment I saw Captain Smith – my skipper – in the water alongside the raft. He was holding up a kid in his arms, and was trying to get the kid on the raft.

'"There's the skipper," I yelled, "Give him a hand," and they did. But he dropped the kid and slid off the raft. We tried to reach him again, but he shook himself free of his preserver and shouted to us, "Goodbye, boys, I'm going to follow the ship." That was the last we saw of our skipper.

'The skipper was a hero, and I can lick anybody who says he wasn't.'[10]

Account 10: Fred Barrett
Here we have an account given by an anonymous 'leading stoker' (undoubtedly Leading Fireman Fred Barrett, who left the *Titanic* in lifeboat 13) who freely acknowledged that he obtained his information about Captain Smith's death from fellow crew survivors:

'This man [the leading stoker] also stated that Captain Smith was seen [by others] swimming in the water holding a child,' a British reporter wrote after interviewing Barrett in England. 'He gave the child to a boat and then swam away.'[11]

Account 11: Fred Barrett
Here an unnamed 'captain stoker' (undoubtedly Fred Barrett again) spoke with a different reporter and repeated the account he'd heard from fellow crewmen:

Just as she was going down we heard some shots fired. I think they were people who preferred to put an end to it themselves. There are men here who saw Captain Smith swimming in the water with a child under his arm after the ship sank. He gave the child to the boat, and then swam away. He refused to get into the boat himself.[12]

Account 12: Margaret Hays
Nine months after the disaster, survivor Margaret Hays spoke with a reporter who relayed her comments about Captain Smith's death:

Speaking of Captain Smith, Miss Hays declares she is positive that he was drowned. 'He did not shoot himself as has been told in the papers,' she said. 'I talked with a man whom I know well, who saw Captain Smith in the water. This man told me that Captain [Smith] could have saved himself on one of the rafts, but he refused to do so. The man told me he saw Captain Smith sink to his death.'[13]

Account 13: George Brereton

George Brereton (a professional gambler who used many aliases) spoke with a reporter who later published his comments in his newspaper:

George Broden [sic], of California, had this to say:

'I was beside Henry B. Harris, the theatrical manager, when he bade his wife good-bye. Both started toward the side of the boat where a lifeboat was being lowered.

'Mr Harris was told it was the rule for women to leave the boat first. "Yes, I know, I will stay," Harris said.

'Shortly after the lifeboats left a man jumped overboard. Other men followed. It was like sheep following a leader.

'Captain Smith was washed from the bridge into the ocean. He swam to where a baby was drowning and carried it in his arms while he swam to a lifeboat, which was manned by officers of the *Titanic*. He surrendered the baby to them and swam back to the steamer.

'About the time Captain Smith got back there was an explosion. The entire ship trembled. I had secured a life preserver and jumped over. I struck a piece of ice but was not injured.'[14]

In truth, George Brereton left the *Titanic* in a lifeboat (probably 15) and was nowhere near Captain Smith when the latter went into the water.

Account 14: George Brereton

George Brereton spoke with a second reporter about the fate of Captain Smith, and the reporter duly shared the story with his readers:

George Brayton [sic], a prominent businessman of Los Angeles, Cal., tells a thrilling story of how Captain Smith met death. It was after a majority of the lifeboats had been filled and Brayton was standing just below the captain when the latter lost his balance and fell from the bridge into the sea.

Smith appeared on the surface of the water and swam toward the sinking vessel. Fifteen yards away was the body of an infant which attracted the struggling sailor and he immediately headed for it. He caught hold of the child and then with his right arm made for a lifeboat. The little one was safely put aboard and the captain resumed his struggle for the sinking *Titanic*.

The women in the boat screamed for the old man to grasp a line which was thrown to him, but he refused it and kept on for the ship. A junior officer lowered a line and the captain was hauled aboard. He was urged to make for a lifeboat, but still he refused and took his place on the bridge again. He was alone when Mr Brayton was taken off in one of the last boats. There was room for the captain, but he responded, 'This is my place and I will remain here and go down with the ship.'[15]

George Brereton apparently left the *Titanic* in lifeboat 15, which was nowhere near the ship during the final minutes of the sinking.

Account 15: Lucy Duff Gordon

Lucy Duff Gordon spoke with a newspaper reporter who relayed her account to his readers:

I did not see Captain Smith after I was put into the small boat, but others told me that when the *Titanic* went down Captain Smith was seen swimming in the icy water. He picked up a baby that was floating on a mass of wreckage and swam with it to one of the small boats. He lifted the baby into the boat, but the child was dead.

The women in the boat, according to the story told me, wanted the captain to get into the boat with them, but he refused, saying:

'No, there is a big piece of wreckage over here, and I shall stick to that. We are bound to be rescued soon.' Nothing more was seen of Captain Smith.[16]

Account 16: Thomas Knowles

Fireman's messman Thomas Knowles survived the disaster, and in later years his daughter wrote a letter to her cousin describing Knowles' experiences during the sinking:

He could not swim, strange to say, but as the *Titanic* gradually sank, he stood on the rails, water over his feet, and Captain Smith pacing the bridge.

Finally father jumped into the sea of chaos and saw Captain Smith lift a baby into a lifeboat, but he refused to be saved himself.[17]

It's unknown whether Thomas Knowles went into the water as described or if he found a seat in a lifeboat (possibly collapsible D), so the truth of his daughter's second-hand account is unknown.

Account 17: George McGough
Seaman George McGough gave the following interview to a newspaper reporter:

Both Capt. Smith and Junior Chief Murdoch were now together on the bridge, the water being up to their armpits. The next I saw of Capt. Smith he was in the water holding a child in his arms. He swam to the raft on which was Second Officer Lightoller and gave the child to the mate. That was the last. He and the ship went down and Murdoch – God help me, don't ask me what I saw![18]

Seaman George McGough left the *Titanic* at 1.30 a.m. in lifeboat 9 and was in no position to see what happened to Captain Smith or First Officer Murdoch fifty minutes later.

Account 18: Various
A lengthy account published in a New York newspaper contained several dubious accounts relating to Captain Smith's death. Rather than dwell on all the erroneous details, misspelled crew names and names that are not listed on the *Titanic*'s crew roster, we'll just reprint the article in its entirety for the reader's edification:

Cyril Handy [unlisted], an able seaman of the *Titanic*, was washed from the forward boat deck at the same time that the captain was swept from the bridge. He found himself swimming toward a lifeboat. As he drew near the boat he came upon a struggling group. It was the captain, swimming with the woman and child.

'We came alongside the boat at the same time,' said Handy. 'The captain asked me to give him a lift. I helped hold the woman while he raised the baby to the boat. Then we both helped lift the woman aboard.

'I put one hand under the captain's shoulder and tried to boost him up. He shook me off. One of the men in the boat caught him by the coat sleeve and held on. The skipper struck at me savagely with his fist. "Get aboard, damn you," he yelled at me, "I'm going back to the ship."

'With a jerk he broke the hold of the man leaning over the gunwale and kicked off from the side of the boat beyond our reach. I was nearly exhausted, and all I remember was someone pulling me into the boat. I lay on her bottom more than an hour, nearly unconscious, they say. When I came to the *Titanic* had gone down.'

Handy's graphic story of the captain's final act of expiation was corroborated by four men who were in the crew of the lifeboat or were picked up by her. It was boat No. 14, from the port side, one of the last to leave the ship. It had about forty women and half a dozen men.

Charles Collins [unlisted], a steward, was the man who took the baby from the captain.

'I was pulling an oar on the starboard side ... We had got only a little way from the ship and she was going down fast, her forward part being under water back to the bridge and her stern high in the air. There was so much crowding in the boat that we couldn't row well.

'Someone shouted that a man and woman were swimming to us and we stopped rowing. Figures drew near, and we saw it was the captain, holding a woman, who clutched something in her arms. When they swam alongside, I reached over and took what I thought was a bundle the captain passed up. It was a child, about two years old. As I lifted it I thought that baby was dead. It wasn't, but it died a few minutes afterward and we buried it during the night, when the women weren't looking.

'The woman was unconscious. She didn't revive until daybreak. Then we learned that she was a second-class passenger. She knew nothing about a child. She said she was not married and didn't remember picking up a baby when she was washed overboard. She must have been half crazed with terror and snatched the baby instinctively.'

Henry Jocklin [Charles Joughin], chief baker, jumped overboard and was picked up by boat No. 14 just as she was pulling away from the side of the ship. He helped haul aboard the woman rescued by Capt. Smith and saw his refusal of rescue.

James Johnson [Johnstone?] and Harry Gunner [unlisted] of the lifeboat's crew told the same story. None of the men knew the name of the woman who was rescued. All agreed that the baby died soon after it was taken on board and was dropped stealthily into the icy sea during the night.

'We couldn't keep it aboard,' said one of the seamen. 'It would do no good and it is bad luck. Then, too, we thought the unconscious woman was its mother and we decided she'd carry on terribly if she came to and found her baby dead, but if she didn't find it she might think it was saved in another boat.'[19]

Account 19: Various

On 20 April 1912 a New York newspaper published an article that touched on the death of Captain Smith:

Arthur McMicken, a steward, who was saved, apparently confirming Seward's story, says he was in a boat which floated near the captain. It was seen that to take the captain into the boat would endanger the lives of all on board. Several men, however, reached out for him, and as they did so he disappeared from view. [Note: McMicken left the *Titanic* in lifeboat 11 at 1.35 a.m.]

'I was in a lifeboat not ten feet away from Captain Smith while he was struggling in the water,' said Alfred Hogg, who was lookout man on board the *Titanic*. 'I saw him clinging to a piece of wreckage. The reports that he shot himself are untrue. I helped lower the boats and helped man one of them. The American women were very brave and helped row the boats. Those who did not row offered to help.' [Note: As previously noted, Hogg left the *Titanic* at 12.40 a.m. in lifeboat 7, the first lifeboat to leave the ship.]

Inquiries among the crew of the *Titanic*, including sailors and stokers, bear out the story that Captain Smith was drowned. Several of the sailors say that the last they saw of him he was standing on the bridge of the *Titanic* and near him were Colonel Astor and Major Butt.

Several said they saw him waist deep in water still on the bridge and that he did not shoot himself.

Details differ as to the death of the captain, but from the reports of witnesses it appears that the commander was on the bridge until the last moment, and that from that point he directed the saving of the passengers. He was calm and collected in manner and gave his orders with firm emphasis.

Everything connected with the death of Captain Smith reveals him in the character of one who maintained the best traditions of the sea. When women hesitated to get into lifeboats while their husbands were not permitted to do so, he expostulated with them, declaring that they must not cause demoralization by their refusal.

There are those who will recall the master mariner, standing erect and firm with the dim light on his whitened hair, shouting orders through his megaphone. His voice was as even as though he were directing maneuvers in calm weather on a summer sea.

His conduct was such that those of his command emulated his example. The captain, despite his advanced years, was a strong swimmer, but he used his skill rather to save the lives of others than for self-preservation.[20]

RUMOUR OF DISAGREEMENT BETWEEN SMITH AND ISMAY

We've already discussed Captain Smith's avowed tactic of speeding his vessels past any ice hazards as quickly as possible. In apparent contrast to Smith's preferred tactic, however, *Titanic* passenger Mary Lines apparently heard shipboard rumours that, if true, would cast a disturbing light on Captain Smith's interactions with Bruce Ismay. 'We had known all day that we were approaching ice,' Miss Lines remembered in later years.

> There had been warnings which … there were some passengers that heard and referred to Captain Smith. And there were some discussions going on of which we heard rumors, and some people overheard these arguments between the captain and Mr Bruce Ismay, who was the managing director of the White Star Line and who was taking the opportunity to make this maiden voyage on this new ship of his line. Captain Smith wished to go south and to slow … and go more slowly. We were taking the fastest route to the United States as we wished to make a fast and quick voyage, and this entailed going, really, very far north, just south of Labrador, the rather northernmost passage. I think usually they had tended to go a little bit south of that area. And particularly in view of the ice warnings, many people felt that we should have immediately turned south.[1]

As will be seen in a moment, it seems possible that the original source of the rumoured Smith–Ismay disagreement might have been Major Arthur Peuchen. In fact, Peuchen may also have been the original source of the rumour that Captain Smith and Bruce Ismay dined together on the evening of 14 April and tarried in conversation below decks until 10 or 10.30 p.m.; Peuchen made these allegations in several post-disaster newspaper interviews[2] and may have spoken about them on board the *Carpathia* as well, because several fellow survivors (e. g., Dorothy Gibson)[3] mentioned the non-existent Smith–Ismay dinner party in their own newspaper interviews.

At any rate, in later years Major Peuchen's nephew, Kendall Peuchen Home, wrote that Peuchen told him about a disagreement between Captain Smith and Bruce Ismay that supposedly took place on the evening of 14 April while *Titanic* was in close proximity to the approaching icefield:

Ismay, the general manager of the line, was to travel on the ship to see that everything went as planned, being connected with the big interests by the magical new wireless telegraph. A secret code was devised to communicate with him as 'Yamsi'. On board, too, was a retiring naval captain [i.e., Captain Smith] who was making his last trip while commanding the unsinkable luxury liner on her maiden voyage in a supreme effort to break the record speed. To make certain of this [and without Smith's knowledge or approval], the spy glasses were taken from the lookouts before leaving England so that nothing would disturb the captain and cause him to alter course. This was the set-up when my uncle got involved.

On account of my uncle's interest in navigation, he had made friends with the captain and dined with him on several occasions. On the evening of the disaster [sic] my uncle was dining with him when news of the ice floe ahead came to him. The captain had confessed his fear of icebergs, and hoped the floe did not have any big ones. Then later that evening the report came from the *California* [sic], the rival American vessel just ahead, that the ship was laying-to until the [ice] floe passed. The captain called Ismay, and when the captain suggested lowering speed and changing course, Ismay became angry and said the captain would suffer severe reprisals if he did so. The ship was unsinkable and the captain had orders to make a record-breaking trip. Meanwhile, below the crew celebrated their record-breaking trip.

When the first mate again reported icebergs, the captain reported Ismay's words. Anyway, it was not long before the lookout called down to say there was an iceberg dead ahead, and the first officer gave orders to turn the ship, but too late.[4]

Where, how and from whom Major Peuchen obtained his information about an alleged Smith–Ismay argument is unknown. However, the fact that Captain Smith dined with the Widener dinner party that evening instead of with Major Peuchen, plus the fact that Smith was back on the *Titanic*'s bridge by 8.55 p.m., makes the premise of a supposed Smith–Ismay argument on the evening of 14 April very tenuous – but not necessarily impossible.

APPENDIX 3

WHAT IF SMITH AND ANDREWS HAD SURVIVED?

The question has sometimes been asked, 'What would have happened to Thomas Andrews and Captain Edward J. Smith if they'd been fortunate enough (or unfortunate enough) to survive the sinking of the *Titanic*?'

In Thomas Andrews' case, it seems doubtful that he would have faced any meaningful condemnation or criticism following the *Titanic* disaster, because he did nothing wrong and had nothing to do with the *Titanic*'s navigation. The great ship he had helped to design and build had been constructed according to the highest standards the firm of Harland & Wolff was capable of achieving, and (during the sinking itself) Mr Andrews quickly ascertained how much damage the ship had sustained and then did his best to help evacuate as many of the *Titanic*'s passengers as possible. These actions were commendable and praiseworthy.

In Captain Smith's case, his actions (after the collision) were just as commendable as those of Thomas Andrews, since Smith likewise inspected the ship for damage and did his best to see that as many passengers as possible were evacuated from the sinking vessel. However, Captain Smith undoubtedly had other considerations in mind regarding his ultimate responsibility for the disaster.

It goes without saying that Captain Smith's navigational decisions on the night of 14 April 1912 would have undergone scrutiny during the American and British *Titanic* inquiries. Of course, Smith would have been acutely aware of that stark fact even while the *Titanic* was in the process of sinking, and his awareness of his unenviable future at the hands of officialdom (plus the heart-shaking fact that the deaths of 1,496 innocent people would be weighing heavily on his soul) might have had a strong influence on his decisions after he swam away from the sinking *Titanic*. Indeed, these two considerations alone would explain why Smith refused to climb onto collapsible B after he handed the Pålsson child up to crewmen who were already sheltering on the overturned lifeboat.

In light of these facts, and in light of Smith's refusal to save his own life by climbing aboard the capsized collapsible B, the reader might be interested to read the texts of two articles that were published less than eight months before the *Titanic* went down. The articles in question discuss several ship captains, some of whom experienced less-serious ship accidents with no loss of life – but who still faced the likelihood of being raked over the coals by the shipping companies that employed them.

Captain Smith undoubtedly knew what lay in store for him if he somehow arrived safely back on shore, and the deaths of 1,496 people who had entrusted him with their lives would have affected his mind-set and might have been the tipping point regarding the question of whether or not he wanted to survive the sinking of the *Titanic*. Although *Carpathia* passenger Dr C. A. Bernard felt that Captain Smith 'likely did what other captains have done – found solace in a pistol shot,'[1] we've shown that the evidence that Smith swam up to collapsible B instead of committing suicide with his revolver is pretty persuasive.

Carpathia passenger Eleanor Danforth shared the present author's opinion about this matter. 'I notice that there have been various stories afloat that Captain Smith shot himself just before the *Titanic* went down,' she told a reporter, 'but this does not appear to be the opinion of a great many of the survivors with whom I talked on the *Carpathia*. The majority of them say that he jumped at the last moment.'[2]

At any rate, let's take a quick look at the fates of several other steamship captains who were unlucky enough to have their vessels involved in collisions or other unfortunate mishaps.

FATES OF CAPTAINS

The White Star line has been among the strictest of the British companies in this regard, as is evidenced in the fate of Captain Inman Sealby, who commanded the *Republic* when she sank in collision with the Italian line steamship *Florida*, on 23 January 1901. No blame was attached to Captain Sealby for faulty navigation or bad seamanship in handling the vessel, and all his career he had been with the White Star Line without being in a wreck. Nevertheless, he was dismissed, afterwards going to the University of Michigan to study admiralty law.[3]

★

THE SHIP CAPTAIN
His Life Pays the Penalty if His Vessel Be Wrecked
SAD TRAGEDIES OF THE SEA
Skillful Mariners Who Went to Death with Heroic Calmness When Disaster Overwhelmed the Craft Committed to Their Care.

For this is the law without excuse
For all of the lords of the sea —
That each must hold his ship from harm,
Whatever the odds may be.

There are many tragedies of the sea that the world knows very little about, or knowing, very soon forgets. These are the tragedies of the men whose lives have been spent in the hard and exacting service which the sea demands, whose long years of toil and skill have brought the high responsibilities of command and whose careers have been cut short by the fault of an hour – yea, even by the error of a minute.

The old rubric that those who never make mistakes have had few opportunities for making them does not apply here. There is never a voyage that does not have its possibility of error, and in many of them arise the sudden emergencies which bring the acid test of presence of mind, cool judgment, expert seamanship and skill. Let these qualities fail the master mariner in his time of need, and, no matter what might have been the stress of body or brain, or of both, his professional career is at an end, if the lapse involves disaster to his ship.

There is that veteran mariner Captain Frederick Watkins. He it was who commanded the *City of Paris* when the old Inman liner came staggering to port with the Atlantic waves swashing about her hold and surging against her bulkheads, the result of a fog-shrouded impact with an iceberg.

The liner was thronged with passengers. The unforeseen danger came near to sending her and her thousand souls to the bottom, but the energy, resourcefulness and skill of her commander brought her safe to port – a deed to be long remembered.

It was remembered up to a few years ago, when a slight miscalculation on the part of Captain Watkins sent his vessel upon the Manacle rocks, on the Cornish coast. Now you may search all of the obscure places of the earth and you may not locate him.

There was the *Prinzessin Victoria Luise* of the Hamburg-American line, which drove hard upon the coral beach at Port Royal, in the island of Jamaica.

The vessel was thronged with tourists, making a jaunt to the West Indies. Fortunately, the sea was calm, and there was no difficulty in getting passengers ashore. When the last had been safely landed the captain went to his stateroom and put a bullet through his brain.

The pitiable part of it all was that he had no need to. It was not the brain he shattered that was at fault, but the Kingston earthquake, which had destroyed the lighthouse.

Captain Griffith of the *Mohegan* stood on the bridge of his fast-sinking ship until the waters engulfed him. Deloncie of the French liner *Bourgogne*, sunk in mid-Atlantic by a collision with the British steamship *Cromartyshire*, was last seen on the bridge, with hand on whistle cord, as his vessel took the long dive. Von Goessel of the *Elbe* went down with his ship, standing with folded arms upon the bridge as the vessel slowly sank.

One of the saddest tragedies of the sea was the wreck of the British steamship *Waiearapa*, which went ashore on Great Barrier Island while on a voyage from Sydney to New Zealand. As the vessel neared the entrance to the harbor of Auckland a thick fog shut in. Captain McIntosh, who commanded her, had been many years in the service of the line and was reputed to be very careful and capable, but while the steamer was groping her way through the mist it was noted that he was exceedingly nervous and depressed.

When night came the fog was so thick that the lookouts could not see half a ship's length ahead. A few minutes past midnight there was a sudden crash, which laid the steamship almost on her beam ends, disabling all of the boats on the careered side. Captain McIntosh was on the bridge at the time. A great wound which had been torn in the vessel's side showed the extent of the disaster. As soon as he realized that his ship must become a total loss the captain strode to the end of the bridge and, exclaiming 'This is the last watch!' plunged overboard to his death. – Waller Scott Meriwether in *Munsey*'s magazine.[4]

BIBLIOGRAPHY

In addition to utilising various primary sources and survivor interviews in 1912 newspapers, the present author consulted the following books:

Barratt, Nick, *Lost Voices from the Titanic*, Palgrave MacMillan, 2010.

Beaumont, J. C. H., *Ships – and People*, Frederick A. Stokes, 1926.

Beesley, Lawrence, *The Loss of the SS Titanic*, Houghton Mifflin, 1912.

Behe, George, *On Board RMS Titanic: Memories of the Maiden Voyage*, The History Press, 2012.

Behe, George, *Titanic: Safety, Speed and Sacrifice*, Transportation Trails, 1997.

Behe, George, *The Titanic Disaster: Final Memories*, Lulu Press (as yet unpublished).

Behe, George, *Titanic Tidbits* (Vol. 2), Lulu Press (as yet unpublished).

Brewster, Hugh, *Gilded Lives, Fatal Voyage*, Crown Publishers, 2012.

Bullock, Shan, *Thomas Andrews – Shipbuilder*, 7 C's Press, 1913.

Davie, Michael, *The Titanic: The Full Story of a Tragedy*, The Bodley Head, 1986.

Duff Gordon, Lucy, *Discretions and Indiscretions*, Jarrolds Ltd, 1932.

Fitch, Tad; Layton, J. Kent; and Wormstedt, Bill, *On a Sea of Glass*, Amberley, 2012.

Gracie, Archibald, *The Truth About the Titanic*, Mitchell Kennerly, 1913.

Halpern, Samuel *et al.*, *Report into the Loss of the SS Titanic: A Centennial Reappraisal*, The History Press, 2012.

Hart, Henry Martyn, *Recollections and Reflections*, self-published, 1917.

Hustak, Alan, *Titanic: The Canadian Story*, Vehicule Press, 1998.

Hyslop, Donald *et al.*, *Titanic Voices*, Southampton City Council, 1994.

Jessop, Violet, and Maxtone-Graham, John, *Titanic Survivor*, Sheridan House, 1997.

Julian, Hester, *Memorials of Henry Forbes Julian*, Charles Griffin & Co., 1914.

Klistorner, Daniel and Hall, Steve, *Titanic in Photographs*, The History Press, 2011.

Lightoller, Charles, *Titanic and Other Ships*, Ivor, Nicholson & Watson, 1935.

Marcus, Geoffrey, *The Maiden Voyage*, Viking Press, 1969.

Marshall, Logan, *The Sinking of the Titanic & Great Sea Disasters*, L. T. Myers, 1912.

Mobray, Jay, *The Sinking of the Titanic*, The Minter Co., 1912.

O'Donnell, E.E., *Father Brown's Titanic Album*, Wolfhound Press, 1997.

Oldham, Wilton, 'The Ismay Line', *Journal of Commerce*, 1961.

Sloper, William, *The Life and Times of Andrew Jackson Sloper*, privately published, 1949.

Taylor, Elmer Zebley, *Jigsaw Picture Puzzle of People Whom I Have Known and Sundry Experiences from 1864 to 1949*, privately published, 1949.

Thayer, Jack, *The Sinking of the SS Titanic*, privately published, 1940.

Wilkinson, Norman, *A Brush with Life*, Seeley Service & Co., 1969.

Williamson, Ellen, *When We Went First-class*, Iowa State University Press, 1977.

NOTES

1: Prelude to the Maiden Voyage

1 Ann O'Donnell, post-sinking newspaper article datelined San Francisco, 19 April 1912.
2 Charles Lightoller, *Titanic and Other Ships* (1935).
3 Bruce Ismay, Senate *Titanic* inquiry.
4 Geoffrey Marcus, *The Maiden Voyage* (1969).
5 Samuel Rule, *St. Ives Western Echo*, 4 May 1912.
6 John N. Smith, *Brooklyn Daily Eagle*, 16 April 1912.
7 David Evans, *South Wales Echo*, 18 April 1912.
8 Mrs L. B. Judd, *Syracuse Daily Journal*, 16 or 17 April 1912.
9 Howard Weber, *Illinois State Journal* (Springfield), 17 April 1912, courtesy of Don Lynch.
10 George Chauncey, *Brooklyn Daily Eagle*, 16 April 1912, courtesy of Don Lynch.
11 J. E. Hodder Williams, 'Captain E. J. Smith Memorial booklet' (1913).
12 J. E. Hodder Williams, *The Land* (New South Wales), 2 August 1912, courtesy of Gary Cooper.
13 W. W. Sanford, *Syracuse Post Standard*, 18 April 1912.
14 J. F. Graham, *Buffalo Courier*, 17 April 1912, courtesy of Don Lynch.
15 Joseph Taylor, *Los Angeles Herald*, 10 April 1912.
16 Captain Anning, *Kalgoorlie Western Argus* (Australia), 30 April 1912.
17 J. P. Grant, *Victoria Daily Colonist* (BC), 17 April 1912, courtesy of Don Lynch.
18 Henry Bucknell, *Brooklyn Daily Eagle*, 17 April 1912.
19 *Ibid.*
20 *Syracuse Herald*, 17 August 1909.
21 Bruce Ismay, White Star Line Special Meeting, 22 April 1912, Minute No. 8424, published by Frankie McElroy in *Death of a Purser*.
22 Dr J. C. H. Beaumont, *Ships – and People* (1926).

23 John Kempster, *Brooklyn Daily Eagle*, 21 April 1912.
24 *Guardian*, 15 April 2016.
25 George Beauchamp told this anecdote to fellow survivor Bertram Dean when they worked together in shipyards in later years. Mr Dean then related the anecdote to Don Lynch in November 1985.
26 US National Archives.
27 Glenn Marston, *Winnipeg Tribune*, 20 April 1912.
28 Glenn Marston, *New York Evening Post*, 19 April 1912.
29 Glenn Marston, *Winnipeg Tribune*, 20 April 1912.
30 *Western Guardian*, 8 May 1912.

2: 10–14 April

1 Note from researcher Brian Ticehurst, 19 May 2005.
2 Except where noted, I would like to thank Chris Daino for his description of the 10 April pre-sailing procedures upon which our summary of Captain Smith's morning activities is based.
3 Roy Diaper, City Heritage Oral History, published by Donald Hyslop *et al.*, *Titanic Voices* (1994).
4 Norman Wilkinson, *A Brush with Life* (1969).
5 Hyslop *et al.* (1994).
6 Daniel Klistorner and Steve Hall, *Titanic in Photographs* (2011).
7 Harold Lowe deposition to the British consulate in New York, courtesy of John Creamer.
8 Thomas Logan's article in the *Philadelphia Inquirer*, 21 April 1912. Note: Colonel Archibald Gracie was said to be the source of Logan's information. However, his article also mentions someone pointing out the Astors on board the ship as the *Titanic* was leaving Southampton. Since the Astors boarded the vessel at Cherbourg instead of Southampton, the overall veracity of this article is open to question.
9 Robert Daniel, *Philadelphia Inquirer*, 21 April 1912.
10 Henry Etches, Senate *Titanic* inquiry.
11 Bruce Ismay, Senate *Titanic* inquiry.
12 *Ibid.*
13 *NYAI Catalogue*, 23 May 1912. 'Elusive Passenger Pens Story' by Daniel Klistorner and Charles Provost, *Voyage*, #63, September 2008, pp. 132–5, courtesy of Daniel Klistorner.
14 Violet Jessop and John Maxtone-Graham, *Titanic Survivor* (1997).
15 *Ibid.*
16 Mary Sloan letter, quoted in Shan Bullock, *Thomas Andrews – Shipbuilder* (1913).
17 Henry Etches, testimony at the Senate *Titanic* inquiry.
18 Bruce Ismay, Senate *Titanic* inquiry.
19 Mrs T. W. S. Brown, *Seattle Post-Intelligencer*, 28 April 1912.
20 Bullock (1913).
21 Elisabeth Lines testimony, limitation of liability hearings.
22 Bullock (1913).
23 John Hart, British *Titanic* inquiry, #10305–11.
24 Bruce Ismay, Senate *Titanic* inquiry.

25 Unnamed British army officer, *The Evening Post* (New York), 20 April 1912.

26 Archibald Gracie, *New York Sun*, 24 or 25 April 1912.

27 Emily Ryerson, limitation of liability hearings.

28 Klistorner and Hall (2011).

29 Don Lynch letter to the present author, 3 April 1986. Information was obtained from Mr Evans' son.

30 Bruce Ismay, British *Titanic* inquiry, #18392–7. Note: the national coal strike that interfered with the routine sailing of British passenger liners had ended on 6 April (four days before *Titanic*'s maiden voyage). In any case, *Titanic* was carrying a nine-day supply of coal – more than enough for a speedy crossing considering the fact that she could get as much coal as she wanted after reaching New York. Indeed, one wonders if Mr Ismay's meeting with Joseph Bell actually might have been for the purpose of easing prior speed restrictions that had been imposed upon the *Titanic* before the maiden voyage began.

31 George Behe, *Titanic: Safety, Speed and Sacrifice* (1997).

32 Ruth Becker letter to *St. Nicholas* magazine, June 1914.

33 E. E. O'Donnell, *Father Browne's Titanic Album* (1997).

34 John Thompson, *New York American*, 22 April 1912. Note: instead of trying to make a record transatlantic crossing, it was merely hoped that the *Titanic* would better the maiden voyage crossing time achieved by her elder sister *Olympic* in 1911.

35 Bruce Ismay, Senate *Titanic* inquiry.

36 Marion Kenyon, oral account tape-recorded at her home in Santa Monica, California, on 6 April 1957, and later partially transcribed by Daniel Klistorner.

37 Marian Thayer affidavit, published in Michael Davie, *The Titanic: The Full Story of a Tragedy* (1986), pp. 51–3. Note: in the *Kingston Gleaner* (Jamaica) of 10 May 1938 survivor Harry Anderson said: 'I don't like talking about the *Titanic*, but there's one lie I'd like to help in nailing down even though twenty-six years have gone. It's still suggested that Captain Smith imperilled his ship because he was drunk. He was not. Even with a friend like me he refused to drink that terrible night. When I insisted, he had a small glass of port, sipped once and left it. And I will swear that's the only drink he touched that night.' Mr Anderson was not a member of the Widener dinner party that night, though, so the specifics of his story about Captain Smith remain unclear.

38 Frederick Ray, Senate *Titanic* inquiry.

39 Henry Etches, testimony at the Senate *Titanic* inquiry.

40 Mike Poirier, 'Piecing together a *Titanic* puzzle: the complex case of Mrs Cassebeer', www.encyclopedia-titanica.org/piecing-together-a-titanic-puzzle.html.

41 Eleanor Cassebeer letter to Walter Lord, 9 November 1955, courtesy of Mike Poirier.

42 Thomas Whiteley, *Newark Star*, 22 April 1912.

43 Bruce Ismay, Senate *Titanic* inquiry.

44 Bruce Ismay, limitation of liability hearings.

45 Thomas Whiteley, *Minneapolis Tribune*, 21 April 1912. Note: the Whiteley account as presented here contains two ellipses, both of which represent deleted sentences claiming that the dinner in question took place on the night of Sunday, 14 April. This was not possible, because on that date Captain Smith dined in the *Titanic*'s à la carte restaurant instead of in the first-class dining room. Even though Thomas

Whiteley was incorrect about the date of the dinner he was describing, we are (charitably) assuming he made an honest mistake about the date and that the dinner in question probably took place earlier during the maiden voyage.

46 Henry Etches, Senate *Titanic* inquiry.

47 Mary Sloan letter to 'Maggie', 27 April 1912, George Behe, *On Board RMS Titanic: Memories of the Maiden Voyage* (2012).

48 Mary Sloan, *Belfast Weekly Telegraph*, 1 June 1912.

49 Mary Sloan letter to 'Maggie', 27 April 1912, Behe (2012).

50 Jessop and Maxtone-Graham (1997).

51 Albert Dick, *Maclean's*, 1 May 1950.

52 Vera Dick, The *Albertan*, 14 April 1960.

53 Albert Dick, *New York Herald*, 20 April 1912.

54 Eleanor Cassebeer, *Binghamton Press*, 29 April 1912, courtesy of Mike Poirier; *Omaha World Herald*, 30 April 1912.

55 Eleanor Cassebeer, *Omaha World Herald*, 30 April 1912.

56 May Futrelle, *Seattle Daily Times*, 22 and 23 April 1912.

57 Henry Frauenthal, *St Louis Globe-Democrat*, 20 April 1912.

58 Hugh Woolner, Senate *Titanic* inquiry.

59 Countess of Rothes, *New York Herald*, 21 April 1912.

60 Jack Thayer, *The Sinking of the SS Titanic* (1940).

61 Charles Stengel, Senate *Titanic* inquiry.

62 Katherine Force, www.charlespellegrino.com/astor-strauss-and-futrelle/.

63 Washington Dodge Jr, 1960s letter to Edward Kamuda, Titanic Historical Society.

64 'The reflections of Edith E. Haisman on the maiden voyage of the RMS *Titanic* recalled on 22 October 1993.'

65 Eva Hart, BBC interview prior to the 1987 Titanic Historical Society convention in Wilmington, Delaware, transcribed in George Behe, *The Titanic Disaster: Final Memories* (unpublished).

66 Eva Hart, Bantam Doubleday Dell Audio Publishing's 1998 audiocassette *That Fateful Night: True Stories of Titanic Survivors in Their Own Words*. Interview was later transcribed by George Behe and published in *The Titanic Disaster: Final Memories*.

67 Robertha Watt, 1981 taped interview by Canadian journalist Robert Bailey, transcribed and published in *The Titanic Disaster: Final Memories* by George Behe.

68 Elisabeth Lines testimony, limitation of liability hearings.

69 May Futrelle, *Seattle Daily Times*, 22 and 23 April 1912.

70 Samuel Halpern *et al.*, *Report into the Loss of the SS Titanic: A Centennial Reappraisal* (2012).

71 *Ibid.*

72 Joseph Boxhall, Senate *Titanic* inquiry.

73 *Ibid.*

74 *Ibid.*

75 *Ibid.*

76 Bruce Ismay, Senate *Titanic* inquiry.

77 Herbert Pitman, Senate *Titanic* inquiry.

78 John Thompson, *New York Sun*, 23 April 1912. Note: the newspaper reporter mistakenly recorded Thompson's first name as being 'James' instead of 'John'. Whereas Thompson said *Titanic*'s engines achieved seventy-seven revolutions on Saturday afternoon, barber Augustus Weikman told the Senate *Titanic* inquiry that

Bruce Ismay had assured him *Titanic* had been limited to seventy-five revolutions several days before the collision. In his own testimony at the Senate *Titanic* inquiry, Bruce Ismay testified that *Titanic*'s engines were indeed making seventy-five revolutions on 13 April, but the reliability of that figure is uncertain due to the fact that Ismay testified elsewhere that: 'I believe that the ship was worked up to 75 revolutions [after leaving Queenstown], but I really have no accurate knowledge of that.' Mr Ismay reaffirmed his statement at the British *Titanic* inquiry when he said, 'I really have no absolute knowledge myself as to the number of revolutions. I believe she was going seventy-five on the Sunday ... seventy-eight I believe was her full [i.e. top] speed.' (BR (British inquiry) 18374–6.)

79 Elisabeth Lines testimony, limitation of liability hearings.

80 Charles Stengel, *Newark Evening News*, 19 April 1912.

81 Unnamed stokers, *New York Tribune*, 20 April 1912.

82 Frederick Barrett, British *Titanic* inquiry, #2302.

83 Esther Hart, *Ilford Graphic*, 10 May 1912.

84 Halpern *et al.* (2012).

85 *Ibid.*

86 Eleanor Cassebeer, 1932 account written for her family, translated from the French by Charles Provost, courtesy of Daniel Klistorner.

87 Madeleine Mellinger Mann, *Commutator*, #31, June 1971, pp. 69A–70. Transcript of interview CBC programme *Something Else*.

88 Madeleine Mellinger letter to Walter Lord, courtesy of Dr Paul Lee, www.paullee. com/titanic/Mellinger.php.

89 Gunnar Tenglin, *Cedar Rapids Daily Gazette*, 25 April 1912, reprinted in Geoff Tibballs, *Voices from the Titanic*. A paraphrased version of the interview appeared in the *Cedar Rapids Evening Gazette*, 26 April 1912.

90 Matt Flynn, *Kansas City Star*, 18 April 1912.

91 Courtesy of the *Rhode Island Sunday Magazine*, 15 April 1962.

92 Archibald Gracie, *Springfield Daily Republican*, 19 April 1912.

93 Halpern *et al.* (2012).

94 *Ibid.*

95 Charles Lightoller, British *Titanic* inquiry.

96 Charles Lightoller, Senate *Titanic* inquiry and British *Titanic* inquiry.

97 Jack Thayer, *The Sinking of the SS Titanic* (1940).

98 Halpern *et al.* (2012).

99 Harold Bride, Senate *Titanic* inquiry.

100 Joseph Boxhall, British *Titanic* inquiry.

101 Halpern *et al.* (2012).

102 *Ibid.*

103 Bruce Ismay, limitation of liability hearings. Note: in light of Mary Lines' story about a rumoured disagreement between Bruce Ismay and Captain Smith, might Smith have given this ice warning to Ismay as a tacit way of reminding him that the icefield ahead of the *Titanic* was dangerous?

104 Thayer (1940).

105 May Futrelle, *Boston Globe*, 17 April 1932, courtesy of Mike Poirier. Note: it's unclear if Mrs Futrelle was describing a personal interaction with Mr Ismay or if she was recalling something she learned about after the disaster.

106 John Thompson, *New York American*, 22 April 1912.

107 Daisy Minahan, *Eugene Morning Register* (Oregon), 28 April 1912. Note: Smith is known to have stated that it was his standard procedure to speed his ships past potential sources of danger as quickly as possible. (Please see the present author's updated edition of *Titanic: Psychic Forewarnings of a Tragedy* for an example of this.)

108 Imanita Shelley account written for the *Powell County Post* (Deer Lodge, Montana), Friday (unknown date), courtesy of Mike Poirier.

109 Lillian Bentham, *Holley Standard*, 25 April 1912.

110 Martha Stephenson and Elizabeth Eustis, *The Titanic: Our Story* (1912), courtesy of Christina Gorch and Jacque Gorch.

111 *New York Times*, 19 April 1912. Mark Chirnside comments, 'This appears plausible as a target for a day's run later during the crossing: we know, for example, that the *Olympic* covered 563 miles during a day's run on a westbound crossing in February 1912 and so another 7 miles would probably mean an additional 0.28 knots per hour over the period.'

112 Henry Martyn Hart, *Recollections and Reflections* (1917), courtesy of Mike Poirier.

113 *New York American*, 22 April 1912. Note: a later article in the *Philadelphia Inquirer* on 23 April 1912 says that 'two sources' denied that Mrs Widener had asked her brother-in-law Joseph Widener to place the substance of this conversation before the Senate *Titanic* inquiry. However, it's unclear whether these two sources were denying the reality of the Widener–Ismay conversation itself or whether they were simply denying that Joseph Widener had informed the Senate inquiry about the conversation.

114 Jack Thayer, *New York Times*, 25 June 1915.

115 Emily Ryerson, 1913 testimony, limitation of liability hearings, US National Archives.

116 Mahala Douglas, Senate *Titanic* inquiry.

117 Emily Ryerson, affidavit quoted in Nick Barratt, *Lost Voices from the Titanic* (2010), pp. 234–5.

118 Archibald Gracie, *Vancouver Daily Province*, 19 April 1912.

119 Archibald Gracie, *The Truth About the Titanic* (1913).

120 Anna Warren, *The Oregonian* (Portland), 27 April 1912.

121 Mahala Douglas, Senate *Titanic* inquiry.

122 Dorothy Gibson, *The New York Dramatic Mirror*, 1 May 1912, courtesy of Randy Bigham.

123 Helen Candee, *Down to the Sea in Ships*, courtesy of Mrs Candee's granddaughter, Mary C. Barker. Acquired by Walter Lord in 1986, charlespellegrino.com/helen-churchill-candee/.

124 Helen Candee handwritten account held by the Paris Museum of Letters and Manuscripts, courtesy of John Lamoreau. Note: although it was rumoured that *Titanic* was trying to set a transatlantic speed record, in reality the vessel was attempting to better the maiden voyage crossing time achieved in 1911 by her elder sister, the *Olympic*.

125 Bruce Ismay, British *Titanic* inquiry, #19051–3.

126 John Thompson, *New York Times*, 23 April 1912.

127 Candee, *Down to the Sea in Ships*.

128 Lucy Duff Gordon, *Discretions and Indiscretions* (1932).

129 Archibald Gracie, *Vancouver Daily Province*, 19 April 1912.

130 Charles Lightoller, British *Titanic* inquiry.

131 Herbert Pitman, Senate *Titanic* inquiry.

132 Harold Lowe, Senate *Titanic* inquiry.
133 Harold Bride, British *Titanic* inquiry; Halpern *et al.* (2012); Senate *Titanic* inquiry. Note: Third Officer Herbert Pitman testified at the British *Titanic* inquiry that the bridge never received this ice warning.
134 Harold Bride, Senate *Titanic* inquiry.
135 Arthur Peuchen, Senate *Titanic* inquiry.
136 Bruce Ismay, Senate *Titanic* inquiry.
137 Bruce Ismay, limitation of liability hearings.
138 May Futrelle, *Boston Globe*, 17 April 1932, courtesy of Mike Poirier.
139 Mike Poirier, 'Piecing together a *Titanic* puzzle: the complex case of Mrs Cassebeer', www.encyclopedia-titanica.org/piecing-together-a-titanic-puzzle.html.
140 *Southern Evening Echo*, 30 April 1912.
141 Hoyt, O'Loughlin and Simpson information comes from an interview with Jane Hoyt, courtesy of Mike Poirier. Dick information comes from Alan Hustak, *Titanic: The Canadian Story* (1998).
142 Hustak (1998).
143 Eleanor Cassebeer, 1955 letter to Walter Lord, courtesy of Mike Poirier.
144 Bruce Ismay, Senate *Titanic* inquiry.
145 Gordon (1932).
146 Rene Harris, *Liberty Magazine*, 23 April 1932.
147 Hugh Brewster, *Gilded Lives, Fatal Voyage* (2012).
148 Daisy Minahan letter to Senator William Alden Smith, 11 May 1912, Senate *Titanic* inquiry. Note: Miss Minahan had apparently forgotten to set her watch back the prescribed time on the previous night, which means she was actually dining at about 6.30 p.m. and that Captain Smith remained in the restaurant until sometime between 8.40 and 9 p.m.
149 Daisy Minahan, Senate *Titanic* inquiry.
150 Ellen Williamson, *When We Went First Class* (1977).
151 Catherine Crosby, *Milwaukee Journal*, 23 April 1912.
152 'Mrs Bucknell Sailed on the Titanic, and Lived to Tell About It', susquehannavalley.blogspot.com/2020/01/mrs-bucknell-sailed-on-titanic-and.html.
153 Arthur Peuchen, *Amboy Evening News* (Perth Amboy, NJ), 20 April 1912.
154 Marian Thayer affidavit, published in Davie (1986).
155 Mary Smith deposition to the Senate *Titanic* inquiry, 20 May 1912.
156 Eleanor Widener, Senate *Titanic* inquiry.
157 Gordon (1932).
158 Antoinette Flegenheim, *NYAI Catalogue*, 23 May 1912. Daniel Klistorner and Charles Provost, 'Elusive Passenger Pens Story', *Voyage*, #63, pp. 132–5, courtesy of Daniel Klistorner.
159 Candee, *Down to the Sea in Ships*.
160 Bruce Ismay, Senate *Titanic* inquiry.
161 Marian Thayer affidavit, published in Davie (1986).
162 Cosmo Duff Gordon, British *Titanic* inquiry.
163 Alfred Omont deposition, UK National Archives.
164 Elmer Zebley Taylor, *Jigsaw Picture Puzzle of People Whom I Have Known and Sundry Experiences From 1864 to 1949* (1949), courtesy of Don Lynch.
165 George Rheims testimony, limitation of liability hearings.
166 Marian Thayer affidavit, published in Davie (1986).

167 Charles Stengel, testimony at the Senate *Titanic* inquiry. Note: in an interview in the *Newark Star* of 19 April 1912, Mr Stengel said, 'Please say for me, in justice to Captain Smith, that he had not been drinking. He smoked cigarettes, but he did not drink.'
168 William Sloper, *The Life and Times of Andrew Jackson Sloper* (privately published, 1949).
169 Mahala Douglas, Senate *Titanic* inquiry.
170 Charles Lightoller, Senate *Titanic* inquiry.
171 Charles Lightoller, British *Titanic* inquiry.
172 Charles Lightoller, Senate *Titanic* inquiry.
173 Charles Lightoller, British *Titanic* inquiry.
174 Charles Lightoller, Senate *Titanic* inquiry.
175 Charles Lightoller, British *Titanic* inquiry. Note: in the *New York Herald* of 19 April 1912, Quartermaster Robert Hichens said Lightoller ordered *him* to phone the lookouts, so it's possible Sixth Officer Moody delegated the job to Hichens.
176 Halpern *et al.* (2012).
177 Joseph Boxhall, British *Titanic* inquiry; also Ryan vs. Oceanic Steam Navigation Company, 20 June 1913.
178 Alfred Shiers, 1913 testimony, limitation of liability hearings, US National Archives.
179 John Thompson, *New York Times*, 23 April 1912. Note: at the Senate *Titanic* inquiry, Leading Fireman Fred Barrett testified that the white 'full speed' indicator light was lit in the *Titanic*'s boiler rooms during the time leading up to the collision. This fact disproves the oft-repeated (but poorly researched) claim that the *Titanic* was not travelling at full speed when the collision occurred, because there's a big difference between 'full speed' and 'top speed' (the latter of which could only be achieved if the *Titanic*'s full complement of twenty-nine boilers had come online – an event that never happened). The *Titanic* was indeed travelling at 'full speed' – that is, she was travelling as fast as her twenty-four main boilers were capable of achieving.
180 Sidney Humphreys, *New York Press*, 21 April 1912.
181 Lawrence Beesley, *The Loss of the SS* Titanic (1912).
182 Charles Stengel, Senate *Titanic* inquiry.
183 Alice Silvey, *Duluth News Tribune*, 24 April 1912.
184 Mary Smith, Senate *Titanic* inquiry.
185 Joseph Boxhall, British *Titanic* inquiry; also 1913 Ryan vs. Oceanic Steam Navigation Company hearing, www.bbc.co.uk/archive/titanic/5049.shtml.
186 Joseph Boxhall, British *Titanic* inquiry.
187 *Ibid.*
188 For a complete survey of these accounts of 'early' icebergs, please see the present author's book *Titanic: Safety, Speed and Sacrifice*.
189 Jay Mobray, *The Sinking of the Titanic* (1912).11.40 p.m.–12 a.m., 15 April.

3: 11.40 p.m.–12 a.m., 15 April

1 Survivors George Thomas, Edith Rosenbaum and Edith Brown all described the collision as having consisted of three distinct 'bumps'.
2 Robert Hichens, as quoted in Mobray (1912). Note: at the British inquiry Hichens said Smith came out of 'his room'. Curiously, in the *New York Evening World* of

19 April 1912 *Carpathia* passenger Dr C. A. Bernard made the cryptic comment that: 'I am sure that Captain Smith was in his cabin smoking a cigar with two friends when he was shunted out of his seat.' Dr Bernard's specificity about Smith's 'two friends' makes one wonder if a bridge survivor might have shared a factual titbit with Bernard that everyone decided to 'forget' later on rather than make it appear that Captain Smith was too busy socialising with friends to be concerned about *Titanic*'s navigation while the vessel was approaching an icefield.

3   Robert Hichens, British *Titanic* inquiry; Robert Hichens, *New York Times*, 20 April 1912; Joseph Boxhall, British *Titanic* inquiry.

4   Joseph Boxhall, British *Titanic* inquiry.

5   Joseph Boxhall, Senate *Titanic* inquiry.

6   Robert Hichens, British *Titanic* inquiry.

7   Unnamed fireman, *Southern Daily Echo*, 29 April 1912. Note: Fireman Harry Senior had a harsher recollection of Captain Smith's order for crewmen to stay away from the boat deck: 'I ran on deck,' he said later, 'and the captain said, "All firemen keep down on the well deck. If a man comes up, I'll shoot him."' (Harry Senior, *New York Times*, 19 April 1912.)

8   Joseph Boxhall, Senate *Titanic* inquiry and British *Titanic* inquiry.

9   Joseph Boxhall, recorded BBC interview, 22 October 1962, transcribed in Behe, *The Titanic Disaster: Final Memories*.

10   Joseph Boxhall, Senate *Titanic* inquiry.

11   Joseph Boxhall, British *Titanic* inquiry.

12   Alfred Olliver, Senate *Titanic* inquiry.

13   Eleanor Cassebeer account of the *Titanic* disaster written for her family, 21 May 1932, quoted in George Behe, *Titanic Memoirs* (Vol. 2) (privately published).

14   Eleanor Cassebeer, *Binghamton Press*, 29 April 1912, courtesy of Mike Poirier.

15   Bullock (1913).

16   Mrs Jacques Futrelle, *The Boston Herald*, 19 April 1932.

17   Bruce Ismay, Senate *Titanic* inquiry; formal statement to the press, *New York Evening Telegram*, 22 April 1912.

18   Jack Thayer, *Philadelphia Evening Bulletin*, 14 April 1932.

19   Bruce Ismay, Senate *Titanic* inquiry.

20   *Ibid.*; formal statement to the press, *New York Evening Telegram*, 22 April 1912.

21   Herbert Pitman, Senate *Titanic* inquiry.

4: 12–12.20 a.m.

1   Robert Hichens, British *Titanic* inquiry. Note: at the Senate *Titanic* inquiry Hichens said that Smith checked the commutator roughly five or ten minutes after the 11.40 p.m. collision, but at the British inquiry he stated that it was after midnight when Smith did so. Note: Seaman George McGough, in *The Evening World*, 20 April 1912, reported a different version of *Titanic*'s alleged list: 'I was on duty; my relief was ready to come up. I heard Captain Smith ordering the carpenter to make the soundings. I heard the report of "Chips," who said: "Ten degrees list to starboard." "My God," cried the captain. "Bosun, pipe all hands on deck."' An interview with Washington Dodge in the *San Francisco Bulletin*, 20 April 1912, contained an even more extreme report regarding the *Titanic*'s alleged list: 'All this

time [during the maiden voyage] the *Titanic* had a slight list to port, but just after the collision Captain Smith, coming hurriedly up and inquiring what the list was and finding it eighteen degrees to starboard, said "My God!"'

2 Joseph Boxhall, Senate *Titanic* inquiry.
3 Robert Hichens, British *Titanic* inquiry, question #1041.
4 Alfred Olliver testimony at the Senate *Titanic* inquiry.
5 Joseph Scarrott, 1933 article he wrote for the *Pier Review*, staff magazine of the Southend Corporation Pier Department. *Southampton Daily Echo*, 2 February 2011, www.echo-news.co.uk/news/8825986.Dramatic_story_of_a_Titanic_survivor.
6 Gilbert Tucker, *Albion Times-Union*, 19 April 1912. Note: Tucker apparently set his watch back the prescribed forty-seven minutes before he went to bed that night.
7 Joseph Boxhall, Senate *Titanic* inquiry, titanicofficers.com/article_22.html, courtesy of Daniel Parkes.
8 Herbert Pitman, testimony at the Senate *Titanic* inquiry; Robert Hichens testimony at the British *Titanic* inquiry.
9 Unnamed deck hand (clearly Harry Senior), *Daily Telegraph*, 29 April 1912, courtesy of Dr Paul Lee.
10 Harold Bride, *New York Times*, 28 April 1912.
11 Courtesy of the *Rhode Island Sunday Magazine*, 15 April 1962.
12 Katherine Gold, *Bathurst Times*, 6 September 1913, p. 6.
13 Dr Fred Douglas (Mary Hélène's husband), *The Standard* (unknown date), courtesy of Daniel Klistorner.
14 Quigg Baxrer entry on *Encyclopedia Titanica*.
15 Dr Fred Douglas (Mary Hélène's husband), *The Standard* (unknown date), courtesy of Daniel Klistorner.
16 Karl Behr, chapter 14 of his privately published 1944 memoir; reprinted in the *Commutator*, Vol. 30, #176 (2006), courtesy of Don Lynch.
17 *Newport Daily News*, 23 August 1912, courtesy of Don Lynch. The identities of the officer and the occupant of the C deck stateroom are unknown.
18 James Johnstone, BR3367–74.
19 Laura Francatelli, letter to 'Mary Ann', 28 April 1912, courtesy of Dr Paul Lee, www.paullee.com/titanic/lfrancatelli.html.
20 Alfred Theissinger, *Washington Herald*, 19 April 1912.
21 Paul Maugé, BR20092.
22 Charles Mackay, BR10696–7. It seems unlikely that Chief Bell would still have been in his cabin after the collision occurred.
23 Edward Dorkings, *Bureau County Republican* (Princeton, IL), 2 May 1912. Note: Dorkings claimed his sighting of Smith occurred after the last lifeboat left the ship, but to the present author the sighting seems more likely to have occurred earlier in the sinking while Captain Smith was beginning his damage inspection below decks.
24 Charles Mackay, BR10696–7.
25 Augustus Weikman, *Camden Post-Telegram*, 19 April 1912.
26 Augustus Weikman, affidavit at the Senate *Titanic* inquiry.
27 James Johnstone testimony at the British *Titanic* inquiry, BR3400–1, 3562.
28 James Johnstone, testimony at the British *Titanic* inquiry, BR3378–400.
29 Samuel Hemming, testimony at the Senate *Titanic* inquiry.
30 Annie Robinson, BR13277–300; Bullock (1913), pp.68–9.
31 Albert Dick, *New York Herald*, 22 April 1912.

32   Pierre Maréchal, *Return of the Savoie*.
33   Elizabeth Allen, *Syracuse Herald*, 21 April 1912.
34   Sidney Collett, *Auburn Citizen*, 23 April 1912.
35   Charles Stengel, Senate *Titanic* inquiry.
36   Charles Stengel, *Philadelphia Evening Bulletin*, 19 April 1912.
37   Charles Stengel, *Newark Star*, 19 April 1912.
38   James McGough, *Philadelphia Evening Bulletin*, 19 April 1912.
39   Spencer Silverthorne, *St Louis Post Dispatch*, 21 April 1912.
40   Pierre Maréchal, 'Matin', *Manchester Guardian*, 20 April 1912.
41   Samuel Rule, *Daily Telegraph*, 29 April 1912.
42   Elizabeth Allen, *Syracuse Herald,* 21 April 1912. Note: Miss Allen stated that the
      above events took place at 'about half past eleven', but, since she also stated that the
      collision occurred at 11 p.m. instead of 11.40, she appears to have put her watch
      back the prescribed forty-seven minutes before she went to bed that night.
43   Violet Jessop and John Maxtone-Graham, *Titanic Survivor* (1997).
44   Algernon Barkworth, *New York Press*, 19 April 1912.
45   Marie Young, *Washington Post*, 21 April 1912.
46   Fernand Omont, affidavit to the British inquiry.
47   Pierre Maréchal, 'Matin', *Manchester Guardian*, 20 April 1912.
48   Isaac Frauenthal, *Toronto Star*, 20 April 1912.
49   Isaac Frauenthal, *St Louis Globe-Democrat*, 20 April 1912; *Toronto Star*, 20 April 1912.
50   Henry Frauenthal, *The Gazette*, 26 April 1912.
51   Nelle Snyder, *Boston Globe*, 20 April 1912.
52   Helen Bishop, Senate *Titanic* inquiry.
53   Dickinson Bishop, *New York Times*, 19 April 1912.
54   Caroline Brown, *Boston Globe*, 21 April 1912.
55   Caroline Brown, *Boston Globe*, 19 April 1912.
56   Isaac Frauenthal, *St Louis Globe-Democrat*, 20 April 1912.
57   Gladys Cherry, 17 April letter she wrote to her mother while the *Carpathia* was
      bound for New York.
58   Karl Behr, *Brooklyn Daily Eagle*, 19 April 1912.
59   Caroline Bonnell, *Trenton Evening Times*, 19 April 1912.
60   Anna Warren, *Portland Oregonian*, 27 April 1912.
61   *New York Dramatic Mirror*, 1 May 1912, courtesy of Randy Bigham.
62   Sloper (1949).
63   *New York Dramatic Mirror*, 1 May, courtesy of Randy Bigham.
64   Archibald Gracie, *The Outlook*, 27 April 1912, courtesy of Randy Bigham.
65   Martha Stephenson and Elizabeth Eustis, *The Titanic: Our Story*, 1912,
      www.encyclopedia-titanica.org/the-titanic-our-story-eustis-stephenson.html.
66   Fred Hoyt, *Springfield Union*, 20 May 1912, courtesy of Mike Poirier.
67   Steve Prentice, *Maclean's*, 23 January 1978.

5: 12.20–12.40 a.m.

1   John Poigndestre, British *Titanic* inquiry, #2874.
2   Charles Hendrickson, British *Titanic* inquiry, #4990.
3   Robert Hichens, British *Titanic* inquiry, #1098.

4   Bruce Ismay, testimony at the Senate *Titanic* inquiry.

5   Bruce Ismay, testimony at the Senate *Titanic* inquiry. Ismay claimed he never saw Captain Smith again after leaving the bridge.

6   Archibald Gracie, Senate *Titanic* inquiry.

7   Charlotte Appleton, *New York Herald*, 20 April 1912.

8   Charles Lightoller, Senate *Titanic* inquiry.

9   Elizabeth Allen, *Syracuse Herald*, 21 April 1912.

10   Harold Bride, *New York Times*, 28 April 1912.

11   This time is based on the new determination *Titanic* ship's time was 122 minutes ahead of New York time (which was 10.25 p.m.).

12   Harold Bride, Senate *Titanic* inquiry.

13   Luigi Finoli, *New York Evening World*, 19 April 1912.

14   Note: Ismay was not in lifeboat 13 or 15.

15   Washington Dodge, *Pittsburgh Daily Dispatch*, 27 April 1912.

16   Joseph Boxhall, Senate *Titanic* inquiry; 1913 Ryan vs. Oceanic Steam Navigation Company hearing, www.bbc.co.uk/archive/titanic/5049.shtml.

17   Charles Lightoller, British *Titanic* inquiry.

18   Samuel Hemming, Senate *Titanic* inquiry.

19   Robert Daniel, *Washington Post*, 22 April 1912.

20   Robert Daniel, *Washington Post*, 19 April 1912.

21   Mrs Norman Chambers, *Syracuse Herald*, 24 April 1912.

22   Woolner said he stood between the two aft-most lifeboats on the port boat deck, but he undoubtedly meant the boats located on the (forward) first-class section of the boat deck.

23   Caroline Bonnell, *Youngstown Telegram*, 19 April 1912.

24   Hugh Woolner, Senate *Titanic* inquiry.

25   Candee, *Down to the Sea in Ships*.

26   Mary Smith, *Huntington Herald Dispatch*, 24 April 1912.

27   *Ibid.*

28   Lightoller (1935).

29   Herbert Pitman, Senate *Titanic* inquiry.

30   Richard Beckwith, *Waterbury American*, 23 April 1912. As unlikely as this information sounds at first hearing, the present author can think of no reason why Officer Pitman would give someone this account of his own activities on the *Titanic* if the story didn't contain at least a kernel of truth.

31   Robert Hichens, British *Titanic* inquiry, #1098–100.

32   Paul Maugé, British *Titanic* inquiry, #20094.

33   Joseph Boxhall, Senate *Titanic* inquiry.

34   Harold Bride, *New York Times*, 28 April 1912. Other survivors do not corroborate Bride's description of an excited crowd existing this early in the proceedings.

35   Harold Bride, official report to the Marconi Company, Senate *Titanic* inquiry. Note: in his testimony at the Senate *Titanic* inquiry, Bride said he found Captain Smith in the wheelhouse instead of out on the boat deck.

36   Albert Dick, *Toronto Star*, 20 April 1912.

37   Albert Dick, *Manitoba Free Press*, 20 April 1912.

38   Albert Dick, *New York Herald*, 20 April 1912.

39   In Bullock (1913).

40   Albert Dick, *Maclean's*, 1 May 1950.

41   Thayer (1940).

42   Jack Thayer testimony at the 1915 limitation of liability hearings, *New York Evening Post*, 24 June 1915.

43   Joseph Boxhall, BR15610.

44   Fred Hoyt, *New York Sun*, 30 July 1938.

45   George Rheims, testimony at the limitation of liability hearings.

46   Katherine Gold and Annie Martin, *Northern Daily Telegraph*, 30 April 1912; *Western Morning News*, 30 April 1912.

47   May Futrelle, *The Boston Herald*, 17 April 1932.

48   Mary Smith, *Washington Post*, 21 April 1912.

49   Harold Bride, official report to the Marconi Company, Senate *Titanic* inquiry.

50   Washington Dodge, *San Francisco Bulletin*, 19 April 1912.

51   Vera Dick, *Washington Post*, 19 April 1912.

52   Albert Horswill, *Post Tribune* (Gary, Indiana), 14 April 1978.

53   Nelle Snyder, *Idaho Daily Statesman*, 26 April 1912.

54   John Snyder, *Minneapolis Journal*, 19 April 1912.

55   *Ibid.*, 22 April 1912.

56   Jane Hoyt, *Amsterdam Evening Recorder*, 23 April 1912.

57   Henry Etches, Senate *Titanic* inquiry.

58   Dorothy Gibson account, *New York Morning Telegraph*, 21 April 1912, from *The Complete Titanic*, by Stephen Spignesi, pp. 97–101.

59   Spencer Silverthorne, *St Louis Star*, 21 April 1912.

60   Elmer Taylor, *New York Evening World*, 20 April 1912.

61   Elmer Taylor, *Atlantic City Daily Press*, 5 May 1912.

62   John Snyder, *Minneapolis Journal*, 19 April 1912.

6: 12.40–1 a.m.

1   Alfred Rowe, 1956 interview with the BBC, web.archive.org/web/2010042 0062740/www.paullee.com/titanic/BBC1956.php.

2   Joseph Boxhall, British *Titanic* inquiry.

3   Joseph Boxhall, Senate *Titanic* inquiry.

4   Alfred Rowe, 1956 interview with the BBC, web.archive.org/web/2010042 0062740/www.paullee.com/titanic/BBC1956.php.

5   Joseph Boxhall, British *Titanic* inquiry.

6   Herbert Pitman, Senate *Titanic* inquiry.

7   Eleanor Cassebeer, *Binghamton Press*, 29 April 1912, courtesy of Mike Poirier.

8   Unnamed steward, *Western Daily Mercury*, 29 April 1912.

9   Eleanor Cassebeer, *Binghamton Press*, 29 April 1912.

10   Sarah Stap, *Birkenhead News*, 4 May 1912, courtesy of Dr Paul Lee.

11   George Harder, *Brooklyn Daily Eagle*, 19 April 1912.

12   Unnamed male survivor, *Boston Herald*, 21 April 1912.

13   Karl Behr, '*Titanic* Disaster' (chapter in his autobiography), courtesy of Don Lynch.

14   Helen Ostby, *Woonsocket Evening Call* (RI), 22 April 1912.

15   Henry Etches, Senate *Titanic* inquiry.

16 W. A. James letter to Bruce Ismay, 29 July 1912, courtesy of Malcolm Cheape. Note: some researchers believe Miss Marsden was in lifeboat 16, but there's zero evidence that Bruce Ismay ever assisted at that lifeboat or indeed that he was ever present on the port side of the ship during the entire evacuation.

17 Nella Goldenberg, *New York Herald*, 21 April 1912.

18 Karl Behr in Mobray (1912).

19 Alfred Crawford, Senate *Titanic* inquiry.

20 Harold Lowe, Senate *Titanic* inquiry.

21 *Ibid.*

22 *Ibid.*, #15983.

23 Augustus Weikman, *Philadelphia Evening Bulletin*, 19 April 1912.

24 Edenser Wheelton, Senate *Titanic* inquiry.

25 Eleanor Cassebeer, 1932 account written for her family, letter translated from the French by Charles Provost. Courtesy of Daniel Klistorner.

26 Charlotte Collyer, *Washington Post Semi-Monthly Magazine*, 26 May 1912.

27 Alfred Crawford, Senate *Titanic* inquiry.

28 Vera Dick, *Los Angeles Times*, 21 April 1912.

29 Vera Dick, *Syracuse Post Standard*, 19 April 1912.

30 Vera Dick, *Manitoba Free Press*, 29 April 1912.

31 Wilfred Seward, *Yonkers Statesman*, 19 April 1912.

32 Samuel Rule, British *Titanic* inquiry, #6442–70.

33 Albert Dick, *New York Herald*, 20 April 1912.

34 Mary Sloan letter written to 'Maggie', 27 April 1912, Behe (2012).

35 Mary Sloan, *The Belfast Newsletter*, 5 May 1912.

36 Bullock (1913).

37 Mary Sloan, *Belfast Weekly Telegraph*, 2 June 1912.

38 Annie Robinson, quoted in Bullock (1913).

39 Ruth Bowker, *Cheshire Observer*, 18 May 1912, courtesy of Dr Paul Lee.

40 Edward Wheelton, Senate *Titanic* inquiry.

41 Joseph Boxhall, British *Titanic* inquiry.

42 Joseph Boxhall, Senate *Titanic* inquiry.

43 Harold Bride, Senate *Titanic* inquiry.

44 Harold Bride, *New York Times*, 19 April 1912. Bride believed Captain Smith returned to the Marconi room and gave his SOS instruction just five minutes after the first distress signals were sent at 12.27 a.m., but Phillips didn't send an SOS message to *Olympic* until 12.57 a.m.

45 Harold Bride, Senate *Titanic* inquiry. Note: the *Frankfurt* is known to have transmitted her position to the *Titanic* (the transmission was overheard by the *Mount Temple*, *La Provence*, *Caronia*, *Ypiranga* and *Birma*), but – for whatever reason – Jack Phillips apparently never received it.

46 Harold Bride, Senate *Titanic* inquiry.

47 *Olympic* wireless PV, Marconi Archive, Chelmsford, England.

48 William Burke, Senate *Titanic* inquiry.

49 Marion Kenyon recorded interview, 6 April 1957, included on the Titanic Historical Society's 1980 Vantage LP album *Titanic II*. The interview was transcribed by George Behe.

50 Marion Kenyon, *New York Press*, 25 June 1915.

51 William Burke, Senate *Titanic* inquiry.
52 Marie Young, *Washington Post*, 21 April 1912.
53 Tillie Taussig, *New York Times*, 22 April 1912.
54 Emma Bucknell, *Philadelphia Inquirer*, 20 April 1912.
55 Dr Alice Leader, *New York Herald*, 19 April 1912.
56 Margaret Swift, *Brooklyn Daily Eagle*, 19 April 1912.
57 Mrs Bucknell, *Philadelphia Inquirer*, 20 April 1912.
58 Alfred Crawford, Senate *Titanic* inquiry.
59 William Burke, Senate *Titanic* inquiry.
60 Marie Young, *Washington Post*, 21 April 1912.
61 Countess of Rothes, *New York Herald*, 21 April 1912.
62 Gladys Cherry letter to her mother, 17 April 1912, published in Hester Julian, *Memorials of Henry Forbes Julian* (1914), and the *Atlantic Daily Bulletin*.
63 Thomas Jones, Senate *Titanic* inquiry.
64 Marion Kenyon recorded interview, 6 April 1957, included on the Titanic Historical Society's 1980 Vantage LP album *Titanic II*. The interview was transcribed by George Behe.
65 Tillie Taussig, *New York Times*, 22 April 1912.
66 Roberta Maioni, 'My Maiden Voyage', *Daily Express*, 1926, posted on the Encyclopedia Titanica website. Also www.reddit.com/r/titanic/comments/14ssonp/titanic_survivor_roberta_maioni_typed_account/.
67 Alfred Crawford, Senate *Titanic* inquiry.
68 Dr Alice Leader, *New York Herald*, 19 April 1912.
69 Thomas Jones, *New York Tribune*, 20 April 1912.
70 Alfred Crawford, Senate *Titanic* inquiry.
71 Unnamed female survivor, *New York Herald*, 19 April 1912.

7: 1–1.30 a.m.

1 Ruth Bowker, *Cheshire Observer*, 18 May 1912.
2 Henry Etches, testimony at the Senate *Titanic* inquiry.
3 Augustus Weikman, affidavit given to the Senate *Titanic* inquiry.
4 Annie Robinson, testimony at the British *Titanic* inquiry; Bullock (1913).
5 Charles Hendrickson, British *Titanic* inquiry.
6 George Symons, Senate *Titanic* inquiry.
7 Walter Wynn, British *Titanic* inquiry.
8 Frank Evans, Senate *Titanic* inquiry.
9 Albert Horswill, WGN radio programme *Headlines of Other Days*, broadcast on 10 May 1934, rrauction.com/auctions/lot-detail/33199100427105-titanic-testimony-albert-horswill.
10 Samuel Rule, British *Titanic* inquiry, #9599.
11 Arthur Peuchen, Senate *Titanic* inquiry.
12 Hugh Woolner, Senate *Titanic* inquiry.
13 Candee, *Down to the Sea in Ships*.
14 Hugh Woolner, Senate *Titanic* inquiry.
15 Ruth Bowker, *Cheshire Observer*, 18 May 1912, courtesy of Dr Paul Lee.
16 Martha Stone, unsigned typed account for William L. Finch, British Vice Consul in Cincinnati, sold by RR Auctions, 16 December 2012.

17 Archibald Gracie, *The Truth About the Titanic* (1913).
18 Mary Smith affidavit, Senate *Titanic* inquiry.
19 Mary Smith, *Washington Evening Star*, 20 April 1912.
20 Mary Smith, *St Louis Post-Dispatch*, 19 April 1912.
21 Mary Smith affidavit, Senate *Titanic* inquiry.
22 Mary Smith, *Pittsburgh Daily Dispatch*, 20 April 1912.
23 Mary Smith affidavit, Senate *Titanic* inquiry.
24 Mary Smith, *New York American*, 19 April 1912, as relayed by Dr L. T. Vinson
    (the family physician) in the presence of Mrs Smith's parents. All three people had
    met Mrs Smith at the pier in New York and heard her tell the story of her *Titanic*
    experiences.
25 Arthur Peuchen, Senate *Titanic* inquiry.
26 Rose Icard, nine-page French memoir of the *Titanic* disaster written 22 August 1951.
27 Arthur Peuchen, Senate *Titanic* inquiry.
28 William Major, *Illinois State Register* (Chicago), 21 April 1912.
29 May Futrelle, *Boston Globe*, 17 April 1932, courtesy of Mike Poirier.
30 Gracie (1913).
31 Helen Candee, *Down to the Sea in Ships*. Note: although Archibald Gracie believed
    Mrs Candee was in lifeboat 6, Hugh Woolner said he placed her in the 'stern-most
    boat on the port side'. Since lifeboat 8 (the rearmost boat in the quad on the port
    first-class boat deck) was launched first, I believe Woolner was describing putting
    Mrs Candee into boat 6 after 8 left the ship.
32 Martha Stephenson, *Cincinnati Enquirer*, 20 April 1912.
33 Charles Lightoller, British *Titanic* inquiry.
34 Lightoller (1935).
35 *The Paterson Morning Call*, 20 April 1912.
36 Lucy Duff Gordon, *Yonkers Statesman*, 19 April 1912. Since there are no reliable
    accounts of panic occurring as early as 1.05 a.m. her statement about the 'last
    lifeboat' suggests that Lady Duff Gordon might have been repeating a story she
    heard on board the *Carpathia* concerning events that happened long after she left the
    Titanic (providing she said these things at all, of course).
37 Edith Chibnall, *New York Herald*, 19 April 1912. We have no way of knowing if
    Mrs Chibnall might have been repeating a hearsay account she heard from someone else.
38 Bertha Mulvihill, *Providence Evening Bulletin*, 19 April 1912. Note: according to
    researcher Tad Fitch, who has researched Bertha Mulvihill's *Titanic* experience,
    Mulvihill told her family she never saw Captain Smith with a revolver. (Tad Fitch
    email to the present author, 17 January 2011.)
39 Renée Harris, quoted in Logan Marshall, *The Sinking of the Titanic & Great Sea Disasters*
    (1912). Note: the veracity of this account of Major Butt's actions is unknown.
40 Washington Dodge, *The Gazette*, 26 April 1912.
41 Mary Compton, *Racine Journal*, 23 April 1912.
42 'The reflections of Edith E. Haisman on the maiden voyage of the RMS *Titanic*
    recalled on 22 October 1993.'
43 George McGough, *Daily Mirror*, 29 April 1912, courtesy of Dr Paul Lee.
44 William Ward, Senate *Titanic* inquiry.
45 Edenser Wheelton, Senate *Titanic* inquiry.
46 Emma Schabert letter, 18 April 1912, from Kyrill Schabert, courtesy of Don Lynch.

47 Walter Bentham (Lillian's brother), *Rochester Democrat*, 21 April 1912.

8: 1.30–2 a.m.

1 Katherine Gold and Annie Martin, *Daily Mirror*, 30 April 1912; *Western Morning News*, 30 April 1912.

2 Annie Martin, *Daily Mirror* (London), 30 April 1912.

3 Hypatia McLaren, *Daily Mail*, 30 April 1912, courtesy of Dr Paul Lee.

4 Kate Gold, *Bathurst Times* (NSW), 6 September 1913.

5 Edith Rosenbaum, *New York Times*, 23 April 1912.

6 Emma Schabert letter, 18 April 1912, from Kyrill Schabert courtesy of Don Lynch.

7 Robert Hopkins, *New York Times*, 23 April 1912.

8 Marie Jerwan, *New York Times*, 19 April 1912.

9 Shan Bullock (1913). Samuel Rule testified at the inquiry that John Stewart left the ship in lifeboat 15, but Frank Evans, who transferred from lifeboat 10 to lifeboat 14, identified Stewart as being one of the three men rescued from the water when lifeboat 4 went back to search for survivors. Despite the fact that Evans described 'young Stewart' being pulled into lifeboat 14, Evans was probably talking about 'young steward' Sidney Siebert instead.

10 Emma Bliss, *Toronto Star*, (6?) March 1959.

11 Luigi Finoli, *Philadelphia Evening Bulletin*, 23 April 1912.

12 Percy Keen, *Western Daily Mercury*, 29 April 1912, courtesy of Dr Paul Lee.

13 Samuel Rule, *Western Daily Mercury*, 30 April 1912, courtesy of Dr Paul Lee.

14 Joseph Boxhall, Senate *Titanic* inquiry.

15 Mary Sloan letter to 'Maggie' on 27 April 1912, Behe (2012); Bullock (1913).

16 Mary Sloan, *Belfast Weekly Telegraph*, 1 June 1912.

17 Joseph Boxhall, 1913 Ryan vs. Oceanic Steam Navigation Company hearing, www.bbc.co.uk/archive/titanic/5049.shtml.

18 Mahala Douglas affidavit, Senate *Titanic* inquiry.

19 Gracie (1913). However, in the *St Louis Times*, 24 April 1912, Miss Allen said the crewman was First Officer Murdoch.

20 Elizabeth Allen, *St Louis Republic*, 24 April 1912.

21 James Johnston, British *Titanic* inquiry.

22 Elizabeth Allen, *St Louis Globe Democrat*, 24 April 1912.

23 Charlotte Appleton, *Brooklyn Daily Eagle*, 19 April 1912.

24 James Johnstone, British *Titanic* inquiry, #3583–89, 3646–703.

25 Joseph Boxhall, British *Titanic* inquiry, #15451–2.

26 Mrs Edward Robert letter to her brother, *Atlantic City Daily Press*, 23 April 1912.

27 Charles Lightoller, British *Titanic* inquiry, #14186.

28 Peter Daly, *Newark Star*, 23 April 1912.

29 Harold Bride, official report to the Marconi Company, Senate *Titanic* inquiry.

30 *Baltic*'s wireless PV, Marconi Company archive in Chelmsford, Essex, England.

31 William Törnquist, *Paterson Morning Call*, 3 May 1912.

32 *The Cleveland Leader*, 19 April 1912.

33 Unnamed fireman, *Western Daily Mercury*, 29 April 1912.

34 Mary Davis, *The Staten Islander (Republican)*, 20 April 1912. Note: although Miss Davis probably heard Captain Smith issuing orders, I believe her reference to

Smith's 'Every man for himself' order was probably something she heard later on the *Carpathia*.

35 Stephenson and Eustis (1912).

36 Nellie Hocking, *Schenectady Gazette*, 22 April 1912.

37 Stephenson and Eustis (1912).

38 Emily Ryerson deposition, limitation of liability hearings.

39 *Ibid*.

40 Ida Hippach, *Chicago Tribune*, 22 April 1912.

41 Nellie O'Dwyer, *Limerick Echo*, 7 May 1912.

42 Text of a cablegram sent by the White Star Line to an official at Harland & Wolff, as reported in *The Irish News*, 22 April 1912. This article was probably the same source Shan Bullock used when describing Andrews throwing deck chairs overboard from the boat deck in his book *Thomas Andrews – Shipbuilder*. However, the *New York Sun* on 24 or 25 April 1912 says that 'the last seen of him he was on deck A throwing steamer chairs overboard, some of which saved the lives of passengers struggling in the water'.

43 An account told by a surviving male passenger to a male 'Stamford survivor', *Hartford Times* (Connecticut), 19 April 1912.

44 *Loss of the Steamship Titanic* (a 1912 booklet published by the United States Senate).

45 George Rowe, Lord-Macquitty Collection, National Maritime Museum, Paul Lee website, www.paullee.com/titanic/gtrowe.html.

46 Emily Goldsmith, *London Advertiser* (Ontario), 24 April 1912.

47 Hugh Woolner, Senate *Titanic* inquiry.

48 George Rowe, Senate *Titanic* inquiry.

49 Arthur Bright, Senate *Titanic* inquiry.

50 Edward Brown, British *Titanic* inquiry, #10518–630. Note: at the British *Titanic* inquiry (BR#18856, 18936) Ismay specifically denied that he ever entered collapsible C in order to assist women and children into the boat and that he did so from outside the boat.

51 Edward Brown, British *Titanic* inquiry, #10518–630.

52 Alfred Rowe, Senate *Titanic* inquiry.

53 Bruce Ismay, *Manitoba Free Press* (Winnipeg), 20 April 1912.

54 Bruce Ismay, Senate *Titanic* inquiry.

55 William Carter, *The Sun*, 22 April 1912.

56 William Carter, *Augusta Chronicle*, 22 April 1912. Note: the Senate *Titanic* inquiry probably questioned Ismay about his entry into collapsible C because of the publication of several other newspaper interviews claiming he'd been invited, ordered or forced to enter the boat. In the *Newark Evening News* of 23 April 1912, Georgette Madill supposedly claimed she saw Ismay enter the 'last lifeboat' after being solicited to do so by Captain Smith himself. (Miss Madill was saved in lifeboat 2, which departed from the *Titanic* before Mr Ismay left the ship; her lifeboat was also on the opposite side of the ship from Ismay's.) Edward J. Schembri (the travelling passenger agent of the White Star Line) may have read Miss Madill's interview, because in the *Syracuse Herald* of 24 April 1912 he claimed Ismay entered the boat only after 'Captain Smith from the bridge called out, "Why don't you get in the boat?" There was no other person around on that deck at the time. There was but one other man in the boat, and Mr Ismay got in.' During his testimony at the

Senate *Titanic* inquiry, Second Officer Charles Lightoller said he was told that Chief Officer Wilde was standing near collapsible C at the time and that Wilde 'simply bundled' Ismay into that boat. On the other hand, Quartermaster George Rowe's Senate inquiry testimony supports Ismay's own claim that nobody invited him to enter collapsible C. For the sake of simplicity, our present book gives precedence to Ismay's own version of his entry into collapsible C, but the truth of the matter may never be known with 100 per cent certainty.

57   Augustus Weikman, Senate *Titanic* inquiry.
58   George Rowe, British *Titanic* inquiry, #17637.
59   Unnamed trimmer, *Hampshire Independent*, 4 May 1912, courtesy of Dr Paul Lee. According to an email from researcher Bruno Piola, fellow researcher Craig Stringer says the man in question was trimmer Albert Hunt.
60   Edward Dorkings, *Arkansas Gazette* (Little Rock), 20 April 1912. Note: the newspaper article mistakenly claims that Ismay left the *Titanic* in the first lifeboat, so if Dorkings' account contains any truth at all, he must have been referring to collapsible C instead.
61   Unnamed fireman, *London Daily Telegraph*, 29 April 1912.
62   Constance Willard, *St Paul Pioneer Press*, 22 April 1912. Note: after the *Titanic's* survivors were picked up by the *Carpathia*, Ismay's comment about the Chinese men was relayed to Miss Willard by William Carter himself.

9: 2–2.20 a.m.

1   Jane Hoyt, *Amsterdam Evening Recorder* (NY), 23 April 1912.
2   Irene Harris, *Liberty Magazine*, 23 April 1932.
3   Irene Harris letter to Clara Butt (sister-in-law of Major Butt), 24 April 1912, Georgia Archives.
4   *Liberty Magazine*, 23 April 1932.
5   Leah Aks, *Norfolk Ledger-Dispatch*, 24 April 1912.
6   *Glen Falls Daily Times*, 11 June 1912.
7   Bridget Bradley, *Glens Falls Daily Times* (NY), 20 April 1912. Note: Bruce Ismay was saved in collapsible C along with four Chinese passengers, but later in her present account Miss Bradley said she didn't learn about any Chinese being saved until after she was on board the *Carpathia* and heard 'stories' about the four men. This suggests that she might not have been in collapsible C with Bruce Ismay, which would leave only collapsible D – the 'last boat' (assuming the details of her newspaper interview are accurate, of course).
8   Unnamed first-class saloon steward, *New York Evening World*, 28 April 1912.
9   Samuel Hemming, Senate *Titanic* inquiry.
10   James McGann, *New York Tribune*, 20 April 1912.
11   Fred Hoyt, *Springfield Union* (MA), 20 April 1912; *The Morning Call* (Paterson, NJ), 23 April 1912.
12   Eustace Snow deposition for the British *Titanic* inquiry.
13   Victor Sunderland, *Cleveland Plain Dealer*, 26 April 1912.
14   Sidney Collett, *Syracuse Post-Standard*, 24 April 1912.
15   *New York Times*, 19 April 1912.
16   *Cincinnati Enquirer*, 20 April 1912.
17   Unnamed reporter, *Daily Express*, 30 April 1912, courtesy of Dr Paul Lee.

18 Kate Buss Willis, 1932 account reprinted in the *Commutator*, Vol. 30, #176, 2006.
19 Charles Judd, *The Daily Herald* (London), 29 April 1912.
20 Edward Brown, British *Titanic* inquiry, #10628–30.
21 *Ibid.*, #10585–7.
22 Frederick Ray, Senate *Titanic* inquiry.
23 Cecil Fitzpatrick, *Western Daily Mercury*, 29 April 1912, courtesy of Dr Paul Lee. In a 27 June 1999 posting on the internet's Titanic Discuss Mailing List, newspaperman Senan Molony writes that Thomas Andrews' Irish friend, David Galloway, was waiting to meet Andrews in New York and subsequently returned to England on the *Lapland* along with most of the *Titanic*'s surviving crew. On 27 April 1912 Galway wrote a letter to Lord Pirrie describing various crew sightings of Thomas Andrews during the evacuation, and among these sightings was one made by an unnamed mess boy (undoubtedly Mess Steward Fitzpatrick), who described seeing Andrews and Smith standing together on the *Titanic*'s bridge right before the end. The boy heard Smith tell Andrews, 'It's no use waiting any longer,' at which point the two men put on lifebelts and then plunged into the sea as the *Titanic*'s bridge began to submerge.
24 Alexander Littlejohn, *The Weekly Telegraph*, 10 May 1912.
25 Thomas Threlfall, *London Globe & Traveller*, 30 April 1912.
26 Alfred White, *New York Sun*, 19 April 1912.
27 James McGann, *The Weekly Freeman*, 27 April 1912.
28 Unnamed steward, *London Daily Chronicle*, 29 April 1912.
29 Edward Brown, British *Titanic* inquiry, #10585–7.
30 Marshall (1912).
31 Unnamed crewman, *St John's Evening Telegram* (NF), 4 May 1912.
32 'C. Q. D.', by Richard N. Williams 2nd, Historical Society of Pennsylvania.
33 *The Star* (Marinette, WI), unknown date 1912, courtesy of Mike Poirier.
34 August Wennerström's personal typed lecture notes, courtesy of Culver and Gerald Wennerström.
35 Charles Judd, *The Daily Herald* (London), 29 April 1912.
36 John Thompson, *New Haven Evening Register* (Connecticut), 22 April 1912. Note: Thompson's claim that Smith was wearing two lifebelts conflicts with the accounts of other survivors who said that Smith was not wearing a lifebelt at all and that he had given his own lifebelt away earlier in the evening.
37 James McGann, *Chicago Tribune*, 20 April 1912.
38 James McGann, *The Weekly Freeman*, 27 April 1912.
39 Harold Bride, Senate *Titanic* inquiry.
40 Robert Daniel, *New York Press*, 19 April 1912.
41 Cecil Fitzpatrick, *Western Daily Mercury*, 29 April 1912, courtesy of Dr Paul Lee.
42 *Ibid.*
43 Harry Senior, *Philadelphia Evening Bulletin*, 19 April 1912.
44 Harry Senior, *The Sketch*, 29 April 1912.
45 Harry Senior, *Philadelphia Evening Bulletin*, 19 April 1912. Senior's account also suggests that Captain Smith might have found another lifebelt for himself after supposedly telling Victor Sunderland that he'd given his own belt away.
46 Jack Thayer Jr, *The Sinking of the SS Titanic* (1940).
47 James McGann, *The Weekly Freeman*, 27 April 1912.
48 Gracie (1913).

49 Isaac Maynard, *The Globe*, 29 April 1912.

50 Carlos Hurd, *Chicago Daily Tribune*, 19 April 1912.

51 Bill Wormstedt, Tad Fitch and J. Kent Layton, *On a Sea of Glass*, p. 33, quotes the *Daily Sketch* of 30 April 1912 as naming Maynard as the man who took a dying child from Captain Smith's arms. The same book (p. 333) quotes the *Shoreman Herald* of 25 July 2009 as saying the story is still current in the Maynard family that Isaac Maynard was indeed the man to whom Captain Smith handed the dying child.

52 Hugh Woolner, *New York Tribune*, 19 April 1912.

53 *The Western Times*, 30 April 1912.

54 *The Western Daily Mercury*, 29 April 1912, courtesy of Dr Paul Lee. Note: according to an interview on page 6 of the *Portsmouth Times*, 4 May 1912, Harris was in lifeboat 14.

55 Fred Barrett, *Ulster Echo*, 30 April 1912. Note: the reporter withheld Barrett's name from his readers so that Barrett wouldn't face repercussions from the White Star Line.

56 Unnamed crewman, *Illustrated Western Weekly News*, 4 May 1912, courtesy of Paul Lee.

57 Elizabeth Nye, *New York Herald*, 22 April 1912. Note: Miss Nye was apparently under the mistaken impression that Captain Smith swam to swamped collapsible A instead of to overturned collapsible B.

58 Harry Senior, *New York Times*, 19 April 1912.

59 Unnamed deckhand (clearly Harry Senior), *London Daily Telegraph*, 29 April 1912, courtesy of Dr Paul Lee.

60 Unnamed deck hand (clearly Harry Senior), *Daily Herald*, 2 May 1912.

61 Harry Senior, *London Daily Telegraph*, 29 April 1912.

62 Harry Senior, *Philadelphia Evening Bulletin*, 19 April 1912.

63 Elizabeth Nye, *Folkestone Herald*, 4 May 1912.

64 Fred Beachler, *New York Herald*, 19 April 1912.

65 Jose Mardones, *New York Times*, 19 April 1912.

66 For a sampling of such accounts, see chapter 20 of the present author's book *Titanic Tidbits*, Vol. 2.

67 John Collins, Senate *Titanic* inquiry.

68 Carl Jonsson, *Manitowoc Herald*, 25 April 1912.

69 For a lengthier discussion of the available evidence pertaining to Captain Smith and the child, please see chapter 20 of the present author's book *Titanic Tidbits*, Vol. 2.

70 Eleanor Smith letter to Frank Hancock, courtesy of Brian Ticehurst; www.encyclopedia-titanica.org/letter-from-captain-smiths-widow.html.

71 J. E. Hodder Williams, quoted in 'E. J. Smith Memorial' booklet (1913).

72 Jessop and Maxtone-Graham (1997).

10: Public Perception of Captain Smith

1 Hart (1917), courtesy of Mike Poirier.

2 Edward Wilding deposition, limitation of liability hearings.

3 Eleanor Smith, *New York Times*, 19 April 1912.

4 Arthur Rostron, *Cleveland Plain Dealer*, 19 April 1912.

5 Ann O'Donnell, post-sinking newspaper article datelined San Francisco, 19 April 1912.

6   Lawrence Beesley, *New York Times*, 29 April 1912.
7   'The *Titanic* Disaster', speech of Hon. William Alden Smith (Government Printing Office, 1912).

11: Public Perception of Thomas Andrews

1   Bullock (1913), p. 78.
2   *Ibid.*, p. 79.
3   Unnamed correspondent, *London Daily Chronicle*, 30 April 1912.
4   Bullock (1913).
5   James Moore, *The London Times*, 22 April 1912.
6   Thomas Andrews Sr letter, courtesy of Craig Sopin.
7   *Ibid.*

12: Public Perception of J. Bruce Ismay

1   William Carter, *The Sun*, 22 April 1912.
2   Carrie Chaffee, *Minot Daily Reporter* (North Dakota), 23 April 1912.
3   John Snyder, *Minneapolis Journal*, 21 April 1912.
4   Mrs Charles Hutchison, *New York American*, 19 April 1912.
5   Unnamed officer, *Philadelphia Evening Bulletin*, 19 April 1912.
6   James Barker, *New York Times*, 19 April 1912.
7   Eleanor Danforth, *Boston Herald*, 20 April 1912.
8   Henry Burke, *Scranton Times*, 20 April 1912.
9   Gordon Gardiner, *Champion of the Kingdom: The Story of Philip Mauro*, courtesy of Virginia Birt Baker.
10 *Magyarorszag* (1980), translation courtesy of Kalman Tanito.
11 Charles Stengel, *Newark Evening News*, 19 April 1912.
12 Unnamed crewmen, *Philadelphia Evening Bulletin*, 19 April 1912; interview was also quoted in Mobray (1912).
13 Charlotte Cardeza, *Worcester Evening Gazette*, 20 April 1912.
14 Thomas Cardeza, *Washington Herald*, 19 April 1912.
15 Mary Fortune, *Hamilton Spectator*, 22 April 1912.
16 Ernest St Clair account, courtesy of Les St Clair.
17 Norman Lynd, *Belfast Weekly Telegraph*, 11 May 1912.
18 *The Toronto World*, 20 April 1912.
19 Marshall (1912).
20 Ben Hecht, *Chicago Journal*, 17 April 1912.
21 John Snyder, *Minneapolis Journal*, 19 April 1912.
22 John Joyce, *Chicago Daily Journal*, 19 April 1912.
23 Unnamed steward, *New York Sun*, 19 April 1912, and *St Louis Globe Democrat*, 19 April 1912.
24 Carlos Hurd, *New York World*, 19 April 1912.
25 Unnamed steward, *Indianapolis Star*, 19 April 1912, and *New York Evening Journal*, 19 April 1912.
26 D. W. McMillan, *Atlantic City Daily Press*, 23 April 1912.
27 *Daily Mirror*, 19 April 1912.
28 J. Bruce Ismay, *New York Tribune*, 20 April 1912.

29 Bruce Ismay, *Baltimore Evening Sun*, 22 April 1912.
30 Bruce Ismay, *Daily Mirror*, 22 April 1912.
31 William Carter, *Baltimore Evening Sun*, 22 April 1912.
32 Christine Elsie Stormont letter, courtesy of Malcolm Cheape.
33 *Ibid*.
34 Elmer Taylor, *Atlantic City Daily Press*, 5 May 1912.
35 Anne Harrison in Barratt (2010), pp. 205–8.
36 *Ibid*.
37 *Ibid*.
38 *Northern Whig*, 15 May 1912, p. 7.
39 Lucile Carter letter, courtesy of Malcolm Cheape.
40 Thomas Ismay letter, courtesy of Malcolm Cheape.
41 W. A. James letter, courtesy of Malcolm Cheape.
42 Edith Russell, a recorded interview given to John Maxtone-Graham for Edward
    Kamuda and the Titanic Enthusiasts of America (later the Titanic Historical
    Society). A transcription of the 1970 taped interview is contained in Behe,
    The Titanic Disaster: Final Memories.
43 Lord Mersey, *New York Evening Post*, 30 July 1912.
44 *The Farmer*, 11 December 1912.
45 Wilton Oldham, *The Ismay Line* (1961).
46 *New York Times*, 19 October 1937.
47 *The Times*, 18 October 1937.
48 Oldham (1961), p. 246.
49 www.bbc.com/news/uk-northern-ireland-17694824.
50 Bruce Ismay, 1914 limitation of liability hearings.

Appendix 1

1 Charles Williams, as related to his friend George Standing, *New York Evening
   Journal*, 20 April 1912.
2 Charles Williams, *New York Press*, 20 April 1912.
3 *Western Morning News*, 29 April 1912. Horswill was saved in lifeboat 1, which left
   the *Titanic* at 1.05 a.m. and was nowhere near the *Titanic*'s bridge at the time of the
   sinking. Horswill undoubtedly heard the story of Smith and the baby from a fellow
   surviving crewman before returning to England.
4 *Western Times*, 30 April 1912.
5 Sidney Collett, *Auburn Semi-Weekly Journal*, 26 April 1912.
6 Anna Hämäläinen, *Detroit News*, 21 April 1912.
7 Thomas Whiteley, *Minneapolis Tribune*, 21 April 1912
8 Unnamed seaman, *New York Herald*, 20 April 1912.
9 George Alfred Hogg, *Brooklyn Daily Eagle*, 20 April 1912.
10 George Hogg, *New York Press*, 20 April 1912.
11 Frederick Barrett, *Manchester Guardian*, 29 April 1912.
12 Fred Barrett, *Manchester Guardian*, 29 April 1912.
13 Margaret Hayes, *Riverside Daily Press*, 23 January 1913, courtesy of Don Lynch.
14 George Brereton, *Cincinnati Enquirer*, 18 or 19 April 1912. Also, Mobray (1912).
15 George Brereton, *Brooklyn Daily Eagle*, 19 April 1912.

16 Lucy Duff Gordon, *Philadelphia Evening Bulletin*, 19 April 1912.
17 Letter from 28 November 1973 contributed by Brian Ticehurst, www.encyclopedia-titanica.org/titanic-survivor/thomas-knowles.html.
18 George McGough, *New York Evening World*, 20 April 1912.
19 *The New York Evening World*, 20 April 1912.
20 *New York Herald*, 20 April 1912.

Appendix 2

1 Mary Lines, *Voyage*, #68, Summer 2009. Note: survivor memories recorded decades after the disaster are not infallible. The *Titanic* was not on the shorter northern steamer track during her maiden voyage as Miss Lines seemed to believe, but her story still hints at the possibility that Captain Smith and Bruce Ismay might have disagreed about the desirability of the *Titanic* steaming hell for leather towards the approaching icefield and beating the *Olympic*'s maiden voyage crossing time. Although no survivor corroboration of this rumoured disagreement exists, might Miss Lines' story explain why Captain Smith remained silent while Ismay was praising *Titanic*'s performance to him on 13 April, declaring that the vessel would surely beat the *Olympic* and arrive in New York on Tuesday night? Or was Mrs Lines' story merely a garbled version of her mother Elisabeth Lines' testimony about overhearing Ismay's conversation with Smith?
2 Arthur Peuchen, *Toronto World*, 20 April 1912; *Manitoba Free Press*, 20 April 1912.
3 Dorothy Gibson, *New York Daily Telegraph*, 20 April 1912.
4 Kendall Peuchen Home, *My Dad*. Note: the present author has serious reservations about Mr Home's account of an alleged Smith–Ismay disagreement and wishes that Major Arthur Peuchen himself was available to shed additional light on this contentious matter.

Appendix 3

1 Dr C. A. Bernard, *New York Evening World*, 19 April 1912.
2 Eleanor Danforth, *Portland Evening Express & Daily Advertiser*, 23 April 1912.
3 *Victoria BC Daily Colonist*, 25 April 1912.
4 *Ogdensburg News*, 20 August 1911.

INDEX

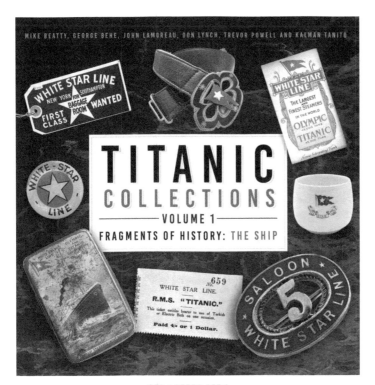

978 1 80399 333 1

Titanic Collections: Fragments of History is a two-part series showcasing rare and important artefacts relating to the history of RMS *Titanic*. Many collectors prefer to hide their treasures away, but the items presented in these beautiful books have been gathered by six well-known and respected researchers, authors, historians and collectors who want to share their acquisitions with the world.

YOU MAY ALSO ENJOY ...

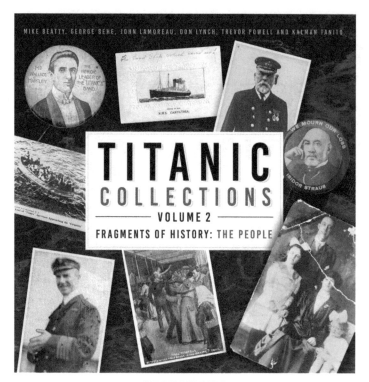

978 1 80399 334 8

'A wonderful gallery of period items related to the *Titanic* and *Olympic*, presented and shared by some of the top researchers and collectors in the field. Many of these items are quite rare or unique, and are not often seen by the general public.'

Bill Wormstedt, co-author of *Recreating the Titanic*